The Global Resurgence of Religion and the Transformation of International Relations

Culture and Religion in International Relations

Series Editors
Yosef Lapid and Friedrich Kratochwil

Published by Palgrave Macmillan

THE GLOBAL RESURGENCE OF RELIGION AND THE TRANSFORMATION OF INTERNATIONAL RELATIONS

The Struggle for the Soul of the Twenty-First Century

Scott M. Thomas

Foreword by Desmond Tutu,
former Archbishop of Cape Town, and winner of the
Nobel Peace Prize

palgrave
macmillan

THE GLOBAL RESURGENCE OF RELIGION AND THE TRANSFORMATION OF INTERNATIONAL RELATIONS
© Scott M. Thomas, 2005.

First published in 2005 by
PALGRAVE MACMILLAN™
175 Fifth Avenue, New York, N.Y. 10010 and
Houndmills, Basingstoke, Hampshire, England RG21 6XS
Companies and representatives throughout the world.

PALGRAVE MACMILLAN is the global academic imprint of the Palgrave Macmillan division of St. Martin's Press, LLC and of Palgrave Macmillan Ltd. Macmillan® is a registered trademark in the United States, United Kingdom and other countries. Palgrave is a registered trademark in the European Union and other countries.

ISBN 1–4039–6112–3 hardback
ISBN 1–4039–6157–3 paperback

Library of Congress Cataloging-in-Publication Data

Thomas, Scott.
    The global resurgence of religion and the transformation of
    international relations / the struggle for the soul of the twenty-first
    century / Scott Thomas.
        p. cm.—(Culture and religion in international relations)
    Includes bibliographical references and index.
        ISBN 1–4039–6112–3—ISBN 1–4039–6157–3 (pbk.)
        1. Religion and international affairs. I. Title. II. Series.
BL65.I55T46 2005
201′.727—dc22   2004057311

A catalogue record for this book is available from the British Library.

Design by Newgen Imaging Systems (P) Ltd., Chennai, India.

First edition: February 2005
10 9 8 7 6 5 4 3 2 1

Printed in the United States of America.

*This book is dedicated to the memory of
Albert J. Lutuli (1898–1967),
former President of the African National Congress of South
Africa, and winner of the Nobel Peace Prize,
to the memory of Beyers Naude (1915–2004),
Afrikaner rebel and prophet, South African patriot, and
global Christian,
and to
my parents,
Beatrice and Marshall Thomas,
for their love, support, and encouragement*

Contents

FOREWORD

Since September 11 a lot of books have been published on terrorism, religion, fundamentalism, and the rise of global religious violence. Here undoubtedly is one that is both helpful and insightful for those of us who feel that there has got to be a better way to promote global security and global welfare. Dr. Scott M. Thomas, by arguing that we need to take culture and religion more seriously in international affairs, chides our conservative friends who feel a firmer military response is what is necessary to win the "war on terrorism," and those of us liberals who have argued that more foreign aid and development assistance are going to solve problems of national security.

What is so refreshing about this book is that it challenges so much of our conventional thinking about religion, terrorism, and fundamentalism. It offers a wider window to see what is going on in international affairs by placing the concerns about religion, terrorism, and fundamentalism in the context of the much larger global resurgence of religion. Dr. Thomas shows that the impact of religion on international affairs today is more wide ranging than Islamic terrorism or religious extremism, and includes the activity of Catholic charismatics, Protestant Evangelicals and Pentecostals, the mainline churches, Western Buddhists, and a variety of "New Age" religions on a whole range of global issues from wars and civil conflicts in Bosnia, Uganda, Liberia, and elsewhere to debates over gender, the family, sexuality, diplomacy, democracy, the environment, and foreign assistance to poor countries.

At a more theoretical level, one of the most important aspects of this book is that Dr. Thomas also places the concerns about religion, terrorism, and fundamentalism in the context of the wider debates going on in theology, social theory, and the study of international relations regarding modernity, postmodernity, and secularization. For most of us these may be big words, ones we are more accustomed to hearing in a university seminar than in everyday conversation.

Dr. Thomas is able to explain that what these words or concepts convey about the here and the now, about how we interpret our own lives and our world, is crucial for our understanding of world politics. Frankly, I'm surprised he was able to bring together insights from so many disciplines in the humanities and social sciences, and I am particularly pleased his concern for ethics and theology shows through in his interpretation of the role of religion in international affairs.

In a way I do not think has been done before, he has applied the social theory of the philosopher Alasdair MacIntyre, and what is called the modern tradition of virtue-ethics to the practical world of diplomacy and international relations. Here he has shown us a new way forward, by calling for a "deeper pluralism" and a "rooted cosmopolitanism," which takes seriously the virtues and practices of faith communities embedded in a variety of religious traditions around the world. What is called for, Dr. Thomas says, are new forms of cultural or public diplomacy, and a type of foreign policy that takes seriously the piety, the faith, and the truthfulness of people's religious convictions in other countries, and how they interpret what this means for their public life—for the protection of human rights, the rule of law, and the like as well as what this means for their private life and family. He shows us in the second part of his book what this might mean in a practical way for promoting international cooperation, for faith-based diplomacy and peacebuilding, and for promoting civil society and democracy, and economic development in poor countries.

It might sound like this is special pleading on my part, as one of those religious professionals who has earned his living talking about God. But my talking about God has been very much about how God is concerned about our world, or what we should really see as his world, as much as he is also concerned about our own lives. Only the relentless secularism of so much of the media and in the social sciences, at least in Western countries, has hidden from view what those of us from Africa or other parts of the developing world are privileged to know so well. A God who is there, in our hope, and in our suffering, in our joy and in our pain as we struggle to help create a world that reflects more closely how we should live with each other as the people of God.

Desmond Tutu
Archbishop Emeritus of Cape Town,
Nobel Peace Laureate
October 4, 2004
Feast of St. Francis of Assisi

PREFACE

In many ways this book on the role of religion in international relations began in South Africa. It was there that I was first confronted in a stark and personal way with what R. Scott Appleby has called the ambivalence of the sacred. This is the way the best and noblest sentiments of religion are often combined with hatred, discrimination, and violence. In between my M.Sc. and my Ph.D. in International Relations at the London School of Economics in the mid-1980s I was teaching in the Department of Political Studies at the University of Cape Town. The black townships were in revolt, the police were using tear gas on the campus, and I remember sitting in my office calmly reading James Rosenau's scholarly account of "linkage politics" and thinking to myself, "this is ridiculous, what am I doing in my office reading about the linkage between domestic and international politics when it is happening right outside my door." This was the beginning of the end of apartheid but we didn't know it at the time.

Now, Americans, you will understand, not even American academics, have a set time in the day for morning and afternoon tea, but the Departments of Religious Studies and of Political Studies did, and at the University of Cape Town they shared the same tea room. I very quickly realized that to really know what was going on in the country I had to partake in tea time because the academics in religious studies were the ones with the closest contacts in the black townships and shanty towns.

I had first gone to South Africa a decade earlier while I was still in high school—after being told at the last minute I couldn't go to Sweden as an exchange student sponsored by the Rotary Club in Milwaukee, Wisconsin. I spent my senior year at an Afrikaner high school in a small town in the Western Cape, less than two hours from Cape Town, but it almost could have been another world. There, in this little Afrikaner town, or *dorp* as they say in Afrikaans, girls were taught how to be young women, boys were taught how to be gentlemen, they worshipped God, and believed in defending their country against liberals, terrorists, and communists.

At this school and by my host families I was nicely, but firmly, indoctrinated into the ethos of one form of religious nationalism— Afrikaner nationalism and the evils of British imperialism. I was constantly reminded that it was the British who created concentration camps during the Boer War and not the Germans. The student who was the head prefect at the high school made clear when I arrived that he was pleased I had come to South Africa. I could now see for myself he declared, "how well we treat our blacks," and so I could help put a stop to all the malicious propaganda in the liberal media.

Most of my schoolmates as well as their parents would no doubt have passed any test of orthodox Christian doctrine, and yet they still supported apartheid. Only in South Africa have I met such kind, generous people, who opened their hearts and their homes to me, and still doubted that the Holocaust against the Jews had taken place (I was told the Dutch Reformed Church was investigating the issue). I met people who genuinely saw themselves as part of a persecuted people—by English-speaking South Africans, by the British, and now the world—some of whom sympathized with Hitler, saying with a soft voice, "You know Scott, just like the Germans were surrounded by the Jews, we are surrounded by the blacks." How can such kind, generous, and God-fearing people believe and do such terrible things?

Reflecting back on this time, I came to see more clearly the dangers of associating God with a particular culture, country, or civilization. It is not only in South Africa—Bosnia, Israel, or Northern Ireland—where it is easy to confuse one's own personal beliefs with biblical faith, and one's cultural preferences with biblical values. If this is true about Christianity it is also true about the other world religions. India, Sri Lanka, and the Islamic world as we now know have their share of violent religious nationalists as well.

A decade later, while I was teaching at the University of Cape Town, Beyers Naude, the dissident Afrikaner who had founded the Christian Institute of Southern Africa after the Sharpeville shootings in 1960, was coming to speak after being unbanned. In other words, according to South Africa's laws in the 1980s restricting civil liberties, he was now allowed to speak in public for the first time in almost ten years. Naude came from a distinguished Afrikaner family. He was a member of the Broederbond (Band of Brothers), the Afrikaner secret society, a moderator of southern Transvaal Synod of the Dutch Reformed Church, and he had dared to call apartheid a sin and a heresy. He was vilified by the Afrikaans media and then banished by them—the same community that had welcomed me so warmly. He became secretary general of the South African Council of Churches after Archbishop Desmond Tutu. Five years after I left he became the only Afrikaner in the ANC's delegation when it opened talks with the South African government in 1990.

On that day he spoke to a huge, overflowing crowd on campus and then came back to the Political Studies and Religious Studies departments for tea. I cannot remember a word he said. What I remember is his presence, a quiet dignity, but also a humility of conviction that transcended politics as much as it was immersed in it, of someone who has not only resisted evil and oppression but also fate and despair. Someone who lived—rather incongruously I thought at the time—in hope because of his faith in the gospel of Jesus Christ.

After my time in South Africa I went back to the London School of Economics. There I learned it was Martin Wight, one of the early founders of the English School of international relations, who had argued in the heady scientific days of the 1950s that hope is not the same thing as secular optimism. It was, as Naude knew from experience, a theological virtue and not a political one, a view not unlike that of Christopher Lasch 40 years later in *The True and Only Heaven: Progress and Its Critics.*

Lasch recalled the research of Eugene D. Genovese and other historians on the religion of the slaves in the antebellum South. The virtue of hope that the slaves displayed did not demand a belief in progress but a belief in justice; they not only believed in but also trusted in, had confidence in, a just, good, and loving God. They had "a conviction that the wicked will suffer, that wrongs will be made right, and that the underlying order of things is not flouted with impunity." This kind of hope "implies a deep-seated trust in life that appears absurd to those who lack it," or cannot see beyond the nihilism or relativism of our postmodern era.

I now realize it was this rather small event, my experience of Beyer Naude's faith and life in Cape Town that day, which made me think that there was a broader research agenda here on the moral force of ideas in world politics—for good or for ill intent—and of those people who come to embody in their integrity those ideas.

The power of religion was being missed by the relentlessly secular theories of international relations, something most scholars are only now coming to grapple with after September 11.

I examined some of the ANC's global religious links in my book, *The Diplomacy of Liberation: The Foreign Relations of the ANC Since 1960,* such as its relations with the World Council of Churches and the World Alliance of Reformed Churches. These interests contributed to a broader research program on the global resurgence of religion at the same time as the issues of religion, culture, and identity became a more important part of international relations. I began to feel that my background in international relations, theology, and ethics provided me with an important combination of academic disciplines with which to interpret these social and cultural changes in international relations.

I was able to bring these ideas together using the social theory of the philosopher Alasdair MacIntyre at the conference on "Religion and International Relations" at the London School of Economics in 2000, in a paper called "Taking Religious and Cultural Pluralism Seriously: The Global Resurgence of Religion and the Transformation of International Society." It was later published in *Millennium*, the LSE's journal of international studies, and presented at the International Studies Association in 2001. It has now been republished as part of Palgrave's series on "Culture and Religion in International Relations" in Fabio Petito and Pavlos Hatzopoulos (eds.), *Religion in International Relations: The Return from Exile* (Palgrave Macmillan, 2003). It is through these contacts that I met Yosef Lapid and Friedrich Kratowchwil—two of my newest dialogue partners—and I am grateful to them and to Anthony Wahl for commissioning this book, and for their patience in helping me to bring it to fruition.

I have also come to realize that books like this one are not really written in isolation but in a community. It may be a less cohesive and more virtual community than a monastic one, but it is a community none the less. It is made up of those people who have given me support, guidance, and encouragement over the years. My former supervisors are a part of it: James Mayall, Jack Spence, and Fred Halliday, as well as my more recent dialogue partners in international relations: Frederich Kratchowil, Yosef Lapid, Jean Bethke Elshtain, Christopher Coker, Raymond Cohn, Roger Eatwell, John Esposito, Nelson Gonzalez, Fabio Petito, Pavlos Hatzopoulos, Brian Neve, Daniel Philpott, Charles Jones, Stefan

Wolff, and David Yost; and in ethics and theology, James Alison, Luke Bretherton, Jonathan Chaplain, David Gill, Ward Gasque, Stanley Hauerwas, Alasdair MacIntyre, and Max Stackhouse. It is also made up of the people whose love and friendship have sustained me: Cynthia Anderson, Joshy Easaw, Vernon Hewitt, Alan Jacobs, Michael Kirwan, James Knight, Daniel LeGrange, Jonathan Lloyd, Tom McGee, Ian Milborrow, Susan Marsh, Piergiovanna Natale, Anthony O'Mahoney, Ivan Schouker, Robert Shelledy, Matthew Titus, Nick Townsend, and Cathy Winnett.

INTRODUCTION: THE STRUGGLE FOR THE SOUL OF THE TWENTY-FIRST CENTURY

T
hree momentous events in international relations—the Iranian Revolution, the rise of Solidarity and the Polish Revolution, and the tragedy of September 11, 2001 indicate how a global resurgence of religion is transforming our understanding of international relations.

The Iranian Revolution—God of Surprises?

Most political scientists and intelligence experts did not predict the Islamic Revolution in Iran because it was not supposed to happen. Certainly, there were observers who thought some kind of social or political upheaval could be in the offing, but not an Islamic revolution.[1] A resurgence of religion—piety, as well as violent religious anger and rage—was not supposed to happen in a developing country participating so thoroughly in modernization and Westernization.[2]

How could so many scholars and policymakers who monitored the politics of Iran have missed the warning signs about what was happening? Zbigniew Brzezinski, President Carter's Advisor on National Security Affairs, has acknowledged that Islamic fundamentalism was a phenomenon largely ignored in U.S. intelligence reports, and the intelligence system allowed the president and his advisors little preparation for the way the Iranian situation so shockingly and suddenly disintegrated.[3]

U.S. intelligence experts, as well as William Sullivan, the U.S. ambassador in Tehran, ignored the particular challenge posed by Islamic fundamentalism. Ayatollah Khomeini was dismissed as a "Gandhi-like" figure with little future role in Iran other than as a venerable sage who had returned to the country (forgetting that Gandhi opposed British imperialism and used the social and religious ethic of nonviolence to force Britain to leave India). They predicted that after the inevitable political upheaval a pro-Western government would be set up, and political continuity with Iran would be maintained. It was mainly Gary Sick, the National Security Council (NSC) officer responsible for Iranian affairs, who argued that the "reformist" policies the Carter administration was then advocating were unlikely to so easily placate the cultural, religious, and social forces unleashed by Ayatollah Khomeini.[4]

After the revolution began, the idea that there was a crucial cultural and religious dimension to the events taking place—that it really was a *religious* reaction to a regime's rapid modernization and Westernization—was dismissed by the policymaking elite. The real causes of the Revolution were still considered to be political, economic, or social opposition to the Shah's autocracy and authoritarianism. One proposed solution was moving the Shah toward a constitutional monarchy or a coalition government with the opposition; another solution—advocated by Brzezinski but opposed on ethical grounds by President Carter and Secretary of State Vance—was strong leadership to crush the revolution.

The Shah's heavy-handedness and oppression were considered to be another cause of opposition and revolutionary upheaval, and so the Carter administration advocated a greater respect for human rights. Respect for human rights and a more open and participatory government were also seen as the only way of limiting the other causes of the revolution. There was anger at the Shah's corruption, and social and economic resentment from the new urban migrants toward the growing gap between the rich and the poor, and there was social resentment on the part of the traditional, bazaar, and merchant classes toward the new class of rising entrepreneurs. Commentators who did not see the Iranian Revolution coming were now surprised at the staying power of a regime based on religion.

The Islamic Revolution is one of the most vivid examples of how the impact of culture and religion was ignored or marginalized in the study of international relations. According to modernization theory—the dominant framework for understanding the politics of developing countries—secularization was considered to be an inevitable part of modernization. The saliency of religion in social and political life was supposed to decline with economic progress and modernization, and so the Iranian Revolution was from the beginning interpreted as a reactionary and fundamentalist response to modernization and Westernization.

The study of culture and religion before the Iranian Revolution was considered irrelevant to political analysis—dismissed by the CIA as mere sociology.[5] The former Iranian hostage Moorhead

Kennedy has argued that senior officers in the Department of State were puzzled about how the issue of religion could have provoked the overthrow of the Shah and the takeover of the U.S. Embassy. Kennedy concluded, "There is no wedge of the pie for religion. . . . Nothing in its long experience prepared the foreign service for a transnational religious movement of the kind led by Ayatollah Khomeini."[6]

The way the revolution was interpreted—as a reactionary response to modernization, was strengthened when Jerry Falwell formed the Moral Majority about the same time. The media and many political commentators also interpreted the rise of Christian fundamentalists in American politics as a reactionary or conservative response to the modernization of American society.[7]

Since the Iranian Revolution religion has still been marginalized in our understanding of international affairs. There is still the attempt by the media or by policy-makers to portray the reformist pressures in Iran only in a secular, liberal, democratic way—a Western way—rather than to recognize that they aim to form a political order that is representative, democratic, and still responsive to traditional values.[8]

Why did the CIA, which helped the *mujahedeen*, the Islamic holy warriors in Afghanistan, fight against the Soviet occupation of their country, not foresee the "blowback" from the Afghan war? Why did they not foresee that the Afghan war would mobilize and radicalize an entire transnational generation of Muslim youths prepared to die for Kashmir, Palestine, Chechnya, and the Taliban's Afghanistan; or that these Islamists would turn on their erstwhile American allies and support other Islamic movements fighting Egypt, Jordan, and Saudi Arabia?[9]

How much better was the analysis of policymakers and commentators in the run-up to the Second Gulf War against Iraq? Many commentators have been willing to acknowledge the impact of Iraqi nationalism, but what of the cultural power of Shiite Islam and the religious legitimacy wielded by Grand Ayatollah Ali Sistani, Iraq's leading Shiite religious leader? How much of a willingness was there to consider his power to influence any of America's plans for Iraq's political future?

The Polish Revolution—God Smiles on History?

The collapse of communism in Eastern Europe is another of the most dramatic events at the end of the twentieth century. The end of communism began in Poland with a workers' strike: the formation of a trade union or social movement that brought together for the first time workers, intellectuals, and the Catholic Church under the leadership of a charismatic, unemployed electrician nobody had ever heard of before. What factors brought the Polish Revolution about, and why did it happen when it did, and the way it did— relatively nonviolently?

A variety of explanations have been offered for the collapse of communism in Poland and the people's revolutions in the rest of Eastern Europe. What most of them have in common is that they leave little room for the role of culture and religion.[10] The first explanation is based on a hard, realist perspective of international relations, and emphasizes military power, Reagan's arms build-up, and great power politics. The United States outgunned and outspent the Soviet Union, and this is what led Moscow to recoil from the use of force in Poland in 1980, unlike what it did in Hungary in 1956 or Czechoslovakia in 1968. These factors eventually led the Soviet Union to let go of Eastern Europe, and this is what contributed to the final collapse of communism in the Soviet Union.[11]

What is called the liberal or pluralist approach to international relations emphasizes that the collapse of communism took place because of growing economic interdependence and the spread of globalization: the widely diffused and yet integrated technologies applied to the global economy, transportation, information, and communications. Deep-seated economic, social, and political transformations were already taking place in these countries because of globalization that showed up the internal, economic failings of communism. In other words, the people's revolutions in Eastern Europe and the collapse of communism in the Soviet Union coincided with the spread of global economic interdependence and the coming of a global society.[12]

Another approach argues that ideas and ethics or morality are fundamental to any explanation for the relatively swift and peaceful collapse of communism in Poland and the rest of Eastern Europe, apart from Romania. The collapse of communism was fundamentally a moral and spiritual collapse because communism eroded the moral or ethical bases of civilization and signaled the end of an era of utopian ideology.[13]

The collapse of communism in Poland and in the rest of Eastern Europe also shows the power of the Roman Catholic Church in the modern world. Religion played a triple-vectored role in the collapse of communism. The Church worked against the alienating of the individual, the totalizing of society, and the sovietizing of society, and in this way contributed to cultural and political resistance in Eastern Europe.[14]

What took place in Poland? At the beginning of the strike of the workers at the Lenin Shipyards in Gdansk in 1980, where Solidarity was born, the first thing the strikers did was to affix to the gateway of the shipyards a large crucifix, an image of the Virgin Mary, the holy icon of Our Lady of Czestochowa, the Black Madonna (which celebrates the defense by Polish nobles of the monastery located there against the Swedes in 1656, with the help of the Virgin Mary), and a portrait of Pope John Paul II. A Catholic mass was said every day, and priests heard confessions just inside the gates of the shipyard.

What did these religious symbols and practices mean, and were these just symbols of hope and inspiration or was something more fundamental going on? If the Catholic Church did have a role in the Polish Revolution, how should it be examined or conceptualized? Does it simply represent the power of symbols or of cultural constructs, or should the role of the Catholic Church be conceived in some other way? We can now see that something more than an appeal to the ideas or symbols of religion took place in Poland.

A series of prior events prepared the way for the Polish Revolution, make intelligible the way the strike unfolded in the Gdansk shipyards, and give birth to Solidarity as the first independent trade union in Eastern Europe.[15] A prior moral, cultural, and religious revolution prepared the way for the Polish Revolution.[16]

We now know that Cardinal Stefan Wyszyński prepared the way with a decade-long and nation-wide program of Marian devotions and pastoral renewal (1956–1966) called the Great Novena of the Millennium to celebrate 1,000 years of Christianity in Poland (966–1966). The Great Novena was a revival of folk religiosity and popular piety, which in Poland meant the power of the Virgin Mary, but it was something more than this as well.

Over the decade of the Great Novena, a three-fold set of activities helped strengthen Poland's national and religious life. First, was the Polish episcopate's emphasis on religious instruction and spiritual formation, the attempt to recatechize Poland, that is to reeducate the entire country in the basic truths of the Catholic faith and the Church's understanding of moral life. Second, there was an emphasis on pilgrimage, with regular visits to the country's major shrines, with preaching, and the call for the country to reconsecrate itself to the Queen of Poland for another 1,000 years. Cardinal Wyszyński's pilgrimage throughout the country became a kind of traveling referendum on Poland's communist government. Third, the greatest pilgrimage, the linchpin of the Great Novena, was undertaken by the icon of the Black Madonna, which was carried throughout the country. Thus, a decade of religious instruction and spiritual formation helped the country to reclaim its national identity and historical memory. The pride, dignity, and memory of Poland as the rampart of Christendom were invoked, this time not against the invading Turks but against the communist domination of the country.[17]

Karol Wojtyla—Pope John Paul II—as the auxiliary bishop and then cardinal archbishop of Kraków implemented the activities of the Great Novena. He used the impending nine hundredth anniversary of the martyrdom of St. Stanislaw to initiate a Synod of Kraków and the archdiocesan study of the teaching of the Second Vatican Council (1962–1965). Over the next decade the "Light and Life" movement of summer camps reached thousands of young Polish people, the leading Catholic weekly, *Tygodnik Powszechny*, built closer links between the Church and the lay Polish intelligentsia, and the Clubs of the Catholic Intelligentsia (KIK) helped deepen the moral, cultural, and religious renewal of the country.[18]

Wojtyla, along with other Catholic clergy, developed close relations with the Workers' Defense Committee (KOR), which brought together workers and intellectuals in an unprecedented fashion and, as the state's oppression increased, came to support not only workers but also anyone whose civil rights were threatened. Adam Michnik, one of KOR's founders, was instrumental in breaking down the barriers between the Catholic Church and the country's left-wing, mainly anticlerical, dissidents and intellectuals.[19]

A key part of the Polish Revolution was the way the Second Vatican Council transformed the Catholic Church in the twentieth century. Karol Wojtyla influenced the direction of key documents of the Second Vatican Council and thus how the Catholic Church would engage with the culture of secular modernity.[20] We now know that for a decade or more Cardinal Wojtyla worked out, as part of his pastoral responsibilities, what a theological understanding of "solidarity" could mean among the Polish people, a people with a deeply felt national and historical religious tradition—the Church, workers, and intellectuals—and then the meaning of solidarity between human beings before Solidarity as a trade union or social movement could be formed.

"It is hard to conceive of Solidarity without the Polish Pope."[21] Only a few months before Pope John Paul II's first trip to Poland, in March 1979, he published his first encyclical, *Redemptor Hominis*, which provided Solidarity with a name and its ideological foundations. It was based on his long reflections on the ideas of the Second Vatican Council regarding freedom of religion, the dignity of the human person, and the concept of solidarity as a middle way between the individual autonomy of capitalism and the collectivism of communism.[22] The Polish Revolution shows the moral, cultural, and religious foundations of change in world politics. It also shows how the interpretation of a religious tradition can have a crucial impact on the type of political action that takes place.

September 11, 2001—Dostoevsky in Manhattan?

Scholars of international relations have had a great deal of difficulty explaining the horrific events of September 11, 2001. The debate over how and why these tragic events happened indicates that there are still many people—scholars, journalists, and members of the public—who are having a great deal of difficulty, as David Brooks has put it, in "kicking the secularist habit," and who still do not want to believe that culture and religion are important for understanding international relations.[23]

The first way culture and religion are marginalized in explanations for religious terrorism or extremism is by arguing that these events occurred because of incomplete modernization. We have already seen that explanations of this kind have been popular among scholars trained in modernization theory since the Islamic Revolution. Modernization is the same as Westernization, for as V. S. Naipaul has argued, Western civilization *is* the universal civilization.[24] Most non-Western cultures have made their peace with the West and with modernity, and they now combine their own cultures with those of the West in remarkable ways. The Islamic world—really the Arab world—is the great exception; this historic rival to the West has not made this accommodation, and there is now one more struggle after the defeat of communism before the West can declare a final victory.[25]

Although genuine security threats exist in the short term that need to be dealt with, over the long haul the spread of religiously motivated terrorism, extremism, or fundamentalism constitutes what Francis Fukuyama has called "aberrations," a few local difficulties in far away countries of which Americans know very little (remembering what British prime minister Neville Chamberlain once said about Czechoslovakia)—such as Iraq, Afghanistan, Pakistan, Uzbekistan, Tajikistan, or Indonesia.

History, meaning the clash of ideologies over how society, politics, and the economy should be organized, is still going the West's way—toward capitalism and liberal democracy. The activities of radical Islamists and terrorists are only "rearguard actions" by disaffected individuals or social groups in "retrograde" parts of the world threatened by modernization and globalization. Once they are sorted out—with more foreign aid, nation-building, or military force—peace, democracy, and free markets can continue to spread around the world.[26]

For many Westerners, this is a very comforting interpretation of the world—liberal modernity—but what if people in the non-Western parts of the world don't want to fit into it? What if they want to gain the advantages of material prosperity, but in ways consistent with their cultural or religious traditions? What if they want to develop without losing their soul?

A second explanation for September 11, one that is popular in the media and among many clerics, scholars, and politicians, is to say that religiously motivated terrorism or extremism is not about religion at all. All of the world religions, in a kind of postmodern cliche, preach a message of peace and goodwill. The roots of the problem are global inequality, world poverty, and social exclusion in poor countries with corrupt rulers and undemocratic governments.

The notion that culture, religion, and theology provide only what Michael Walzer has called the "colloquial idiom of legitimate rage" is, as he has acknowledged, simply part of "the inability of leftists to recognize or acknowledge the power of religion in the modern world."[27] Commentators argue that religious terrorist groups are using religion only as a cloak to hide more tangible, secular, material, or economic interests.[28] It has almost become a truism to say that terrorism ferments in cultures of poverty, oppression, and ignorance, and so eliminating these conditions through free trade, foreign aid, and economic development is now an important part of the war against global terrorism.[29]

There is simply no reason to believe that foreign aid is going to turn Islamists into liberals. Many commentators have pointed out that poverty, social exclusion, and a lack of civil liberties are not on Osama bin Laden's list of grievances, nor on that of al-Qaeda. Many of the September 11 highjackers were well educated and from middle-class backgrounds—doctors, lawyers, engineers; they were familiar with the West because they were often educated there. They did not come from poverty-stricken countries but from Egypt or Saudi Arabia, neither of which is poor by international standards. Contrary to popular myths about terrorism, this is in keeping with the fact that most terrorists do not come from poor backgrounds, are not ill-educated, and are not suffering from some kind of personality disorder or socioeconomic grievance.[30]

Something else is going on in the world. A more global perspective on religious violence is needed. In 2001 over half of the 34 serious conflicts around the world had a religious dimension to them. A rise in religiously related conflict or terrorism by new religious non-state actors has taken place over the last 20 years; they do not rely on the support of sovereign states (which is what distinguishes global terrorism from international terrorism), nor do they seem to set any constraints on the limits of their violence.[31]

A third type of explanation for September 11 that marginalizes culture and religion argues that religious extremism is really no different from other forms of ideological extremism in the twentieth century. The motives, and to some extent the methods, of radical Islamic groups are similar to a variety of the "anti-liberal" and "anti-modernist" ideologies of the Left and the Right that were also opposed to modernity and liberal rationalism—Russia's communist insurgency going back to World War I, the Italian fascists, the German Nazis, and the crusade by General Franco to reestablish the Reign of Christ the King in Spain.

President George W. Bush, speaking to Congress shortly after the attacks on New York and Washington, D.C., used this analogy when he argued that al-Qaeda and its supporters were the heirs of all the murderous, totalitarian, ideologies of the twentieth century.[32] Some liberal political and cultural critics have accepted this explanation for the September 11 tragedy as well. The reason why the United States is hated is because a new breed of religious fascists and totalitarians are opposed to the dynamism of a liberal culture and civilization.[33]

The only difference is that today antiliberal ideological extremism is connected to religion—radical Islam. Concepts such as political religion, fascist religion, totalitarian religion, Islamic fascism, and clerical fascism to describe the Taliban, al-Qaeda, and Iran's mullahs, are all concepts that emerged in political science almost a generation ago to understand the appeal of fascism and totalitarianism. The idea now is that there is a connection between the "religious" nature of fascism and what is "fascist" or "totalitarian" about certain forms of religion.[34]

September 11 is now connected to the Right's fascism and terrorism or the Left's revolutionary terrorism.[35] Osama bin Laden and his supporters are thought to be no different from the violent and fanatical nihilists, anarchists, and extreme Marxist revolutionaries of a century ago. After the UN compound in Baghdad was blown up and the train bombing in Madrid, many commentators denied that these attacks had anything to do with religion and said it was all about nihilism and violence. "How do you negotiate with nihilism?"[36]

Therefore, so the argument goes, we should stop reading the Koran or studying Islam, or thinking about culture and religion, and go back to reading the revolutionary nihilism in Joseph Conrad's novel, *The Secret Agent* or Dostoevsky's *Notes from the Underground*.[37] Recall that in Dostoevsky's *The Demons* an entire provincial city is set ablaze amidst its inhabitants' nihilism and romanticism. The French philosopher, Andre Glucksmann, emphasized how nihilism is connected to this kind of violence when he titled his essay on the wider implications of September 11, *Dostoevsky in Manhattan*.[38] What we notice about these explanations for September 11 is that even after these horrific events there is still a refusal to take culture and religion seriously in international relations.

What Can We Learn from these Events?

The first theme indicated by these momentous events is the overall message of this book. There is a global resurgence of religion taking place throughout the world that is challenging our interpretation of the modern world—what it means to be modern—and this has implications for our understanding of how culture and religion influence international relations.

Consequently, the global resurgence of religion, as this concept is set out in chapter 1, is a far more wide-ranging phenomenon than religious terrorism, extremism, or fundamentalism.[39] The global resurgence of religion taking place in the developed world—charismatic Catholics and Catholic conservatives, evangelicals and Pentecostal

Protestants, New Age spiritualists, Western Buddhists, and Japanese traditionalists—is part of a larger crisis of modernity in the West. It reflects a deeper and more widespread disillusionment with a modernity that reduces the world to what can be perceived and controlled through reason, science, and technology, and leaves out the sacred, religion, or spirituality.

The global resurgence of religion also can be seen in the way authenticity has come to rival development as a key to understanding the political aspirations of the non-Western world. Authenticity refers to ways of gaining economic prosperity and fashioning political, economic, and social systems that are consistent with a country's moral base, its cultural heritage, and its religious tradition. It is one of the results of the failure of the secular, modernizing, state to produce democracy or development.

What if there are multiple paths to being modern, keeping with the cultural and religious traditions of societies rooted in the main world religions? What is called the postmodern world opens up this possibility, and this is why the twentieth century may turn out to be the last modern century. Postmodernity challenges the idea that in our era there is still a grand narrative—the Western concept of modernity—a single overall character and direction to the meaning of progress, modernity, or development for all countries; and this narrative or framework, most importantly for social scientists, is sufficient to explain the impact of culture and religion in international relations.

The second theme of this book is that the global resurgence of religion indicates international relations needs to consider the wider debates in social theory over modernity, postmodernity, and secularization. "[T]he attacks of September 11," Robert Keohane has admitted, "reveal that all mainstream theories of world politics are relentlessly secular with respect to motivation. They ignore the impact of religion, despite the fact that world-shaking political movements have so often been fuelled by religious fervor."[40]

The global resurgence of religion and the challenge of post-modernity help us to see one of the reasons for some of the most recent blind spots or blowback in U.S. foreign policy—Iran, Iraq, Egypt, Pakistan, Afghanistan, for example—may be the way culture and religion have been marginalized in international relations. What is needed is not only more facts—to gather more intelligence or better information—but better concepts, theories, and assumptions to interpret the impact of culture and religion on international affairs. Chapter 2 examines the set of concepts and assumptions in social theory that have marginalized culture and religion in international relations—modernization theory, secularization, positivism, and materialism.

If religion has been ignored or marginalized in international relations—and, is now returning from exile, then another question is how should religion be brought back into the study of international relations?[41] Does religion need to be brought into the existing concepts, theories, or paradigms of international relations or are new ones required? A more disquieting suggestion is that what is required is a new concept of theory and what it is supposed to do in international relations.

These questions are examined in chapter 3. What each of these momentous events brings out is an issue that has been emerging for quite some time in international relations theory. After the Cold War we now recognize the focus of realists on the distribution of military or hard power resources, and the emphasis of liberals on economic interdependence has to be supplemented by the role of what Joseph Nye has called soft power—ideas, belief systems, and ideologies—or more broadly the role of culture in explaining and understanding international relations.[42]

The way questions about religion, soft power, and culture are usually framed is to ask how do ideas or beliefs in religion have their causal capacity and influence policymaking? There is a now a great deal of effort underway to try and determine how much ideas matter as causes of political outcomes.[43] This book questions whether religion can be defined as simply a set of ideas or even symbols that constitute a cultural form of soft power. It also questions the way research programs involving culture and religion are framed in international relations because they often involve unstated assumptions about the nature of religion and liberal modernity.

These momentous events show that religion often does far more than provide the colloquial idiom of legitimate rage or the motives for some of the world-shaking political movements in international relations. Religion often helps to constitute the very content of a social movement's identity, and religious values, practices, traditions, and institutions really do shape their struggles, encourage mobilization, and influence their type of social or political action.[44]

Many scholars and commentators seemed far more surprised by the rise of al-Qaeda and its role in September 11 than they ought to have been. The study of international relations has recognized for some time that new types of non-state actors or nongovernmental organizations (NGOs) can influence international relations. However, religious non-state actors, apart from some early studies of the Catholic Church, have not been investigated with any consistency in contrast to a variety of other types of non-state actors—the IMF, the World Bank, multinational corporations (MNCs), and relief and development agencies. It is one more example of the way religion has been marginalized in the study of international relations.

Therefore, another theme of this book examined in chapter 4 is the way globalization has facilitated a constantly evolving role of religion in international relations. There is a whole array of what are called new religious movements in the sociology of religion that are shaping the global cultural, religious, and political landscape. What may be distinctive about religious groups and communities, which the theory of international relations has so far not been able to fully incorporate, stems from the way religion is rooted in and constitutive of particular types of local faith communities, as well as being part of a variety of global non-state actors in international relations. They are as much a part of world politics as the NGOs that are considered to be part of an emerging global civil society. They will also play an important role in shaping the contours of world politics in the twenty-first century.

If religion is brought back into the study of international relations, how will it transform our understanding of some of the substantive global issues that confront all of us—international conflict and cooperation, diplomacy and peacebuilding, and the promotion of civil society, democracy, and economic development? The second part of this book examines what it means to take religion seriously in some of these global issues.

Chapter 5 examines what it means to take religion seriously as a source of international conflict. It is no use saying people who use religion to legitimate hatred and violence are simply abusing or misinterpreting religious traditions for their own misguided purposes. Most disturbingly, there has always been what R. Scott Appleby has called "the ambivalence of the sacred" in each of the great world religions. The noblest expressions of religion and spirituality can also produce hatred, violence, and intolerance.[45] What the theory of violence and the sacred developed by the French literary theorist and anthropologist Rene Girard help us to understand is that the ambivalence of the sacred is an inherent part of culture and religion. The cultural and religious dimensions of finding scapegoats—other individuals or social groups to persecute or marginalize, is the way most societies have promoted social cohesion and political stability.

Therefore, while a political solution is necessary to resolve ethno-religious or national conflicts in failed or collapsed states, it will not be sufficient to promote long-term political stability or reconciliation. Something more is required because politics will not solve the problem of scapegoating violence. It will simmer beneath the surface calm, and at the right moment will erupt again in a variety of political religions or sacred nationalisms because what Girard calls the underlying "sacrificial crisis" in failed states or deeply divided societies has not been resolved.

Chapter 6 explains that the study of culture and religion has not been a central part of mainstream theories of international cooperation or regional integration. These theories argue that power politics or economic interdependence can explain international cooperation. However, culture and religion may not be as marginalized from international cooperation as the theories suggest is the case. It can be argued that a prior or deeper agreement among states may be necessary to develop the rules, norms, or institutions of international society. In other words, a deeper understanding may be necessary for the interests and rationality of states to foment international cooperation. This can be seen in the role of Protestantism in shaping the nature of American hegemony in the Bretton Woods postwar international order, and in the way European integration was, and for many Europeans still is, a political project of Christian Democracy and Catholic social thought.

The global resurgence of religion and globalization have contributed to new wars and internal conflicts in ways that call into question the adequacy of inter-state or conventional diplomacy to resolve them. Chapter 7 examines the role of religion in what is called multitrack diplomacy, which involves a variety of non-state actors in diplomacy, peacebuilding, and conflict resolution.

Peacemaking has been an activity of many religious traditions because pacifism and nonviolence has been central to their religious message and witness. However, the ideas, concepts, and theories in these areas often have been developed within discourses and practices that rely on secular reason, even if there is a religious motivation behind them.

There is no naked public square in international politics any more than there is one in domestic politics.[46] What the global resurgence of religion and the changing nature of international conflict indicate is that diplomacy, peacebuilding, and conflict resolution are now confronted with many of the same problems of multiculturalism that confront the liberal democracies in the West. What is called faith-based diplomacy has arisen over the last decade as one of the types of multitrack diplomacy to handle these new multicultural challenges to diplomacy and peacebuilding. Rather than relying on ideas or concepts rooted in secular reason, it deliberately relies on the virtues, discourses, and practices of different religious traditions as a vital part of diplomacy.

Since the end of Cold War promoting civil society and democracy has been a major feature of foreign aid programs, and after September 11 nation building has come back as a priority of U.S. foreign policy. Chapter 8 shows that our past efforts to promote civil society, democracy, and nation building do not augur well for the prospects of these policies in weak or failed states today. It turns out that a foreign aid policy that supports a narrow range of NGOs that fit the accepted secular, rational, and utilitarian concept of civil society is not the same thing as supporting democracy or civil society.

This is not surprising since the role of religion in the rise of democracy and civil society has been ignored in much of the political science literature. Building civil society is not a value-free technique for Western donor governments and aid agencies to promote freedom, democracy, or economic development. Culture and religion cannot be ignored so easily. Any concept of civil society that does not integrate religion into a broader discourse on what civil society is, how it functions, and how it may be supported, misunderstands what constitutes civil society and what makes it sustainable in developing countries.

Chapter 9 examines how culture, religion, and economics are increasingly a part of the debate over a more holistic concept of economic development taking place in a variety of international organizations. This is another less widely recognized aspect of the global resurgence of religion. The World Bank, for example, has indicated that religious leaders and institutions—churches, mosques, and temples—are often the most trusted associations in developing countries, and provide the best infrastructure in poor communities. This means faith-based organizations have a key role in alleviating world poverty and promoting sustainable development.

The War on Terrorism

What does bringing religion back into international relations mean for our understanding of the war on terrorism? Our attempts to rebuild failed states or promote freedom, democracy, or economic development will not be successful if they do so in ways that unleash the same kind of disruptive forces of social change that we have not been able to cope with in our own countries, which have stronger social and political institutions. Therefore, the promotion of civil society, democracy, and development requires a more active public and cultural diplomacy that takes seriously the moral and religious debates over social, political, and economic life taking place in the developing world. The concerns of faithfulness and cultural authenticity have to be a part of foreign policy or else our policies to promote democracy or development will not only lead to policy failure, but may also contribute to instability, revolution, or even more terrorism.

It is often said the war on terrorism is also a war of ideas, in daily contests over words, images, and sounds that global telecommunications are now spreading around the world. The cultural battle today is not a rerun of the cultural battles of the Cold War, with the battle mainly being waged, as Paul Berman suggests, in the big cities and universities in Europe or the United States—the leading capitals of thought.

A battle for faith and life is not the same thing as a battle over competing secular ideologies. This is a struggle that is being fought in the schools, mosques, churches, and temples in the West as well as those in the dusty villages and burgeoning cities of the non-Western world. It is a struggle that takes place in private prayer as well as in public life. It is a struggle over what it means to build communities of character in a postmodern world. A struggle over the soul of the new world order is taking place, and taking cultural and religious pluralism seriously is now one of the most important foreign policy challenges of the twenty-first century.

How is this Book Different?

At the outset, scholars of international relations and interested readers in foreign affairs may be suspicious at the references that have already been made in this book to the disciplines of theology, religious studies, and the sociology of religion. One might think that a study of the impact of culture and religion in international relations is by its very nature an interdisciplinary area of inquiry, and yet in practice there often has been very little dialogue between these disciplines regarding religion and foreign affairs. September 11 dramatically demonstrated the importance of an interdisciplinary approach to the study of religion in international relations. This book is written with that spirit in mind, and so it engages in a variety of debates in ethics, theology, sociology, and history as well as in international relations.

One of the things that distinguishes this book from many others is that it is rooted in the key concepts of what is called the English School of international relations, which for many years was associated with the London School of Economics.[47] This term is used to describe a group of scholars, mainly historians, philosophers, theologians, and former diplomatic practitioners, who in the late 1950s gathered together to form the British Committee on the Theory of International Politics.[48]

This book seeks to revitalize the dialogue that some of the early English School thinkers—Martin Wight, Herbert Butterfield, and Donald MacKinnon—started a generation ago between theology and international relations. The reason for this is that the early English School took seriously the impact of religious doctrines, cultures, and civilizations on international relations at a time when they were ignored or marginalized in the mainstream study of the discipline because it was preoccupied with the Cold War. The kind of questions they asked about culture, religion, and identity have now become some of the most important ones in the study of international relations.[49]

Another caveat is in order. Although this book is about the way religion has been ignored or marginalized in the study of international relations, it is important to remember that this omission is part of a larger problem. Religion has been marginalized for some time in the humanities and social sciences. The religious dimension of many world-shaking political events has been hidden from history until recent changes in scholarly outlook opened up this dimension—the American revolution, the civil war, the civil rights struggle, the role of religion in the theory of civil society or in democracy theory, and the role of religion in the spread of democracy and in the Cold War are only some of the areas in which the role of religion is now more widely acknowledged.

PART ONE

BRINGING RELIGION BACK INTO INTERNATIONAL RELATIONS THEORY

CHAPTER I

"THE REVENGE OF GOD?" THE TWENTIETH CENTURY AS THE "LAST MODERN CENTURY"

The concept of religion was invented as part of the political mythology of liberalism and now has emerged as a universal concept applicable to other cultures and civilizations. This understanding of religion is used to legitimate a form of liberal politics that considers the mixing of politics and religion to be violent and dangerous to reason, freedom, and political stability. The global resurgence of religion, however, challenges the concepts of social theory that interpret public religion in this way. It challenges the idea that secular reason can provide a neutral stance from which to interpret religion, and it opens up the possibility of multiple ways of being "modern," making "progress," or being "developed" consistent with a variety of cultural and religious traditions.

The Invention of Religion

The concept of religion used in this book refers to the primary world religions—Judaism, Christianity, Islam, Hinduism, Confucianism, and Buddhism, along with Sikhism, Jainism, Taoism, or Shinto—which comprise about 77 percent of the world's population.[1] There is something that is both concrete and illusive about the concept of the world religions. On the one hand, what is concrete about the concept is that it refers to what are identifiably global religions that have adherents around the world. On the other hand, what is illusive about the concept is that identifying the main world religions as one of the subjects of this book does not settle what it is about religion that is being examined, nor why the world religions are important for the study of international relations.

Some of the most important questions in international relations theory that have been asked since September 11 include the following: were these horrific events about religion, or were they about something else? What are the root causes of Islamic terrorism and Islamic fundamentalism, and what can we do to prevent this kind of activity in the future? The problem with the way these questions are asked is that they seem to assume there is a social activity out there in the world that can be identified by a universal category called "religion," it is a phenomena that seems to occur in all societies, even though it was supposed to decline with modernization, and this seemingly universal human activity can be studied in a way that can give satisfactory answers to these questions.[2]

What has been remarkably odd following September 11 is that many of the same kind of questions political scientists and scholars of international relations are now asking about culture and religion, scholars of early modern Europe have been asking about the "wars of religion" for more than a generation. Therefore, understanding the nature and causes of the wars of religion in Europe—the civil war between Catholics and Protestants in France (1550–1650), and in the Thirty Years' War that engulfed all of Europe in one of its most bloody and devastating conflicts (1618–1648), is crucial for the way culture and religion are interpreted in international relations today.

History, it is often said, is a fable agreed upon, and the fable in this case is the political mythology of liberalism surrounding the wars of religion. The fable liberal political theorists tell us about the wars of religion is central to the way most people still interpret the mixing of religion and politics, and so it is central to the way that concepts such as fundamentalism, political religion, or religious extremism are constructed.

According to this political myth, what the wars of religion indicate is that when religion is brought into domestic or international public life—when religion is politicized or de-privatized as a type of political theology or political religion, it inherently causes war, intolerance, devastation, political upheaval, and maybe even the collapse of the international order. Therefore, the story goes on to say, the state—the liberal or secular state, is needed to save us from the cruel and violent consequences of religion. The modern state, the privatization of religion, and the secularization of politics arose to limit religion's domestic influence, minimize the affect of religious disputes, and end the bloody and destructive role of religion in international relations.[3] Thus, the political mythology of liberalism is the myth of the modern secular state as our savior from the horrors of modern wars of religion or clashes between civilizations.[4]

The only problem with this myth is that it is historically untrue, but like many myths, it stays with us because its totemic power tells something we want to believe about ourselves as modern men and women. Most scholars of early modern Europe now recognize that the debate and confusion over the role of religion and other political, social, or economic forces in the wars of religion in Europe—like we see being reproduced right now in many of the debates on the role of religion in ethnic conflicts or terrorism, was based on retrospectively applying a modern concept of "religion," as an ideology or set of privately held beliefs or doctrines, to societies which had yet to make this kind of social and cultural transition.

What many historians and anthropologists of early modern Europe now recognize is that no universal concept of religion applicable to all societies and cultures is possible, despite the attempts since the Enlightenment to find one, and not only because the elements of religion are historically specific. Most importantly, the concept of religion is itself the historical product of the discursive practices and history associated with one particular culture, religion, or civilization—Latin Christendom—which has now become the liberal modernity of Western civilization. These social changes then went on to influence ideas about the state, the nation, nationalism, and international society. In other words, at the outset we have to recognize that the very concept of religion is itself the invention of liberal modernity.

The "modern" reading of religion has distorted our understanding of what the wars of religion in early modern Europe were all about, and given the global resurgence of religion, it continues to inhibit our understanding of the role of religion in ethnic and internal wars or in international conflicts today. If we interpret the wars of religion as a backward and barbarous period of European history when people killed each other over clashing religious doctrines—such as the real presence of Christ in the Eucharist— then we will probably also misinterpret the role of religion in the Balkans wars, the Middle East, or anywhere else in the world. This does not mean religion was an unimportant part of the wars of religion or that it is unimportant in wars or ethnic conflicts today. At issue is the *meaning* of religion in early modern Europe, and how this has influenced our understanding of religion in international relations today.

Scholars have come to adopt a social definition of religion, which they believe is compatible with how people understood their religious, moral, and social lives at that time. "Religion" in early modern Europe should be interpreted as a "community of believers" rather than as a "body of beliefs" or doctrines as liberal modernity would have it. Therefore, what was being safeguarded and defended in the wars of religion was a sacred notion of the community defined by religion, as each community fought to define, redefine, or defend the social boundaries between the sacred and the profane as a whole.

How does this social definition of religion help us to better understand the contemporary international order and the pressures that the global resurgence of religion has placed upon it? What this section seeks to show is what I call the invention of religion, as a set of privately held beliefs or doctrines, was a product of state-building—necessary for the rise of the modern state, modern nationalism, and the rise of modern international society.

How did the transition from religion as a community of believers to religion as a set of privately held beliefs and doctrines take place? The full story of this transformation has been told elsewhere.[5] What are important here are those elements of a social theory of religion, which help us to recognize the way the invention of religion has framed the kind of questions we ask about religion in international relations.

During the Middle Ages the term, *religio*, referred to the monastic life, or it was used to describe a particular "virtue" supported by practices embedded in the Christian tradition, as part of an ecclesial community (called the church). In other words, this social definition of religion, as a community of believers, meant the virtues and practices of the Christian tradition were not separated from the tradition and community in which they were embedded and which sustained them.[6] This social understanding of religion can also be called mainstream or "traditional religion," and this is what Christianity signified for most people in early modern Europe.[7]

As a result of the modern concept of religion, the virtues and practices of the Christian tradition come to be separated from the communities in which they were embedded. The modern concept of religion in Latin Christendom begins to emerge in the late fifteenth century, and first appears as a universal, inward impulse or feeling toward the divine common to all people. The varieties of pieties and rituals are increasingly called "religions," as representations of the one (more or less) true *religio* common to all, apart from any ecclesial community. A second major change takes place in the early sixteenth or seventeenth centuries when *religio* begins to shift from being one of various virtues, supported by practices of an ecclesial community embedded in the Christian tradition, to a system of doctrines or beliefs that could exist outside the ecclesial community.

Religion was embedded in the practices of power and discipline regulated by the authoritative structure of the ecclesial community—the Roman Catholic Church in Latin Christendom. What did the rise of the state and rise of nationalism mean for this social understanding of religion? "Religion," as a set of moral and theological propositions, had to be made compatible with the power and discipline of the new monarchies of Europe, by detaching them from the virtues and practices embedded in the religious tradition embodied in the ecclesial community. Religious belief, conscience, and sensibility were privatized by the secularization of politics, and the previous discipline (intellectual and social) of religion was taken over by the state, which was now given the legitimate monopoly on the use of power and coercion in society.

The invention of religion—as a body of ideas—is presupposed rather than critically examined when scholars try to evaluate the impact of religion or theology in early modern Europe, in the rise of nations and nationalism in ethnic or internal conflicts, on promoting international cooperation, or the beginning of modern international society. The growing civil dominance over the Catholic Church by princes and the rise of state power and state churches in Latin Christendom incorporated a transition from a social to a privatized or nationalized concept of religion. For the state to be born, religion had to become privatized and nationalized. The state used the invention of religion to legitimate the transfer of the ultimate loyalty of people from religion to the state as part of the consolidation of its power—the process of state-building and nation-building, which we have come to call internal sovereignty.

The shift to a modern concept of religion was fundamental for the creation of modern international society. For international society to be born religion had to be privatized and nationalized by the state, which is what the princes legitimated as part of the Treaty of Westphalia that ended the Thirty Years' War, and helped to create

European international society. The new concept of religion, allowed the state to discipline religion in domestic society, and the agreement not to interfere in the religious affairs of other countries was used to secure the external sovereignty and independence of states in European international society.

The problem with applying the modern concept of religion to the study of many of the societies in central Europe, central Asia, and most of the non-Western world is that they have still not entirely made, or are struggling not to make, this transition to a modern concept of religion. The privatisation or marginalization of religion is not entirely a part of the Greek Orthodox world, nor is it a part of many non-Western societies incorporated (through colonialism and imperialism) into the modern international society. This is why strong religions and weak states still characterize much of the developing world. These states and faith communities are being forced more than ever before, to define, defend, or redefine the social boundaries between the sacred and the profane in the face of modernization and globalization.[8]

The Global Resurgence of Religion

The global resurgence of religion, as the concept is used in this book, can be defined in the following way:

> the global resurgence of religion is the growing saliency and persuasiveness of religion, i.e. the increasing importance of religious beliefs, practices, and discourses in personal and public life, and the growing role of religious or religiously-related individuals, non-state groups, political parties, and communities, and organizations in domestic politics, and this is occurring in ways that have significant implications for international politics.

The global resurgence of religion describes the ways religion and politics are being mixed together around the world. What is increasingly being challenged is an idea that is part of the political mythology of liberal modernity. This is the idea that religion is, or should be, privatized, restricted to the area of private life in domestic and international politics.

The global resurgence of religion is about what Robert Wuthnow has called the "restructuring of religion" in a global era. A focus on the remolding or restructuring of religion may provide a better way of interpreting how the forces of social and cultural change are coming together because of globalization to bring about a long-term cultural shift in domestic and international politics.[9]

The global resurgence of religion is global in a geographic sense because it is not confined to any particular region of the world, the American South, Central Asia, or the Middle East, and from a comparative politics or comparative religion perspective, it is happening in countries with different types of political systems, and it is occurring in each of the main world religions.[10]

The global resurgence of culture and religion is also taking place in countries with different religious and cultural traditions and in countries at different levels of economic development. This means it is not limited to failed states such as Somalia, Liberia, or Afghanistan, or poverty-stricken regions such as Sudan or Bangladesh, nor those with low levels of economic development, such as Egypt, Sri Lanka, or Thailand.

The global resurgence of religion occurs in oil-rich Saudi Arabia as well as some of the most successful of the Newly Industrialized Countries in the Pacific Rim, such as South Korea, Malaysia, Indonesia, and the Philippines, and in the countries with emerging markets in Latin America. Religion, of course, remains an important feature of politics in the United States, the most modern country in the world.

The idea of a religious resurgence in cultures and countries around the world at different levels of economic development can be understood in an empirical sense and in a theoretical sense. In other words, religion—rituals, practices, ideas, doctrines, discourses, groups, or institutions, in an empirical sense was a dormant, marginal, or less important part of politics during the 1950s and 1960s—the heyday of the theory of modernization. It is now a more observable part of people's private and public lives, and so scholars, if often reluctantly, now acknowledge religion to be a global aspect of politics in the late twentieth century.

Unfortunately, as we also discover in this chapter, an empirical approach to the global resurgence of religion cannot be separated from a theoretical approach, which examines the concepts and assumptions scholars bring to the study of culture or religion in international relations. Another possibility, to put the matter most starkly, is to say religion has always been a part of politics and society in developing countries because the concerns of religion are an inevitable part of what it means to be human. Religion is as much a part of human life as any other aspect of society or culture.[11]

However, on this reckoning, religion is more obvious today only because social scientists have taken off the kind of ideological blinders, which have hidden the role of religion from politics and history. Social scientists are looking at the same phenomenon they were always looking at, but with new or different lens, no longer colored or distorted by the ideologies that have dominated the social sciences—materialism, positivism, and Marxism. This book takes what might be called an intermediary position. There is a global resurgence of religion, but this global and cultural shift is also prompting scholars to rethink their theories and assumptions regarding the study of religion in international relations.

The Levels of Analysis

Among scholars of international relations the concept of the level of analysis was developed to help them sort out the multiplicity of actors, influences, and processes useful for explaining events in international relations. The various levels of analysis—global, inter-state, the state and society levels, and the individual level, that is, the role of key individuals—are perspectives that brings together the actors, influences, and processes at each level of analysis.[12] This framework is set out in figure 1.1.

The impact of the global resurgence of religion on international relations can be seen at each of these levels of analysis. In using this framework it is possible to indicate more fully some of the various aspects of the global resurgence of religion examined in this book.

Global Level

The global or world level of analysis seeks to explain the out-comes in international relations in terms of global natural, social, or

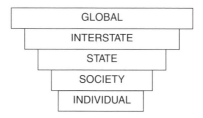

Figure 1.1   The levels of analysis

technological forces that transcend the relations between states at the level of analysis of the international system. It is this level of analysis that is becoming increasingly important because of the integrating and fragmenting effects of globalization on international relations.

Many of the world religions—religious institutions and communities, such as Sufi orders, Catholic missionaries, and Buddhist monks, have had a global influence for centuries. In more recent times this influence was often intermingled with trade, imperialism, religious pilgrimage, and proselytizing or evangelism. What is called transnational religion describes the crossing of state boundaries of religious individuals, institutions, and movements. This activity, like the activity of most religious non-state actors, sometimes predates and increasingly transcends the division of the world into the states that make up the interstate level of analysis.

Many scholars consider the global resurgence of religion to be a part of globalization. Globalization refers to a set of technological processes affecting the world economy, telecommunications, information technology, travel, and growing economic interdependence between states and peoples that is altering our sense of time and space, and is creating the possibility that the world will become a single social space.[13]

Globalization, it is argued, has created a "shrinking world," and so the metaphors abound—spaceship earth, our global neighborhood, global society, global civil society, and global international society. It is argued globalization is rapidly dissolving the social and economic barriers between states, transforming the world's diverse populations into a uniform global market, and at the same time ethnic, religious, and racial hatreds are fragmenting the political landscape into smaller and smaller tribal units. Thus, according to some theorists of globalization, the global resurgence of culture and religion is coming about in response to the paradoxical interdependence of these social forces. Globalization is creating a more unified and a more fragmented or pluralistic world at the same time.[14]

At the global level of analysis the resurgence of religion around the world can be identified as one of the "megatrends" of the twenty-first century. It is one of a number of large scale social and cultural changes taking place across many cultures and countries at the same time that can be examined at the global level of analysis.[15]

Globalization is changing the religious landscape throughout the world. First, globalization is rapidly changing what religion is, and what constitutes religious actors in international relations. Ever since Samuel Huntington popularized the notion of the "clash of civilizations" most accounts of religion in international relations have followed an analysis of the static and rather well-delineated blocs that make up the main world religions and civilizations— Judaism, Christianity, Islam, Buddhism, and Hinduism. However, this assumes a stability in the global religious landscape, and a rather static approach to religious non-state actors that is quite at odds with the reality of religion in the twenty-first century. Scholars concerned about change in international relations also need to be concerned about how globalization is changing religion as well, and what effect this may have on international relations.[16]

There is a constantly evolving role of religion in international relations. Rapid religious and social changes are taking place in the Islamic world, which has produced a variety of the Islamic non-state actors we see in the newspapers every day now—al-Qaeda, Hamas, Islamic Jihad, and so on—but there are a variety of Islamic non-state actors that are not terrorist groups, and a variety of new non-state actors in all of the other world religions as well.

There is a whole array of what are called new religious movements in the sociology of religion—such as the Fulan Gong and Pentecostalism—which have millions and millions of followers around the world. They are also shaping the global cultural, religious, and political landscape on which states and non-state actors operate. Pentecostalism, for example, is at the cutting edge of Christian growth in China, Korea, Thailand, and Vietnam. Although this region is constantly referred to as the Pacific Rim, how would it change our image of world politics if we recognized that it could also be called the "Christian arc" above Indonesia, the country with the largest Muslim population in the world?[17]

Second, globalization is helping to create or expand the existing ethnic and religious diaspora communities around the world. The mass migration across state boundaries, usually for economic or political reasons—to flee poverty or oppression, or in the case of slavery, as a result of oppression—has been going on for several centuries. Although there are other factors, such as the aftermath of war, globalization is helping to create and expand religious diaspora communities around the world.

Religious diaspora communities are one of the most significant types of non-state actors in world politics in the twenty-first century. It is already complicating the issue of security and global terrorism—for example, in Europe is Hamas a social welfare organization or is it a terrorist organization? The fact that al-Qaeda can use the *hawala* network, the global, informal networks of Islamic finance, to move money around the world does not make this form of finance illegitimate; it only speaks to the pervasiveness of Islamic diaspora communities in world politics.[18]

Another aspect of religious diaspora communities is the changing nature of global missions. Missionary activity, as a North–South activity, has long dispersed new or different religious and cultural ideas and values around the world. What is new, facilitated by global travel, with the vibrancy of religious life in developing countries, is that missionary activity is becoming a South–North phenomena, with a variety of Buddhists, Hindus, Muslims, and Christians from developing countries promoting America's and Europe's re-evangelization. The way more radical, militant, conservative, or extremist forms of religion (there are no neutral terms to use here) have appeared in the West is only one aspect of this global phenomenon—what Felipe Fernandez-Armesto has called "counter-colonization." If he is correct, then the spread of Hinduism, Buddhism, and "New Age" spiritualities in the West is also another aspect of it, and is part of the "revenge of the East" that is transforming the notions of religion and spirituality in Western modernity.[19]

Third, globalization is facilitating the more rapid spread of cultural and religious pluralism. One of the most commented on features of globalization is the way diverse cultures and religions are no longer in exotic, faraway places of which we know very little. Most of us now live in communities with a variety of churches, mosques, temples, and synagogues, and their worshipers are our friends, neighbors, coworkers, and classmates. It is an inherent part of what we identify as the postmodern world.[20]

Fourth, the large-scale religious changes in world politics are being accompanied by the global vitality and growth in Islam and Christianity. The media often casts Islam as the defining religion of the developing world, but this can be contested. The global spread of Christianity is shifting its center of gravity from the industrialized countries to the developing world. The majority of Christians in the world by 2050 will be nonwhite, non-Western, will be from the developing world, will espouse forms of Christianity that are far more emotive and charismatic than those found in the West, and many of them will be living as minorities under non-Christian and often hostile regimes.[21] The support for freedom of religion has become a key aspect of U.S. foreign policy (as opposed to supporting these elements as an overall human rights foreign policy). This shift in U.S. foreign policy, as we see in chapter 8, partly emerges from these changes in global religion.

What happens when the vitality of Islam and Christianity meet in countries throughout the developing world? This social and political situation is unprecedented in world politics, and scholars have not even started to think through its consequences for international relations. A similar situation has not existed since the Middle Ages. There were crusades and wars of religion, but as any study of Thomas Aquinas shows, it was also the last time intellectuals in the West took Islam seriously—its ideas, values, culture, and civilization.[22] This is the other side of the story of the clash of civilizations.

Fifth, the spread of new religious movements has hardly had any impact on the study of non-state actors in international relations theory. Much of the study of non-state actors, as we see in chapter 4, is still dominated by the notion that NGO coalitions and new social movements are forming a brave new world of global civil society.

This kind of partial vision has missed the full impact of the revival of Islam and Christianity in the global South and the spread of new religious movements that are also creating global religious subcultures, which may play as important a role as transnational NGO coalitions—on human rights, the environment, or world poverty, in shaping the future of world politics, world civilization, or global civil society.[23] In the aftermath of the Cold War, it is all of these types of global subcultures that are going to be part of the contested and competing meanings of world politics in the twenty-first century.[24]

Interstate Level

The global resurgence of religion can also be examined at the more common level of analysis of the international system. At this level there is a more conventional understanding of states and their interests, including foreign policy—military power, arms races, alliances, the balance of power, and the spheres of interest, as well as the role of states in conflict and international cooperation.

The general issue at this level of analysis is that religion was no longer supposed to be a part of international politics because of the "Westphalian presumption" in international society. This is the notion that religious and cultural pluralism cannot be accommodated in international public life, and is part of the political mythology of liberalism surrounding the wars of religion.

The origins of the modern international system goes back to the Treaty of Westphalia (1648) that brought the Thirty Years' War to an end. These treaties ended the legitimacy of religion as a source of international conflict among the states of Christendom. The new Westphalian system recognized the state as the dominant actor, replacing the transnational authority of the Catholic Church, and it established political realism and the secular principle of *raison d'etat* (reason of state) as the main principles of statecraft by replacing religion as the basis of foreign policy.

However, for some time now religion has been returning from exile, overturning the Westphalian presumption in international relations. This can be seen in less spectacular ways than the Iranian and Polish Revolutions or in the rise of global religious violence. It can be seen, as part two shows, in the rise of faith-based diplomacy, the World Faiths Development Dialogue started by Dr. George Carey, the former Archbishop of Canterbury, and James Wolfensohn, the president of the World Bank, in the role of the world's religious leaders at the United Nations, and at the annual meetings of the World Economic Forum in Davos, Switzerland, and in the growing role of religion in peacemaking and conflict resolution.

The early English School, as we see in chapter 6, argued that the various international systems in history have been based on a common culture—most often influenced by religion, such as the ancient Greek city–state system. It drew attention to the cultural foundations of the working of the balance of power in European diplomacy, and more generally, to the role of culture and religion in international cooperation.

Questions about the meaning of the cultural or religious foundation of a state system has surfaced with the debate Jacques Delors, the former president of the European Commission, started over the idea of the "the soul of Europe," and it is part of the debate over the place of Europe's Judeo–Christian heritage in the European Constitution. The role of culture and religion also surfaces in the debate over Turkey's membership—as an Islamic state in the new Europe after the fall of communism.

The early English School posed the question about the cultural foundations of state systems during decolonization, when more and more countries were gaining their freedom and independence. What had been a European international society was expanding to become a global international society. What would be the common culture underlying this global international society? The answer they gave, during the heyday of modernization theory, was that Western modernity would provide the culture of global international society. However, developing countries have reacted to the way the culture of Western modernity is being imposed on their societies. This can be seen in the debates at the UN conferences on human rights, women, and population, and in the way religion continues to influence foreign policy.

State and Society

These levels of analysis considers the types of social, economic, or political actors that influence the state's domestic and foreign policies, and the wider political culture in which these actors and influences are embedded. The politics of ethnic conflict and nationalism, the resurgence of religion in states at different level of economic development, the religious challenge to the secular state, or the impact of the military–industrial complex are located at these domestic levels of analysis.

At the state and society levels of analysis global religious communities and subcultures are starting to complicate multi-faith relations in the West on a host of social policy and public policy issues. They challenge the way religion has been separated from the public square. Religion has become one of the new types of what are called "intermestic" policy issues in international relations, that is, issues that symbolize the merger of domestic and international politics. This concept has mainly been used to examine the way domestic economic issues have an international dimension, such as when American shoe companies want lower tariffs on Japanese imports of American shoes, but it also increasingly applies to multiethnic as well as multi-faith relations.[25]

The uproar among British Muslims regarding Ayatollah Khomenei's *fatwa* against Salmon Rushdie, and the issues it raised regarding freedom of speech, religious toleration, and the laws on blasphemy is only the most prominent example of the way multi-faith relations has become an intermestic issue in world politics. French foreign policy toward Algeria is closely related to French domestic policy toward North African immigrants. Young French

Muslims, for example, who were born in France, but whose parents may come from Algeria or Morocco, are coming to recognize in Islam a transnational identity. In France they may be a minority, but in pan-Islamic unity with other Muslims around the world they perceive themselves to be in the majority.

Multi-faith relations have become an intermestic issue in Britain. This can be seen in the problem of so-called "honor killings" among Muslim families in Britain and Pakistan. If young Pakistani women in Britain choose a husband on their own without the approval of the more traditional family, there are instances when she or her husband or boy friend are murdered by members of her family. This issue combines globalization with problems of murder, immigration, individual freedom, and religious freedom, and with the broader issue of how religious and cultural traditions are interpreted.

A number of other multi-faith issues are becoming intermestic issues in world politics as well because of the way what are perceived in the West as minority religious communities are really a part of global religious subcultures. The politics surrounding the ritual slaughter of animals is one such increasingly emotive issue in multi-faith relations. At issue is whether in democratic and pluralistic societies are there ways in which religions are above the law or a law unto themselves? The particular Jewish and Muslim regulations for the *kosher* and *halal* ritual slaughter of animals can come into conflict with animal rights activists, or possibly even secular society's general guidelines regarding the humane treatment of animals.[26]

The issue of young girls wearing the Islamic veil in schools erupted in France right after the Rushdie affair, and, in the aftermath of September 11, it has made headlines again with France's ban on wearing conspicuous religious symbols—headscarves, skull caps, turbans, or crosses. It is argued French law protects freedom of religion and conscience, but such symbols contradict the French principles of *laïcité* (secularization), which seeks to exclude religion from public life, allegedly in the interests of religious toleration.

What is at issue in many of these examples is the way liberal modernity has invented religion as a system of private belief, and so religious freedom is interpreted as an aspect of freedom of conscience, and is defended by European human rights provisions in this way. However, there is still a social dimension to many global religions, and so private belief and public practice and observance cannot be so easily separated. The way multi-faith relations has become an intermestic issue in world politics illustrates the ideological assumptions behind what are often thought to be the state's neutral notions of religion and toleration, and the way these notions are challenged by the global resurgence of religion.

Individual Level

The individual level of analysis covers the perceptions, choices, values, and beliefs of individuals, and the impact they can have on international relations. Globalization has facilitated the role of individuals in world politics, and explanations at this level of analysis probe how different individuals, with different beliefs or characteristics make different choices.

A cautionary note is in order. The individual level of analysis emphasizes the role of individuals, personality traits, education, socialization, and cognitive or psychological factors that influence individuals and their decision-making. However, there are often unstated assumptions at this level of analysis, as we see in chapters 2 and 3, regarding liberal notions of "the self," individual freedom, and autonomy. These assumptions, and the rational choice theory on which they are sometimes based, examine individual decisionmaking quite apart from the cultural or religious traditions in which such notions of choice and rationality are embedded.

Many scholars have not recognized until recently that respected religious leaders or individuals—Ayatollah Khomeini, Pope John Paul II, the Dalai Lama, Martin Luther King, Oscar Romaro, Desmond Tutu, Gandhi, or Aung San Suu Kyi can become actors in international relations. Some of these people are what Peter Paris has called "moral exemplars in global community," and have had an impact on the ideas and values in world politics.[27]

Ordinary people also can become actors in international relations at extraordinary times—A. T. Ariyaratne, a teacher who became the founder of the Sarvodaya community development movement in Sri Lanka, Lech Walesa, the unemployed electrician, who played a key role in Solidarity, or Beyers Naude, the Afrikaner who founded the Christian Institute, and sat with the ANC delegation when it met with the South African government for the first time.

We are now more aware of what Thomas Friedman, the foreign affairs columnist at *The New York Times*, has called the angry, "super-empowered individuals," who are involved in terrorist activity, but this underplays the role of a Gandhi, a Rosa Parks, a Martin Luther King, or a Albert Lutuli, and how their efforts influenced the ANC in South Africa, aboriginal struggles in Australia, and countless other struggles for nonviolent political change around the world. Now, after September 11, we may be more aware that individuals as non-state actors can have a devastating impact on world politics. However, righteous or indignant, committed individuals, if not super-empowered ones, are also involved in world politics, and they will always be there, as long as people feel compelled as active citizens to work peacefully for social justice and political transformation. Globalization can facilitate the positive action of individuals in world politics as well.

Explaining the Global Resurgence of Religion

The concept of the global resurgence of religion raises some of the same kind of analytical difficulties Samuel Huntington encountered when he examined the global spread of democracy.[28] If the concept can be defined by what social scientists call a similar or general type of event occurring in different places and in different cultures or religions at about the same time, then the global resurgence of religion may be explained in a number of ways.

It is important to be clear about the phenomena this book is trying to explain or understand in international relations. The dependent variable in this book is not greater religiosity per se, for in that case it would be a book about comparative religion or the sociology of religion. What is being explained is how the greater levels of religiosity or even spirituality are taking place in public life, and doing so in ways that have an impact on international relations. It is for this reason the concept of the global resurgence of religion is broader than religious extremism or fundamentalism.

Huntington has said that the following types of explanation are not exhaustive, nor are they mutually exclusive, nor do they have to be contradictory. They all may be at work in various ways. What these different types of explanation bring out is the importance of the different levels of analysis for understanding the global resurgence of religion.

Single Cause

If the global resurgence of religion is occurring within separate, or diverse states, societies, cultures, or religions—the Islamic Revolution in Iran, the rise of the Moral Majority in the United States, or the global spread of Pentecostal Christianity, then this may indicate that there is a single cause or a common influence on these events. It may indicate a single cause within a particular region of the world, or maybe even a single cause within a particular religious tradition.

If there is a global resurgence of religion as the concept has been defined in this book, then the first questions to ask about it are, "What is the phenomena that is being explained by the global resurgence of religion," or "Is this a coincidental trend?" The global resurgence of religion is far from cohesive in its goals, objectives, or tactics. It includes an Islamic resurgence in both Arab and non-Arab Muslim countries—Iran, Saudi Arabia, Egypt, Malaysia, and Indonesia, the growth of evangelical Christianity, liberation theology, and Pentecostal Protestant Christianity in Latin America, Jewish revivalism, and the growing role of spirituality in corporate America as well as Hindu and Sikh activism in India.[29]

Possibly, in a more direct sense, it is easier to see this single cause explanation operating within particular religious traditions rather than influencing all of them at once. The global impact of Vatican II, for example, leading to a change in the Catholic Church's support for democracy rather than authoritarianism influenced the spread of democracy in Catholic countries, particularly in Poland, the Philippines, in Latin America, and elsewhere.[30]

Remarkably, the global spread of Pentecostal Christianity that may be transforming the possibilities for democracy and economic development in Latin America began with a single cause, the Azusa Street revival in Los Angeles at the beginning of the twentieth century. A group of poor, down and out black and white hymn singers, itinerant evangelists, domestic servants, janitors, and day workers in a run down section of Los Angeles believed a new Pentecost was happening, a new outpouring of the holy spirit in today's world.[31]

The defeat of the Arabs in the Six Day War in 1967, is another single cause, which led to a crisis in Arab nationalism is often seen as one of the main factors contributing to the rise of Islamic fundamentalism. It should be remembered, however, that this had at first a greater impact on Arabs than it did the broader Muslim world (although with the globalization of Islam this is changing).

Parallel Development

The global resurgence of religion may be caused by a parallel development in separate states, societies, cultures, or religions. In other words, the same independent variables manifest themselves almost simultaneously in different countries. Huntington's example of this type of explanation is the idea that a country is likely to develop democracy once it passes certain thresholds in economic development.

This type of explanation for the global resurgence of religion goes to the heart of the contemporary debates among scholars regarding the causes of the September 11 tragedy and the spread of religiously motivated terrorism or fundamentalism. It is the idea that there may be a common independent variable or a common influence in these separate states or societies, which is behind the cultural antagonism that causes religious extremism, fundamentalism, and terrorism.

Scholars disagree over what may be the common cause explaining the global resurgence of religion as a parallel development in different societies or communities—social exclusion, world poverty, or the absence of democracy. It is this latter explanation, for example, that is behind the analysis of the Arab Human Development Report.[32]

This chapter argues that the common influence leading to the parallel development of the global resurgence of religion is the impact of globalization on a wide-ranging cultural revolt against secular modernity (here, please note the adjective, secular, in front of modernity). What this book defines as the global resurgence of religion is often rather narrowly identified by many scholars as religious extremism, terrorism, or fundamentalism, and is identified with a fundamentalist revolt against modernity. The problem with this explanation is that it is based on unstated and often unchallenged assumptions regarding religion, modernity, and secularism that are a part of the political mythology of liberalism.

Snowballing Effect

The global resurgence of religion might be the result of a snowballing effect, in which the religious revivalism in one country starts to affect other countries. The possibility of this explanation is increased by globalization because knowledge of social or political events in one country can trigger off events that are comparable in other countries.

In other words, demonstration effects, or what scholars have called "emulative linkages" are more likely because global information and telecommunications more closely link together states and societies around the world.[33] After the Iranian Revolution there was a fear among Western policymakers that "Iran-style" popular religious upheavals could spread to other Arab or Islamic countries. The way the Indian army stormed the Sikh's holist shrine, the Golden Temple at Amritsar in Punjab, which led to prime minister Indira Gandhi's assassination, angered the global Sikh community.

Now, there is a concern that suicide bombing may become a type of emulative linkage in world politics. It may be copied by sympathetic Islamic groups in other countries (Bali, Madrid, Israel), or as we see in chapter 5, in the violence between Amal and Hezbullah in Lebanon (and maybe now in Iraq among the Shiite groups), suicide bombing and terrorism were copied as part of the rivalry between religious groups.

Prevailing Nostrum

Another possibility is that the global resurgence of religion may have taken place because of changes in the prevailing nostrum, or the prevailing remedy—in this case modernization. It is possible that the immediate causes of the global resurgence of religion differ significantly in each country, but that these different causes prompt a common response if the elites in a country or possibly, even the mass population, share a common enough belief in the efficacy of the *zeitgeist*'s prevailing remedy or nostrum.

A break-down in the *zeitgeist* is the opposite possibility, and so a common belief develops that something else should be tried—Arab nationalism, Hindu nationalism, and so on. The specific individual causes for the global resurgence of religion act on a common set of beliefs, or in this case, a breakdown in the common set of beliefs.

Democratic transitions, for example, may have taken place in different countries to cope with a variety of problems—military defeat, inflation, a breakdown in law and order, or deepening economic recession. The global resurgence of religion may be a response to the crisis of the liberal state in the West as well as the crisis of the secular and modernizing state in the developing world.

Questioning the Secular State

The global resurgence of religion can be seen as one of the results of the failure of the secular, modernizing state to produce democracy or development in the developing world. Developing countries, since the period of colonial occupation, have been confronted with a dilemma: should they emulate the West and spurn their own culture in order to gain equality in power, or should they affirm their own cultural and religious traditions but remain materially weak?[34]

In many countries this dilemma of identity and development was resolved in the first years after independence by emulating the West—development, modernization, and Westernization all appeared to mean the same thing. The first generation of Third World elites that came to power beginning in the late 1940s— Nehru's India, Nasser's Egypt, Sukarno's Indonesia (and going back to the 1920s, Ataturk's Turkey)—espoused a similar "modernizing mythology" inherited from the West based on the rather taken-for-granted superiority of Western scientific, technological, pluralistic, and democratic values and assumptions based on the Enlightenment.

The modernizing mythology was based on the notions of democracy, secularism, socialism, and nonalignment between the superpowers in foreign policy. The elites believed strong states could promote political stability and economic development, and this would be undermined if religion, ethnicity, or caste dominated politics.[35] This modernizing mythology failed to produce democracy or economic development. There was a general failure of the modernizing, secular state, evident by subsequent "political decay," the decline of politics into corruption, authoritarianism, and patrimonialism, since the late 1960s, and by the rise of failed or collapsed states since the late 1980s.[36]

What is called political religion or politicized religion emerges out of a perceived failure of secular, state-run, nationalism to produce democracy, and the failure of the neo-liberal prescription of free markets and open economies, which produced more inequality than development. The conflict between religious nationalism and secular nationalism intensified to became one of the most important developments in the politics of developing countries in the 1990s. This can be seen in a variety of conflicts from Sri Lanka to India to Central Asia, and, of course, in the Balkans, Egypt, Israel, and Palestine.[37]

Authenticity and Development

The global resurgence of religion can also be seen as part of the search for authenticity and development in the developing world.

The global resurgence of religion in developing countries can be seen as part of the "revolt against the West." Three "waves of revolt" can be identified; the first, from the 1940s through the 1960s, was the anticolonial struggle for independence and sovereign equality, but this revolt was expressed within a Western intellectual discourse— the ideas about freedom, democracy, and self-determination came from the West; the second, from the 1970s through the 1980s, was the struggle for racial equality—seen most vividly in the struggle against apartheid in South Africa, and in the struggle for economic justice—the call for a North–South dialogue; and now the third— the struggle for cultural liberation— is the reassertion of traditional and indigenous cultures in the developing world.[38]

The third wave of revolt, or global "struggle for authenticity," became more powerful in the 1990s. In developing countries the modernizing, secular state has failed to provide a legitimate basis for political participation and a basic level of economic welfare for its citizens. In many developing countries secular nationalism, Arab or African socialism in Algeria, Egypt, Zambia, and Tanzania during the 1960s, or Afro-Communism in Angola, Ethiopia, and Mozambique in the late 1970s failed to produce economic development and extend political participation. Thus, authenticity has begun to rival development as the key to understanding the political aspirations of the non-Western World. In the search for a more authentic political system the debate is increasingly about how to mix political and religious authority as well as promote economic development.[39]

Conclusion:
Religion in a Postmodern World

The global resurgence of religion can be seen as part of the larger crisis of modernity. The resurgence of religious faith is a type of cultural critique of the kind of world modernity has brought us. It marks the end of a certain kind of modern faith in the idea of progress, and an optimism about the ability of science and technology to solve the problems created by the modern world. The global resurgence of religion does not signal an end to a belief in reason, but it does indicate the end to a belief in secular reason.

The roots of the struggle for authenticity and the questioning of modernity go back to what Gilles Kepel has called, "the revenge of God," the great reversal of the 1970s when faith in science and technology, along with modernity and progress in the West, and in the modernizing mythology espoused in developing countries lost their totemic power and started to go into reverse.[40] A new religious approach began to take shape in the 1970s based on the search for authentic identity, meaning, and economic development. In the West there had been earlier attempts to "modernize" Protestantism—the creation of liberal Protestantism, which tried to help Protestant Christianity come to terms with the Enlightenment and to adapt religion to the modern world. A similar attempt to "modernize" Catholicism—liberal Catholicism—also took place in the nineteenth century, but it was resisted until the Second Vatican Council.[41] However, the point of departure for these efforts at religious modernism was a recognition that religion had to come of age, and had come to terms with the fact that science, technology, and progress had created a new form of life—called modernity, which was now the global home of all of us.

What can be defined as the global resurgence of religion results from a collapse in the faith of modernizing religion, and is motivated by the desire of people of different faiths and cultures to rethink and reevaluate how religion and modernity are related. It reflects a deeper and more widespread disillusionment with a modernity that has reduced the world to what can be perceived and controlled through reason, science, technology, and leaves out the sacred, religion, or spirituality.

Thomas Friedman tapped into this phenomenon while traveling around the United States to promote his book on globalization. People kept asking, he says, "[e]ven if we get the right politics, geopolitics, geo-economics and geo-management for sustainable globalization, there is another, less tangible, set of policies that need to be kept in mind—the olive tree needs in us all: the need for community, for spiritual meaning and for values with which to raise our children. Those have to be protected and nurtured as well for globalization to be sustainable."[42]

Gilles Kepel has identified this disillusionment with modernity as part of the resurgence of Judaism, Christianity, and Islam around the world. "Like the workers' movement of yesteryear," he goes on to say, "today's religious movements have a singular capacity to reveal the ills of society, for which they have their own diagnosis." He continues to explain,

> Our working hypothesis will be that what these movements say and do is meaningful, and does not spring from a dethronement of

reason or from manipulation by hidden forces; rather it is the unde-
niable evidence of a deep malaise in society that can no longer be
interpreted in terms of our traditional categories of thought.[43]

At this point Kepel's analysis is close to that of William James,
who believed it was the "sick souls" rather than the optimistic,
"healthy-minded" ones who had a "profounder view" of the modern
situation.[44] It was, as Charles Taylor has observed, an Augustinian
insight, which James built his theory of religion on, "that in certain
domains love and self-opening enable us to understand what we
would never grasp otherwise, rather than just following on understanding as its normal consequence."[45] What if the global
resurgence of religion can no longer be interpreted within the
traditional categories of social theory? Such a perspective has
hardly made any inroads in the mainstream study of international
relations.

What this suggests is that the global resurgence of religion
cannot only be interpreted as a "fundamentalist" or "anti-modern"
reaction to the inevitable and inexorable spread of modernization
and globalization. Like Kepel, Casanova argues, "Against those
evolutionary theories which prefer to interpret what I call the
'deprivatization' of modern religion as anti-modern fundamentalist
reactions to inevitable processes of differentiation, I argue that at
least some forms of 'public religion' may also be understood as
counterfactual normative critiques of dominant historical trends, in
many respects similar to the classical, republican, and feminist
critiques."[46] Thus, the global resurgence of religion can be understood as a parallel development in the developed world and
in developing countries that is part of a wider, already existing,
critique of global modernity, authenticity, and development.

A postmodern perspective begins with a recognition that modernity's discontents have shown us that the Enlightenment's promise
of freedom, autonomy, and meaning through rationality and knowledge has turned out to be a hallow one.[47] It shares a basic insight
with those artists, theologians, and cultural critics who recognize
the limits to the disenchantment of the world, a trend foreseen by
George Simmel over a century ago, who worried that the growing
attachment to this "world of things" would steadily devalue the
human world.[48]

At least in the developed world, from the United States or
Europe to the Pacific Rim, with rising affluence, the renaissance of

the arts and culture, represents this perspective, and is another one of the "megatrends" of the twenty-first century. The arts are contributing to a deeper, may be even spiritual, examination of life, and so what it means to be human is expressed in a variety of cultural and literary revivals in different regions of the world.[49] Thus, the postmodern world is turning out to be a post-secular world as well. It is giving rise to what is increasingly called post-modern theology and spirituality, which recognizes that identity is linked to relationships with the family, society, and the natural world, which can be seen as part of a larger divine reality.[50]

What a postmodern perspective opens up is the possibility that there may be other ways of being "modern," making "progress," or being "developed." Although postmodernity can mean a lot of things, in this sense it suggests that rather than there only being one path to modernity—Westernization, there may be multiple paths, "multiple modernities," or multiple ways of being modern appropriate to the different cultural and religious traditions in the developing world.[51] This is one of the promises of what is called a postmodern world.

For all these reasons the twentieth century may be the "last modern century."[52] It may be very misleading to view the global resurgence of religion through such lenses as the "clash of civiliza-tions," "fundamentalism" or religious "extremism"—as if the global resurgence of religion is an aberration in an otherwise "modern" world. A truly multicultural international society is being formed for the first time, and finding out what it means to take cultural and religious pluralism seriously is one of the most important aspects of international politics in the twenty-first century.

CHAPTER 2

BLIND SPOTS AND BLOWBACK: WHY CULTURE AND RELIGION WERE MARGINALIZED IN INTERNATIONAL RELATIONS THEORY

The learned have their superstitions, prominent among them is a belief that superstition is evaporating.[1]

—*Garry Wills*

Religion can no longer be ignored. Did the tragic events on September 11 have something to do with culture and religion or were they about something else? If this is an important question to answer—and, another question is whether or not this is an important question (Paul Berman, for example, argues that we have to defend ourselves regardless of why people are attacking us)—then how should we go about trying to answer it? What kind of implications does the answer we come up with have for the conduct of U.S. foreign policy, the war on terrorism, national security, or Western security more generally? Another set of questions are about the implications of the answer we come up with for promoting a dialogue between civilizations, international cooperation, and international development. What the right questions to ask about the impact of culture and religion in international affairs are, and how we should go about trying to answer them is now one of the most important questions in the study of international relations.

Why is this the case? It is increasingly apparent some of the same assumptions about culture, religion, and secularization theory that social theorists have used to try to answer the many questions people have asked since September 11 resemble the earlier assumptions and theories social scientists used to explain Christian fundamentalism and evangelical Christianity.[2] Asking why people are attracted to religious extremism or fundamentalism is similar to one of the main questions asked after World War II, "Why were people attracted to fascism in Italy and Nazism in Germany?" or "Why were people attracted to communism?"[3]

Many social theorists accept the idea that secularization is a simple, inherent, linear process leading to progress, modernization, and development. Adopting what is variously called traditional religion, religious extremism, or fundamentalism is considered to be like other forms of "irrationalism," ideological extremism, or reactionary politics—fascism or Nazism. They are all considered to be a way of coping with various kinds of desperation, declining social status, or economic and social exclusion.[4]

What if this explanation turns out to be mistaken, or at least it is inadequate to explain the robust, and persistent impact of religion in the United States, the most modern country in the world? What if it turns out to be a mistaken explanation for the mega-churches in the burgeoning megacities in many parts of the developing world—Seoul, Manila, Sao Paulo, Lagos, and Nairobi, and so on? Well, then it may have a limited ability to explain the impact of religion in international affairs.

Conceptual Maps

It is a problem of using the correct conceptual maps to interpret what is taking place. Using the wrong conceptual map—or theory or paradigm—can be just as misleading (and maybe even more dangerous for your security) than using the wrong geographical map—one of the Rocky Mountains in the western United States—to navigate your way around the Alps in Europe. The point is not only that such maps indicate inappropriate routes, but that they can hide or distract a researcher from observing those features of the religious and political landscape that do require attention.[5]

Any analogy can be pressed too far. In this case it is not only a matter of competing maps, but in social theory using a general map called "mountains" that can be used as a guide to any particular mountain range. This is, of course, what scholars have done since the late seventeenth and early eighteenth century with what I called the "invention of religion" in the last chapter as a universal concept of modernity. Religion has become a type of common human experience related to divinity or the sacred applicable to all societies, without acknowledging the assumptions about modernity that lay behind this conception.

Max Weber also did this with his concept of "ideal-types" that could then be set against multiple examples of reality. Modernization is conceived of borrowing from the West, and the degree of social change is determined by the proximity to which values, ideas, and institutions—supposedly perfected in the West, such as an inner-worldly asceticism, the separation of church and the state, rule of law, or the nuclear family are accepted in society. The existing culture and religion—traditional society, is from this perspective a barrier to be overcome if social change and modern ways of thinking and acting are to occur.

At issue here is a particular conceptual map developed by the main founders of social theory, which posited a strong relationship between a decline in religion with secularization, modernization, and globalization. In other words, in terms of the map analogy, is a decrease in religion a necessary feature of the modern landscape, and so the outcrops of fundamentalism or religious extremism are its residual features, leading for the moment to extremism and terrorism, but in time they will be warn away by the pressures of modernization and globalization?

Is a decline in religion an intrinsic or inherent part of modernization, or is it an extrinsic part of it in the sense that it occurs in some countries and not in other ones? If this is the case, then might there be what Eisenstadt has called "multiple modernities"—multiple maps in a global and multicultural society—and so we should not make the same assumptions about culture and religion for all societies, communities, or states in international relations?[6]

It was Europeans, of course, the founding fathers of sociology—Weber, Durkheim, and Marx—who developed secularization theory. This is the origin of the belief that what occurred as part of Europe's modernization will happen in time everywhere else in the world, and it is the origin of the conviction that as the world modernizes, it will necessarily secularize.

What happens to our analysis of the global resurgence of culture and religion if Europe—rather than the United States—turns out to be the exceptional case, as Peter Berger and a number of prominent European sociologists have now argued? In other words, what happens if it turns out that the assumption that secularization is an inherent feature of modernization may only be applicable in some sense to "European religion," and is not a model for export as we try to understand the resurgence of culture and religion in the politics of countries in the rest of the world.[7] This proposition may be very difficult for many Europeans; indeed, perhaps, many Westerners, to accept since—if, the truth be told—they are used to having *their* culture or civilization as the main exemplar of what modernity means for the rest of the world.

Is Western Modernity the Global Home for Us All?

The first reason why the global resurgence of religion was unexpected is because of the way culture and religion were neglected or marginalized in social theory. It might seem like this is an odd thing to say, given the important studies of religion by Weber, Durkheim, and other scholars who developed the sociology of religion. However, as Robert Wuthnow has emphasized, the main assumptions of social theory helped to explain religion away, rather than to explain its significance in social action.[8] If this is the case, then it should not be so surprising that culture and religion were marginalized in the study of international relations.

Culture and religion came to be neglected or marginalized in international relations because of the impact of modernization theory. The classical sociologists analyzed culture and religion in the context of the original transition from "traditional society" to "modern society," the society created by capitalism and industrialism that emerged in Western Europe, spread to North America, and is now spreading around the world.

The main U.S. foreign policy debates after World War II focused on two areas. The first focused on how to conduct the nuclear arms race and was confronted with the security dilemmas of European geopolitics (i.e. the Berlin crisis and the debate over massive retaliation or flexible response in nuclear strategy). The second focused on the struggles in the developing world for political independence and economic development.[9]

The ideas on culture and religion from the classical sociological tradition influenced the theory of modernization that was developed by American social scientists in response to the nationalist pressures for decolonization at the start of the Cold War. In other words, modernization theory provided from the start what was meant to be—in Walt Rostow's memorable phrase—"a non-Communist manifesto," a way to promote political and economic development as part of the struggle against communism in the third world.[10]

Modernization meant the complete transformation of the economic, social, cultural, and political infrastructure of developing countries. The characteristics of modern society seemed conspicuously to match those of the United States, if not always those of Western Europe. "Although it has been the subject of much criticism, its assumptions continue to under gird much of our conventional wisdom about religion and politics."[11] Therefore, it is important to examine modernization theory's assumptions since this conventional wisdom still informs the view of culture and religion taken by many scholars of international relations.

Modernization theory focuses on what was referred to as the level of analysis of the state and society rather than the analysis of the international relations in chapter 1. It focuses on what is wrong with developing countries rather than what is wrong at the level of analysis of the international system—the constraints or opportunities provided by international politics or the global economy. Modernization theory reemerged in the literature and policy debates on democracy, civil society, and good governance in 1990s because of the way poor governance, and political instability had clearly undermined the economic development of Africa. An active civil society was an important part of the democratic changes in Latin America, Eastern Europe, and Southern Europe.[12]

The first assumption of modernization theory is that a "modern society" can be clearly distinguished from a "traditional society," or at least a society in the process of becoming modern through economic development. Scholars already recognized by the late 1960s that the distinction between traditional and modern society was not as clear-cut as the theory indicated, but this conception still bedevils our understanding of a religious tradition as something static and monolithic, rather than something dynamic and changing. Although it was recognized that traditional society was more complex and not a static or monolithic unity, an ongoing, public role for religious personnel and religious institutions in society was still considered to be part of a traditional and not a modern society.

The second aspect of modernization theory is that modernization is conceived to be a linear, progressive conception of social change, a universal theory, applicable to all non-Western societies that were in the process of becoming "modern," that is they were making an inevitable transition toward a common end. The existing differences between societies were considered to be "residual" or temporary obstacles that would gradually be overcome as these societies became more modern. This aspect of modernization theory has now crumbled to the ground as thoroughly as the Twin Towers. John Gray argues that September 11 did more than kill thousands of people and demolish the World Trade Center. It also destroyed the West's ruling myth—the belief that modernity, that is, Western modernity, is a single global condition, the global home for all of us.[13]

Secularization is the third aspect of modernization theory, and it is social theory's assumptions about secularization that have had the most negative implications for the study of culture and religion in international relations. Generally, it has been widely assumed since the eighteenth century that secularization was, and remains, an inherent feature of modernization.

Although secularization theory has become a more contested concept than is often realized by scholars of international relations, for a long time it has been the conventional wisdom since the social sciences were created. It is in some ways an empirical claim— although Robert Bellah, as we will see, considers it to be a myth about the way society is organized.

The general proposition of secularization theory was straightforward. It is argued that the numbers of people who declare themselves to be believers and who regularly attend religious services will steadily decline as a country modernizes since the kind of cultural pluralism modernity creates undermines the stability of belief. There will also be a steady retreat of religion from the public square, as social, economic, and political institutions are transformed toward religious and ideological neutrality and lose their religious identity.[14] In a modern society religion continues to be influential only if it is "modernized," that is, it conforms to modern norms, such as rationality, relativism, and pluralism, and makes compromises with the modern secular state, science, and economics.[15] It is argued today that this is what has happened with the rise of liberal Protestantism and liberal Catholicism, and it has yet to happen in Islam.[16]

It is now recognized that that even if there is growing separation—or, differentiation in sociological language, between religion and the state, that is, political secularization, and even if there is growing social and cultural pluralism—it does not necessarily lead to the full-scale secularization of society.[17]

Chapter 1 referred to Robert Wuthnow's concept of the "restructuring of religion" in a global era to describe the religious change now taking place in the world. Similarly, Peter Berger has called this kind of religious change a shift in the institutional location of religion. Berger, one of the early theorists of secularization, now argues that pluralism and modernity affects the "how of religious belief," how religion is structured, but not necessarily the what,"[18] the content of religious belief. Another problem with secularization theory is that it is increasingly recognized that it is based on an inaccurate reading of European history, one that is deeply influenced by the Enlightenment's assumptions about religion. Although there is still an ongoing debate about these matters, the Middle Ages was never a great "age of faith" from which religion has now declined because of the triumph of the "age of reason," science, education, and the Enlightenment.[19]

A more contentious part of the debate is the notion that "Christian Europe" never existed. It appears that one way of understanding Christian Europe is to say that it was little more than an elaborate patchwork of state churches, supported by converted political and intellectual elites that established official rituals of conformity, but made little effort to fully Christianize the mass of the peasant population. The myth of past piety and a belief in the decline of religion are a product of wishful thinking and, as Garry Wills has stated, a superstition of the learned that goes back to the Enlightenment, but one that may not have much basis in history.[20]

The persistence of secularization theory despite the global resurgence of culture and religion is rooted in modernization theory. It would seem "modernist" explanations themselves are indicative of a form of faith—in a certain understanding of rationality, secularism, and modernity. Secularization theory links the decline in religion to certain beliefs—for that is what they are—about the nature of rationality, modernization, and progress, and so it includes powerful images and assumptions of what many people in the West want to believe modernity is.

This is why Robert Bellah argues secularization could more properly be called a "myth" rather than a theory. Its social function is mythic, for it provides an emotionally coherent picture of a modern world in which religion and spirituality are not "real forces" in world politics, but are residual, reactionary, or epiphenomenal forces that can be explained away as responses to various types of deprivation, whether they are social, political, economic, or psychological.[21]

It would appear that these are the assumptions behind the idea that foreign aid and economic development will turn radical Muslims into good liberals, but if modernization theory is wrong, then economic development is not going to resolve these cultural and political issues between the West and the Islamic world. It will simply provide the financial and other kinds of resources for a further intensification of the conflict later on. In other words, modernization theory provides a way for Western policymakers to see militant religion as a short-term problem of national security, and to avoid taking cultural and religious pluralism seriously.

The "Westphalian Presumption" in International Relations

The second reason the study of international relations has marginalized religion goes back to the history of international relations and the rise of the modern international society. Religion is no longer supposed to be a part of international politics because of the Westphalian presumption in international relations, which as we have seen is part of the political mythology of liberalism surrounding the European wars of religion. This is the notion that religious and cultural pluralism cannot be accommodated in a genuinely global multicultural international society. Religion must be disciplined by the state—privatized, marginalized, and nationalized as a form of order and social cohesion, or religion must be overcome by a global or cosmopolitan ethic as the basis of international order.

The origins of the modern international system goes back to the treaties of Westphalia (1648) that brought the Thirty Years' War to an end, and fundamentally altered the assumptions diplomats and princes made about the basis of the international order. What were purported to be religious atrocities were so appalling that the concept of Christendom itself was discredited and led to a new political theory or even theology of international relations.

A new order of national states was already developing out of Middle Ages. These treaties ended the legitimacy of religion as a source of international conflict among the "new states" of Christendom that emerged from the fragmentation of medieval Europe.[22] The new Westphalian state system recognized the state as the dominant actor, replacing the transnational authority of the Catholic Church. Pope Innocent X famously declared the treaty "null, void, invalid, iniquitous, unjust, damnable, reprobate, inane and devoid of meaning for all time."[23] Westphalia also established political realism and the secular principle of *raison d'etat* (reason of state) as the main principles of statecraft by replacing religion as the basis of foreign policy.[24]

A key aspect of the Westphalian settlement has come to be known as the nonintervention norm in international relations. Both the Peace of Augsberg (1555) and the Treaty of Westphalia a century later, by adopting the principle of *"cujus regio, ejus religio"* (the ruler determines the religion of his realm) made religious toleration and noninterference (on religious grounds) in the domestic affairs of other states—in other words, pluralism among states— one of the main principles of the modern international order.[25]

It can be argued that the Westphalian settlement established a political theology for modern international relations. It is a doctrine that prescribes what the role of religion and political authority should be in domestic and international politics that has lasted for 300 years—from the seventeenth century until the end of the twentieth century.[26]

Perhaps, the rejection of religion was stronger in the study of international relations than in many other areas of the humanities and social sciences because of the way this political theology of international relations undermined the study of religion in this academic area. The Westphalian system—the emphasis on the state, the state-system, nonintervention, and a concept of security narrowly defined as military security was accepted in early modern Europe as part of the political mythology of liberalism, which in terms of international relations was also an argument about security—to end the wars of religion. Religion on this reckoning was considered to be the ultimate threat to order, civility, and security.[27]

The Paradigms of International Relations

The third reason culture and religion have not been a part of the study of international relations is because these social forces were marginalized in the main images, paradigms, perspectives, or traditions of thought used to study international affairs. The study of international relations has been dominated by the perspective called realism, neorealism, or structural realism. Realism has been able to marginalize religion because it focuses on states and the interaction between states in international society, on military power as the dominant form of power in international relations, and national security as the main issue confronting states in international relations.

Realists argued that conflict and cooperation take place in international society under the structural conditions of international anarchy. This concept points to the lack of a central, common, or overarching power in international politics. Power—military and economic capabilities—are distributed among autonomous, self-interested, and independent states or powers, with each one pursuing its own national interests, and this is what makes power politics a colloquial phrase for international politics. International politics is considered to be a self-help system since each state in the final analysis is responsible for its own security, and cannot rely on other states. The key concepts realists have used to explain and understand the world include national security, vital interests and national interests, power, alliances, the balance of power, and spheres of interest.[28]

Clearly, the impact of non-state actors, including the role of religious actors, is marginalized from the core of this approach to international relations—they became illegitimate international actors after Westphalia. If the role of religion is regarded at all in the realist tradition, it is mainly as the state has invented it, as an aspect of state power, as Lucretius and Machiavelli both observed. Religion was simply "superstition," although sometimes a useful one, as a type of ideology the state can use to gain legitimacy, promote social cohesion, and so maintain its power.

What distinguishes neorealism from classical forms of realism is the emphasis on the rationality of states as unitary actors, and as we see later, a more functional or structural conception of the international system. States are rational actors in so far as they rank their goals, existing capabilities, and policy options before they make rational choices regarding foreign policy decisions that compete in an anarchical international system.[29]

Realism's early non-Christian roots can be found in the works of the ancient Greek historian, Thucydides, in his account of the Peloponnesian War between Athens and Sparta, and in early modern political theory in the writings of Machiavelli, Richelieu, and Hobbes (an early translator of Thucydides). Apart from Thucydides they characterized the political changes in their day as a departure from classical Christianity, and its political embodiment in medieval Christendom, and argued that states would flourish by affirming this departure.[30]

Religion was not always marginalized from the realist tradition of international relations. The classical or modern realist tradition dating back to the 1940s and 1950s was rooted, at least to some extent, in religious perspectives before the full impact of positivism and the behavioral revolution was felt in the study of political science in the United States.

The religious dimensions of political realism, with the emphasis on sin, or the limits of human nature, or on human knowledge, on the likelihood of irony or tragedy in political outcomes, and on the limits of what politics can accomplish, begins with the rediscovery of St. Augustine for the Realist paradigm, who is often called the first political realist for this reason.[31]

St. Augustine's ideas were introduced into the American study of international relations by the Protestant theologian, Reinhold Niebuhr, the only theologian in the canon of classical realism who contributed to the development of realism in the twentieth century.[32] Unfortunately, it might be argued, too many scholars of international relations seem to have interpreted St. Augustine second handed, through reading Niebuhr, and this has distorted the elements of the Augustinian tradition within realism—how to work in the earthly city to achieve the lesser good. It might be time to revisit the Augustinian tradition as part of a broader study of Christianity and world affairs.[33]

Niebuhr deeply influenced George Kennan whose Christian realism is a lesser acknowledged aspect of his political thought.[34] It is widely acknowledged that Niebuhr educated an entire postwar American generation of scholars and politicians who made American foreign policy.[35] David Brooks has recently argued that that his kind of insights on the fragility of what can be accomplished through politics, even with the best of intentions, and the inevitably corrupting use of power are deeply needed in U.S. foreign policy today.[36]

It was pointed out in the introduction that the role of religion in international relations was also a key part of some of the early thinkers in the English School of international relations—Martin Wight, Donald MacKinnon, and Herbert Butterfield. These scholars were responsible for one of the most distinctive features of the English School: the historical sociology of different state-systems showing the importance of religion and world history for the study of international relations. They were, however, also "soft realists," aware of power, but also the ambiguities inherent in the use of power, and so they were also concerned about diplomacy and the ethics of statecraft.[37]

Unfortunately, their contribution to the English School, that is, its willingness to take culture and religion seriously, has been marginalized in much of the English School's current research program. However, its comparative approach to state-systems in world history, and, as we see in later chapters, its concepts of diplomacy and of international society, are continuing to be the basis for much research.[38] Thus, the role of religion in the realist tradition is a complex one, rooted in changing philosophical assumptions as well as the changing methods for studying international relations. We pick up on some of these other reasons for religion's marginalization in the realist tradition in the next section—positivism and materialism.

The other dominant perspective in international relations is variously called pluralism, liberalism, or neoliberal institutionalism because of its focus on the prospects of morality, international law, and international institutions promoting international cooperation. The pluralist emphasis of this perspective focuses on how a variety of non-state actors, including the IMF, the World Bank, private foundations, terrorist groups, and the Roman Catholic Church, can influence outcomes in international relations. We see in chapter 4 that the pluralist tradition, given its willingness to include a variety of other actors in world politics, is at least more open than some forms of realism to the possibility of religious non-state actors in international relations.

Unfortunately, what pluralists open up with one hand—religious non-state actors, they close with the other one. The main emphasis in pluralism has been on how the changing nature of power—to include economic as well as military power, has expanded the agenda of international relations. Many pluralists still argue that the state is the main actor in international relations, but states increasingly have to operate in a world of economic interdependence. They argue a broader concept of international security is needed, one which includes a variety of social and economic issues that have an impact in the global arena, such as human rights, energy and natural resources, the environment, and world poverty. Military power is now intermingled with economic power, but pluralists are still hesitant to talk about the power of culture and religion. We also see in chapter 4 that the closest they have come is seeing culture as a form of soft power in international relations.

Living in a Rationalist World: Positivism, Materialism, and International Relations Theory

The fourth reason culture and religion have not been a part of the study of international relations is because of two sets of limiting assumptions—positivism and materialism—that have influenced the main paradigms of international relations, and way the social world of international relations should be studied. These assumptions are part of what is often called the second great debate over theory and methods in international relations.

The second great debate is often seen—at least in the United States—as a triumph of positivism and behavioralism, the scientific study of international relations, over the stodgy traditional methods of diplomatic history, jurisprudence, and political philosophy, which were vigorously defended by the English School.

Another casualty were a set of Christian perspectives on international relations, briefly examined in the last section, ranging from relatively secular neo-Thomism to sterner forms of Augustinian realism. The Thomist positions, mainly although not exclusively, from within the Catholic Church, have continued to inform the debate on foreign affairs within the churches, and among the wider public, particularly in relation to just war theory and nuclear deterrence (during the Cold War). Perhaps, the weight of these arguments was greater in the United States than in Britain where religion plays a larger role in political culture, but even their role there should not be overstated.

They were, however, until recently marginalized within the study of international relations. The situation is now changing because of the global resurgence of religion, and religion has been returning from exile in international relations. What this means is that positivist approaches to the study of international relations are now doubly outflanked, with postmodernism on one side, and a religious resurgence on the other side.[39]

Rationalist assumptions have limited the idea of what good theories are, and what they are supposed to do in international relations. We have seen that until recently they have also limited the role of ideational factors of all kinds in international relations—ideas, ideals, passions, aspirations, ideologies, belief systems, norms, and collective identities. These two sets of limiting assumptions can be conveniently combined under the heading of rationalism because they provide the basis of neorealism and neoliberalism, the two positivist, mainstream approaches to the study of international relations. The first set of limiting assumptions has to do with the prevailing epistemological basis for the study of international relations, that is, the main way knowledge is created within the discipline.

Positivism is loosely used to mean the way the scientific method used to study the physical and natural world is applied to the study of human affairs. The scientific view of the world is one in which the world is made up of unconscious particles in mechanistic interaction. In the scientific method, the approach to theory and methods developed to examine the natural or physical world, what theory is supposed to do is explain events that are observed through the senses from the outside, that is, the actual events are external to the theories we have produced as humans about the natural world.

At the outset this explanatory or scientific approach to theory, can be contrasted with the interpretative approach to theory found in the humanities and in some of the more critical or postmodern approaches to the study of international relations, which is examined in chapter 3. This approach to theory recognizes that there is a distinction between studying an unconscious world of atoms or a range of mountains, and the conscious world of human beings with emotions, thoughts, and intentions that are capable of representing the world to each other in meaningful ways. Therefore, this interpretative approach to theory seeks to understand human or social action from the inside, that is, within an intersubjectively understood context of the motives and meaning of social action for the actors themselves.

In social theory, not surprisingly, there is a long debate about the adequacy of this description of how the social world differs from the natural world, and this debate has become an important part of what is called the third great debate over the nature of theory in the study of international relations.[40] This chapter and the next one only engage with this debate in so far as it is helpful to indicate what is at stake for how religion is studied in international relations.

Positivism is the first assumption of rationalist approaches to the study of international relations, and is based on naturalism. Naturalism assumes that there is a unity of science and a single logic to explanation. There is only one reality out there in the physical, natural, or the social worlds, and so the methodology of scientific investigation using systematic techniques of observation and measurement is the same for both worlds.[41]

The single logic of explanation means that both the natural and the social worlds are capable of being known in the same way. Accordingly, there is not a great deal of difference between forming theories to account for a natural event—a volcanic eruption or an earthquake, and theories of social action to account for political eruptions—like the Iranian Revolution, the Polish Revolution, the rise of Christian or Islamic fundamentalism, the fall of Marcos in the Philippines, or the Zapatista uprising in the Chiapas, Mexico.

The second assumption is that facts can be separated from values because for the social world—like for the physical or natural world—there is something "out there"—some absolute conception of "the way the social world really is." So observable phenomena—data, facts, or events—are external to and independent from the different or competing theories or interpretations we develop about them. It is this assumption that is behind the attempts by rationalist scholars to isolate ideas or beliefs from their contexts, to come up with methods—process tracing, counterfactual analysis, and so on, to separate the "subjectively" perceived "interests" of actors from what is considered to be "objectively" going on around them in order to try and find out how much ideas matter in specific political outcomes.[42]

The third assumption of positivism is that for the social world there are general laws, patterns, or regularities like in the natural or physical worlds that can be "discovered" by the appropriate theories, and "tested" with the appropriate methods against the evidence out there, that is, outside or external to the theories we develop of the social world. Therefore, explanatory theories seek to discover covering-law or general regularities, and predicable patterns among events that are observed (i.e., theory as it is defined by the nomological-deductive method).

Thus, it is these assumptions that constitute what is called the explanatory or social scientific approach to theory in international relations. Explanatory theories are based on an essential truism, that any time someone generalizes beyond one example or event, some idea of a theory is being used. According to its adherents this is what makes explanatory theories different from historical summary or generalizations based on the study of history.

We can now see the assumptions behind the way religious fundamentalism or terrorism are studied in international relations.

A general type or class of event is defined—"religious fundamentalism"—with a given set of specified characteristics. If a new example of this type of event is found—the Iranian Revolution, the Polish Revolution, the rise of the Moral Majority, the BJP in India, and so on—then what it means to explain any of these events in the social sciences is to deduce that the new event taking place is an instance of the general type of event—fundamentalism. Thus, what we can see so far is that the integrity of the explanatory theory hinges on correctly specifying the general type or class of event and its specific characteristics at the beginning of the investigation. And, as we come to see, this is the problem.

The second set of limiting assumptions have to do with the impact of materialism on international relations. Any discussion of the so-called "root causes" of the tragic events of September 11, Islamic fundamentalism, global religious violence, or the global resurgence of religion more generally is based on some evaluation of materialism.

The general materialist assumption is that the various forms of life exist regardless of our perceptions or interpretations of them. What can be observed taking place is a reflection of material causes, and this means that ideas or ideology, including culture and religion, are epiphenomenal forces. They are the result of more basic material, economic, or technological forces in society. Therefore, they have no independent role in any explanation. Culture and religion are part of the ephemeral realm of values, beliefs, attitudes, and feelings, and are an *effect* of the more obdurate and observable and measurable facts of social life—income inequality, unemployment, fertility rates, or crime—and are not a *cause* of social or material life.[43]

It has been argued that this general view of materialism was one of the few orthodoxies of the American academy during the 1960s, and it remains prevalent in American political science today. It informs the social theories of rational choice and functionalism. For realists, outcomes are determined by how hard power resources are distributed among states, and for liberals outcomes are determined by the economic and technological forces of globalization. The foreign policy implications of materialist assumptions are simply for more foreign aid to promote economic development as the remedy for most political problems—civil war, social unrest, secession, revolution, and so forth.[44]

It is important to recognize that this kind of argument has been around for a very long time, and Martin Wight probably gave one of the clearest responses right after World War II, arguing that common material interests still do not resolve the problem of power in an anarchical international system.[45] It will only be noted for the moment that the materialist assumptions that inform this kind of approach to foreign aid policy is hardly adequate to explain the ethno-national motives for secession in relatively prosperous countries such as the demands of the Slovaks for separation from the Czechs, or of French-speaking Canadians from the rest of Canada, nor Scots from the rest of the United Kingdom.

In the Marxist tradition materialist assumptions mean that culture and religion remain little more than an ideological subterfuge, and are a part of the ideology of the superstructure that masks the material conditions that determine thoughts and actions. Marxists, strictly speaking, emphasize the fear and coercion that maintain the prevailing capitalist order.[46]

Antonio Gramsci has provided another version of this Marxian idea that has become influential in the study of international relations. Going back to Machiavelli, with his emphasis on consent as well as coercion, he emphasized the role of the working class's consent in its own oppression. He accomplished this through his concept of hegemony, which emphasized that the working class was kept down by the legitimating of the existing order through the moral, political, cultural, and religious values of the dominant group in society.[47] At this point we will only observe that both versions of Marxism are based on the way liberal modernity has invented the concept of religion as a belief system or set of ideas that the state can manipulate.

Explaining Culture and Religion in International Relations

How have the rationalist perspectives of neorealism and neoliberalism marginalized culture and religion in international relations? The answer to this question brings together the main paradigms of international relations and the approaches to theory in the social sciences. It makes use of the distinction that was made earlier between explaining international relations from the outside, and understanding the social world of international relations from the

	EXPLAINING social events from the outside	UNDERSTANDING social action from the inside
HOLISM "top–down"	I SYSTEMS STRUCTURE international system	II SOCIETY international society
INDIVIDUALISM "bottom–up"	III UNITS AGENTS "rational choices"	IV ACTORS

Figure 2.1   Approaches to social investigation in international relations

inside in order to discover the motives and meaning of social action. The explanatory or social scientific approach to theory is the one that has dominated the study of international relations.

We use the main perspectives of social investigation as they have been introduced into international relations set out in figure 2.1. There are difficulties in using diagrams like this one because they cannot handle the complexity of the issues involved, but its main purpose is to highlight the key assumptions about social theory that have implications for how culture and religion are studied in international relations.[48]

Holism

The first perspective is called holism, and it is a top–down or structural approach to social inquiry. It seeks to account for individual agents or actors by referring to some larger whole, and the explanation for social events is determined by an appeal to the structural and material forces of the system—power politics, economic inter-dependence, and globalization.[49] According to this perspective the basic features of the international system are determined by the structural determinants of international anarchy, and this is what explains the actions of the individual units—in this case states—in an international system (quadrant I of figure 2.1).

Rationalist approaches emphasize the objective aspect of the social bond that constitutes what is called the international system by holding a functional, structural, or even material conception of international politics. For neorealists international outcomes—what happens in international relations—is determined by the distribution of the mainly military capabilities among states, and the polarity or arrangement of the actors, unipolarity, bipolarity, or multipolarity, in an anarchical international system.

Neorealists focus on one of the aspects of international anarchy, that is, survival, the distribution of the capabilities of hard power—mainly military might, and the ever present possibility of the use of force—and how this affects the calculations of states, which is their primary concern. This means that what is important to states is not only how much states might gain from cooperation in some absolute sense, but in relative terms, that is, in relation to other states, because the states with whom they cooperate with today they may go to war with tomorrow.

If states cooperate, such as when alliances are formed, when they decide to join an international organization like the United Nations, or join an international regime like the Law of the Sea or the Bretton Woods international economic order, international cooperation is explained from the outside, as a rational and func-tional response to threats to security, even though variously detailed distinctions can be made as to why, and under what conditions cooperation takes place. When structural change takes place in the international system it is because of the changes in power politics, military power, alliances, and the balance of power.

Neorealist theory marginalizes the impact of culture and religion in international relations. Religious extremism, fanaticism, or nationalism are considered to be epiphenomenon of the interna-tional system, that is, a result from the growing disorder among states caused by the anarchical structure of the international sys-tem. It is anarchy and not the impact of culture, religion, or nation-alism that forces states to be concerned about security and violent disorder in the post–Cold War world.[50]

Thus, the prescription of neorealism to deal with the impact of culture and religion is similar to what we have called the Westphalian presumption in international relations. Religion, as we saw in relation to the wars of religion and the Treaty of Westphalia, has to be put back in its place and disciplined by the power of the state—religion has to be privatized, nationalized, and modernized if there is going to be domestic and international order.

In theories of neoliberalism realist assumptions about the way states often dominate in international politics, and a materialist conception of state interests are shared with neorealism, but the focus is on a different aspect of international anarchy. Here the concern is with how international anarchy affects the ability of states to reach and keep agreements even when common interests do exist among states. Cooperative arrangements need to be devised to reduce the impediments to reaching and keeping agreements and over come the defects of anarchy.

Neoliberals marginalize culture and religion because economic interdependence and globalization are the main determinants of international outcomes. The common interests among states and international cooperation are explained from an objective, top–down approach by the increasing density of contacts, interests, and interdependence caused by the social, economic, and technological forces of globalization operating in the international system. We can, so it is argued, see this process at work in the laws of war formulated as the Geneva Conventions, in the trade rules of the World Trade Organization, and in the Law of the Sea.

In the view of neoliberals it makes little difference whether or not peoples or states share a common culture or civilization. International society can evolve as a rational and functional response to the logic of international anarchy without preexisting cultural or moral bonds between states. Culture and religion do not need to be a part of our analysis of international cooperation.

Thus, both neorealist and neoliberal theories in the rationalist world of international relations have similar analytical foundations that contribute to the way culture and religion are marginalized in international relations. The holistic or top–down approach to neorealist and neoliberal theories emphasizes the functional, structural, and material aspects of international relations. Any explanation for the behavior of the units or states is based on these structural principles of the international system.

Individualism

The second rationalist approach to social investigation is called individualism, and it is a bottom–up approach to social inquiry. This approach is also often called methodological individualism, and is a bottom–up approach to social inquiry that examines human or social action in an atomistic or individualistic way. It seeks to explain or understand the actions of separate actors, units, or agents in terms of simple or discrete components that can influence the larger system or structure.

This bottom–up approach emphasizes that the nature or composition of discrete or individual units—the actors, agents, ethnic groups, states, or even individuals—is what determines the basic structure of their relations in the social system, the social structure of a domestic society, or the basic structure of relations between states in the international system (quadrant III of figure 2.1).

In methodological individualism social action or outcomes are considered to be a product of the rational choices of individuals or separate units. Agents, units, or individuals, as rational actors, efficiently match available means to their desired ends. Rational choice approaches marginalize the importance of any kind of behavioral norms, and any concept of the actor's identity because norms play no independent role apart from the strategic choices of actors. The explanation for an actor's behavior focuses on the agents that respond to an objective environment, whether it is market prices, security, or welfare.

Rational choice theory does not theorize about why or how the interests and preferences of actors are formed in the first place. There is a refusal to recognize—in a way that goes back to Aristotle—that normative concerns are an inevitable part of politics. Politics is a part of the moral life, and so understanding values and beliefs are crucial to explaining or understanding political action. Rational choice theory also does not consider how the interests or preferences of actors can be transformed, something we consider in chapter 7 on peacebuilding and faith-based diplomacy.

Now, what should be recognized is that rational choice theory emerged because of a frustration over the emphasis in behavioral political science on only observable behavior, with its search for general patterns of behavior (the nomological-deductive method). The behavioral approach, with its search for tangible and observable law-like general patterns left little room for the psychological processes of decisionmaking.[51]

However, another core assumption of rationalist theories, one which goes back to the Enlightenment, is that rationality is independent of social and historical context or cultural or religious tradition, and it is independent of any specific understanding of human nature or purpose of human flourishing. Alasdair MacIntyre, as we see in chapter 3, fiercely criticizes this concept of rationality because of the relationship between rationality and social tradition. This is a part of his well-known critique of liberal modernity, which he calls the Enlightenment project.

Neorealists emphasize that concerns about identity (ethnicity, religion, or even gender) are unimportant in international relations. The objective and external conditions of international relations—the anarchical structure of the international system, creates like units, that is, the units or states tend to become more homogeneous in their interests because all states are confronted with the same objective concerns regarding security.

Neoliberals emphasize that in an increasingly interdependent world it is important for states to put their relations on a stable basis through predicable and enforceable procedural rules that can limit transaction costs, build confidence, and increase the possibility of mutual gain for all. Therefore, neoliberals point to a variety of rational choices states can make for greater cooperation without any appeals to ethics, altruism, or the common good. They have provided a theory that seems to use realist assumptions for idealist ends.

Thus, both rationalist perspectives of neorealism and neoliberalism, from a bottom–up perspective, assume that the actors—states or individuals—are solid or unitary actors with fixed, given, or stable identities, whether they are ethnic, religious, or national identities, and their interests and preferences are already a given part of their identities. Identity is an exogenous, external condition on which the theories are based. For the theory to explain the rational choices of agents or actors—states or individuals—the interests and preferences of the actors are considered to be a given part of the theory.

Conclusion

Bringing culture and religion back into the study of international relations requires a number of changes in the theories of international relations, some of which have been taking place for some time. In the first instance there has been a growing recognition since the 1970s that a variety of actors other than states—non-state actors—can be important for determining international outcomes. During the Cold War this started to happen with the rise of non-state actors, interdependence, and transnationalism. This reinforced the arguments of theorists in the liberal or pluralist perspective who claimed that there is a close linkage between domestic policy and foreign policy, and that a growing number of transnational actors can influence outcomes in international relations. Chapter 4 examines the rise of religious non-state actors and religious transnationalism.

In the second instance normative theory also started to come back into international relations, overcoming the positivist predilections of mainstream theorists, partly in response to the ethical dilemmas emerging from the Vietnam War and global issues, such as world poverty and the abuse of human rights. We have seen that religion or theology provides one of the traditions of ethics available for normative theory which, until recently, has been neglected in the study of international relations.

In the third instance bringing culture and religion back into international relations is part of a wider effort to bring ideas, values, more broadly, ideational factors back into the study of international relations. The role of liberal ideas of democracy and freedom in helping to bring about the end of communism and the Cold War has helped to bring about a wider recognition that ideas can cause or influence political outcomes in international relations. There are forms of power other than military power or even economic power—the soft power of ideas, ideologies, morality, culture, and religion—that can play a role in international relations. However, there are limits to what these approaches can accomplish. Religion cannot be reduced to one of a variety of ideational factors without losing the meaning and significance of religion for social action in international relations. Therefore, bringing culture and religion back into the study of international relations requires rethinking or expanding on what a good theory is and what it is supposed to accomplish in international relations, and this is one of the main topics of the next chapter.

CHAPTER 3

IN THE EYE OF THE STORM: EXPLAINING AND UNDERSTANDING CULTURE AND RELIGION IN INTERNATIONAL RELATIONS

We theorize and construct in the eye of the storm.

—*Ernst Troeltsch*

Politics is a practice of the imagination. . . . We are often fooled by the seeming solidity of the materials of politics, its armies and officers, into forgetting that these materials are marshaled by acts of the imagination. How does a provincial farm boy become persuaded that he must travel as a soldier to another part of the world and kill people he knows nothing about? He must be convinced by the reality of borders, and imagine himself deeply, mystically, united to a wider national community that stops abruptly at those borders.[1]

—*William T. Cavanaugh*

In chapter 2 we saw that it was a common set of assumptions about religion in social theory as well as the main theories of international relations that were at least partly responsible for the way culture and religion were marginalized in the study of international relations. What if it may not only be a matter of using the correct conceptual maps—theories or paradigms—to interpret what is taking place in world politics? The social scientific approach to the study of international relations assumes that there is an objective social world "out there" waiting to be discovered by the mapmaker or social scientist. All that is needed is study leave from teaching, enough funding, and an appropriate methodology.

What if the social world is not like the natural world and cannot be discovered and mapped in quite the same way? What if trying to map the social world as if it was like the natural world can also lead the mapmaker or social scientist to miss important and possibly even dangerous features of the international landscape? Is it possible this is why American policymakers were surprised by the Islamic Revolution in Iran, or why they failed to foresee the "blowback" in the form of global Islamic militancy from their support for the *mujahedeen* in Afghanistan?

A failure of intelligence is also a failure of the political imagination—a failure of judgment and interpretation. The issue is not only getting better and more data, facts, and details of events, but also better theories, paradigms, and frameworks through which they are interpreted. However, what if even this may not be sufficient to understand the impact of religion in international relations?

Henry Dunant, Osama bin Laden, and the "third debate": Why Better Concepts and Theories Aren't Enough

What some scholars have tried to do for the last decade or more is incorporate culture and religion into the existing paradigms of international relations. It was argued that culture and religion, if these social forces were considered at all, needed to be more clearly related to our key concepts, and as we see in chapter 4, this is how most scholars have tried to bring religion back into the study of international relations—as a form of soft power, as non-state actors, as social movements, as transnational ideas, as epistemic communities, or as pressure groups in foreign policy, and so on.

Tinkering with the main concepts of the discipline or coming up with better theories or paradigms may not be the only way of bringing culture and religion back into the study of international relations. What Robert Wuthnow called attention to a decade ago in sociology is that the general debate over theory and methods in the social sciences has crucial implications for how culture and religion are studied. At this point his argument is similar to the those posed by the "third debate" over the nature of theory in international relations in what Yosef Lapid has called the "post-positivist" era.[2] It is only now, however, in the aftermath of September 11 that the full implications of this debate for the study of culture and religion may be taken more seriously.

There is a growing willingness among scholars of international relations to consider what Wuthnow suggested a decade ago. What if more is required than simply getting better data or facts about culture, religion, human intelligence, and so on? What if we need to do more than adapt the existing concepts or paradigms of international to account for the influence of religion in international relations? A more challenging possibility, central to the third debate, is that our concept of what theory is, and what it is supposed to do in international relations needs to be revised to better account for the impact of culture and religion on international affairs.

Wuthnow argues that the existing approach to theory has difficulty in incorporating the impact of culture and religion because it is unable to account for the meaning and significance of social action. An interpretative approach to theory may be required if we are to go beyond examining religion as epiphenomenal, and begin to take seriously the global resurgence of religion in international relations.

The way cultural meanings are shaped in and by religious movements or by religious and political change is an important part of the global restructuring of religion. What an interpretative approach to theory brings to the study of international relations seems to be more widely recognized in the wake of the events of September 11, although this approach has been widely used in religious studies and in the sociology of social movements for some time. One of the main reasons for this is that interpretative theory may be one of the best ways to research the meaning and significance of social action since the interests and demands of religious groups are framed within socially and historically grounded religious beliefs and identities.

Many scholars of international relations are often frustrated by the fact that interpretative theory does not produce the kind of general conclusions or law-like propositions that emerge from explanatory theory in the social sciences. There is an absence of predictive capacity in interpretative theory, but this does not mean it is irrelevant to policy analysis. Interpretative theory, at least in its narrative form, does help to locate those points of decision where different actions might have produced different results or a different ending, and so it can show up areas where more information is useful, and where possible policy interventions may help to produce different outcomes.[3] It is argued in part two that it is by trying to identify some of these decision points and decisive actions that a narrative approach to theory—one which takes seriously the religious beliefs, virtues, and practices of faith communities—may be relevant for policy analysis regarding international conflict and cooperation, cultural diplomacy, and peacemaking and conflict resolution.

Some scholars of international relations may find it difficult to acknowledge what Wuthnow contended at the end of the Cold War: "If recent events in Eastern Europe have undermined Marxist theories, as Westerners would like to think, they have perhaps undermined the empirical positivism that grew out of the scientific revolution as well."[4] Wuthnow, however, continues with remarks that are as prescient today as they were over a decade ago for the state of theoretical confusion regarding the study of culture and religion in international relations.

> If the Middle East continues to produce surprises, these surprises are not simply failings in the capacity of our theories to predict the location and timing of the next political crisis. They are instead surprises that betray a deeper bewilderment and confusion. We do not understand when a Muslim leader [i.e. Ayatollah Khomeini] calls the United States the "infidel". Nor do we understand when a television preacher [i.e. Jimmy Swaggart] in our own society weeps publicly begging God for forgiveness. We do not understand because our theories provide no basis from which to understand. They expect rationality and produce cynical interpretations based on assumptions about self-interest. *They stress cause and effect, but leave no room for meaning and significance.*[5] (Emphasis added)

Over a decade later we still cannot understand why devout Muslims crash airliners into skyscrapers to the glory of God, believe terrorism against "infidels" will assure a Muslim "a supreme place in heaven," or why another Muslim leader has declared not only war but a *jihad*, a holy war, against "infidels"—mainly meaning the United States—because foreign workers and American troops in Saudi Arabia pollute "the land of Muhammad," a phrase Osama bin Laden used repeatedly in 2001. We also do not understand why middle-class British Muslims from prep schools and with a university education become willing recruits for al-Qaeda. The only explanations we seem to be able to come up with are the same ones modernization theory has used to explain religious fundamentalism.[6]

The United States prior to September 11 had poor information about the identity and location of terrorist networks within the United States and outside the country. Perhaps, as Robert Keohane has argued, it was due to something else as well, something that is really part of the third debate in international relations. The failure of domestic or foreign intelligence agencies to connect the dots in the activity that led to September 11 was also the result of an "asymmetry of beliefs" as well. The United States was "unable to process coherently the information that its various agencies had gathered because *religious beliefs are an unintelligible part of a conventional understanding of politics* (emphasis added)."[7]

Keohane, like many scholars of international relations after September 11, has started to acknowledge what Wuthnow has been arguing within the discipline of sociology. We are still in a state of confusion about how to study culture and religion in political science or international relations.

Perhaps, amidst this theoretical confusion, it is not surprising many scholars and commentators still deny that culture and religion — religious ideas, doctrines, or concepts — have any kind of explanatory power in international politics. There is still skepticism that religion can be part of a causal explanation for what happened on September 11, 2001, which, as we saw in chapter 2, is for many scholars the only kind of explanation there is in international relations.[8]

The attempt to explain the global resurgence of religion with reference to religion is considered to be a crude form of reductionism. It can be argued, however, the reason some scholars seem to think the explanatory power of religion can be reduced or marginalized is a form of secular reductionism. Religion is often considered to be part of a cultural system, and simply provides an open menu of choice, readily available religious ideas or texts for political actors to choose from to support whatever actions or policies they want to.[9]

In a less dramatic way the story of Henry Dunant and the founding of the International Committee of the Red Cross also points to the limits of explanatory theory, with its concern for cause and effect and utility maximization for understanding the meaning and significance of certain types of social action in international relations. The issue in this case is the role of Christian morality in the rapid adoption of moral principles in warfare.

> There is no rational, functional, consequentialist reason for Henry Dunant to spend three days helping the war wounded, write a book about the experience, print it at his own expense, and spend months trying to persuade governments of the rightness, not the utility, of his cause. Such moral concerns about the rightness and justice are more easily accommodated within some social–structural account that links Dunant's actions and those of the statesmen who signed the Geneva Conventions to Christian morality and Western civility.

Dunant and others claimed to act as if they did because these actions were required of them as civilized Christian gentlemen.[10]

What is remarkable is the way Martha Finnemore in this account seems to underplay the role of Dunant's personal faith and the religious revival in Switzerland as well as the more general notion of Christian morality in Europe at the time his ideas were formulated. What we can see more broadly, however, is that there is a problem with explaining and understanding culture and religion, whether it is the spread of religiously based terrorism or humanitarianism in international relations. Underlying these perspectives are key, unstated premises and underlying assumptions about religion and liberal modernity that belong to the third debate in international theory.

What this chapter argues is that if religion is to be taken seriously in international relations, then at least some of the implications of the third debate over theory in international relations will have to be accepted. This means it will not be sufficient to bring religion into our existing concepts, or to simply add religion or some proxy variable as an approximation for some aspect of religion (church attendance, questionnaires about beliefs, etc.) into our existing concepts or theories of international relations.[11]

At one level, this leads to a fundamental problem of mis-specification. It is to mis-specify religion as a variable, to reduce religion to one of a variety of ideas, ideologies, or belief systems that have an impact on international life. It is to also examine religion as simply another type of pressure group or non-state actor in international relations.

To accept the conventional approach to the way religion is often examined in the study of international relations is to accept in an uncritical way that social theory is itself what postmodernists call a hegemonic discourse. It is to accept that social theory establishes a regime of truth that provides the means for assessing and evaluating whether statements about culture and religion are true or false, or whether they may even be nonsense. It is also to accept that social theory establishes particular modes of legitimate reasoning that are capable of determining conclusions about culture and religion in international relations.[12] However, the political philosopher William Connolly, has in a similar way as this book rejected secularism as a single, authoritative basis for public reason and public ethics.[13]

Many of the approaches to international relations with an inter-pretivist orientation toward social reality—critical theory, post-modernism, social constructivism, as well as the English School—have similarities with the movement in contemporary Christian theology known as radical orthodoxy.[14] Both traditions of theology and international relations theory would now acknowledge the distinction introduced in chapter 3 between (objectively) explaining events and (inter-subjectively) understanding social action in international relations. They would also broadly accept the contention that social theory no longer provides a neutral, rational, or universal account of society, history, or social reality, including the social world of international relations.[15]

What many secular social theorists may not want to acknowledge is what radical orthodoxy argues are the implications of this interpretivist approach for the study of religion in social theory. Social theorists, who in the past tried to ignore or marginalize religion by explaining it away in terms of some other natural, social, or material reality or by privileging an account of social theory based on secular reason are themselves insufficiently self-critical or aware of their own philosophical (if not also quasi-religious or theological) assumptions, which no appeal to such secular rationality can justify any longer.[16]

Secular reason or social theory do not provide a kind of objective or nonideological space, a "view from nowhere," from which to study the world or from which competing paradigms can be compared; and nor does theology or any religious tradition, many social theorists would quickly add. Radical orthodox theologians would agree with them. For, in our very discourse about history, politics, or social life we are saying at the same time something about ourselves as well. Rudolf Bultmann recognized this a long time ago, although he was caught up in his own existentialist approach to theology.

> [T]he essence of history cannot be grasped by "viewing" it, as we view our natural environment in order to orient ourselves to it. Our relationship to history is wholly different from our relationship to nature. Man, if he rightly understands himself, differentiates himself from nature. When he observes nature, he perceives there is something objective which is not himself. When he turns his attention to history, however, he must admit himself to be a part of history; he is considering a living complex of events in which he is essentially involved. He cannot observe this complex objectively as he can

observe the natural phenomena; for in very word which he says about history he is saying at the same time something about himself.[17]

It is for this reason, as we saw earlier, Robert Bellah has argued that the theory of secularization is not so much a theory as it is a powerful myth, a powerful story we tell ourselves about how we want to be in the world. Now, if social reality is only available to us as *interpreted* reality, then it comes to us structured and narrated by our fundamental stories. The most significant of which has been the powerful story of enlightenment and progress told by secular or liberal modernity in chapters 1 and 2, although fewer people seem to be as convinced of this story today.[18]

The contention social theory no longer provides a neutral, rational, or universal account of society or history is accepted by most scholars working within an interpretivist orientation. What they might disagree with is radical orthodoxy claim that although liberal modernity cannot be refuted, it may be "out-narrated" by a deeper, more coherent, and persuasive account of the impact of culture and religion international relations.

Therefore, if religion is to be examined as a fundamental category in international relations, as Martin Wight, and the early English School suggested, this means one cannot get behind it to some more fundamental category, such as the "social," "class," or the "economic," and those who claim to be able to do so end up turning social theory into an alternative theology, although of a secular kind. When this happens, what social theory has become is the substitution of one *mythos* of salvation for another.[19] Jacques Derrida has argued in a similar way that the claim to separate or restrict religion from politics is itself a theological–political claim.[20] We can now see more clearly that this is exactly what has happened, as we saw in chapters 1 and 2, with the invention of religion by liberal modernity as a parable about the way the liberal state and the Westphalian settlement has saved us from the power of religion in international relations.

We may not inhabit the kind of rationalist world, as we saw in chapter 2, through which many scholars have wanted to explain in a social scientific way the events in international relations. What for some is so troubling is a nihilistic and relativistic world of competing, incommensurable truth claims, each one claiming adherents, in the struggle for power or influence, and now theology and religion have come back from exile and are as much a part of the political game as any other discourses in international relations.

It is for this reason that social theory, as Wuthnow indicates, cannot explain what it means to be an "infidel" civilization, or what it means to say "infidel" troops are occupying the "sacred" soil of Saudi Arabia because these terms come from a different framework entirely. To understand them requires moving away from a conception of social theory as a privileged discourse with respect to other discourses, and to recognize the value of methodological pluralism—multiple discourses or a diversity of paradigms, in which each one illuminates the meaning of social events or actions in different ways.[21]

Following Ruggie, Lapid, and Kratchowil, however, this is not a plea for chaos in methodology or epistemology. What narrative theory may indicate is that the alternative to explanatory theory is not chaos even if narrative theories of social action remain underdeveloped in the study of international relations. Although the notion of chaos does seem at times to be celebrated in this way by scholars of postmodernism in international relations.[22] As Wuthnow says,

> Moving beyond the impasse in contemporary [social] theory . . . requires us to adopt an interpretative stance toward the role of theory and a more appreciative stance toward religion. I do not mean that we must abandon rigor, or the desire for objectivity, or view religious fanaticism with sympathy. But we must try to interpret the significance of contemporary events in terms of the hopes and aspirations of their participants, including their hopes for salvation and spiritual renewal, rather than trying to mold these events to fit some preconceived views about the secular movement of history.[23]

Taking culture and religion seriously in international relations means we need to do what Fouad Ajami admonishes us to do. "It is easy," he says, "to judge but hard to understand the ghosts with which people and societies battle, the wounds and memories that drive them to do what they do. Even if we disagree with people's choices of allegiance, we must understand the reasons for their choice, the odds they fight against, the range of alternatives open to them."[24] We need to take the hopes and aspirations as well as the rage, anger, self-pity, fears, and wounds of people or civilizations seriously, and, like the prophet Jeremiah, recognize that they cannot be healed lightly.[25] We return to this vital point in chapter 7 when we examine the role of religion in diplomacy and peacebuilding.

How do people in other parts of the world live out their moral and social lives in what are the real existing religious communities in which they live? Although this will adds greater indeterminacy to our models of history or theories and paradigms of international relations, trying to answer this kind of question can lead to a truer, more accurate perspective on world politics.

Social Constructivism: Understanding Culture and Religion in International Relations?

We have seen that according to Wuthnow one of the problems with the explanatory approach to theory is that its emphasis on rationality, interests, and utility maximization leaves little room for the meaning and significance of social action. What a state or non-state actor's interests or preferences are (much of the theory so far deals mainly with states), social constructivists argue, partly depends on what they value, and what they value is related to their identity, national history, and how the state was formed.

However, constructivists argue the identities, interests, and international institutions in which states are embedded are mutually constituted, and so they are shaped or formed through social interaction with other states and non-state actors in international society. States can redefine their interests not only because of external threats or the demands of pressure groups in domestic society, but also because international norms and values can shape state interests in ways that structure and give meaning to the whole of international society. Therefore, if we are going to understand what states want—their interests and preferences—then we have to understand the social structure, that is, the dense networks of transnational and international social relations that make up international society and shape their perceptions of the world and their role in it.[26]

Social constructivists recognize that actors—individuals, states, as well as non-state actors—need to know who they are before they can know what they want, or how they can best pursue their interests in international relations. What kinds of power and security do states or other actors seek in international politics and for what purposes? Do the meanings these actors given to power and security help to explain their behavior or social action?[27]

Yosef Lapid has called this problem the absence of "meaning-related content"—culture, religion, and identity—in international relations theory.[28] At issue is having the right analytical tools for the right kind of job. This is why Wuthnow considers an interpretative approach to theory, one which is concerned with the meaning and significance of social action, is appropriate for the study of culture and religion in international relations.

If we return to figure 2.1 introduced in chapter 2 on the approaches to social investigation in international relations we may be able to see more clearly the positive aspects of social constructivism for understanding the role of culture and religion in international relations. This framework was introduced in chapter 2 in relation to explanatory theory. It is elaborated on here in relation to interpretative theories for understanding culture and religion in the social world of international relations.

Holism

Recall that holism is a top–down, systemic, or structural approach to social inquiry. Constructivists are holists in so far as they emphasize the social characteristics of international society. They argue that the rationalist theories of neorealism and neoliberalism have an under socialized view of international relations. The larger whole or the international environment in which states operate not only consists of the kind of hard, observable, material factors that William Cavanaugh mentioned in the epigraph to this chapter— such as military power, foreign aid, and foreign investment—but also social facts, acts of the social and political imagination: ideas, values, culture, and religion. In other words, as constructivists would put it more formally, there is no choice between "ideas" or material factors in foreign policy. Ideas constitute interests for it is through such ideas that the world is interpreted and interests are constructed.[29]

The social world of international relations influences not only the incentives for different kinds of state behavior, but also the identity of states, that is, the basic character of states in international society. In other words, the identity of states as well as their social action is explained by an appeal to the systemic or structural dynamics of what can be called international society.[30]

The early English School and social constructivists recognize that a prior, deeper agreement or intersubjective bond or understanding among states exists, which suggests that they form an international society rather than only an international system

	EXPLAINING social events from the outside	UNDERSTANDING social action from the inside
HOLISM "top–down"	I SYSTEMS STRUCTURE international system	II SOCIETY international society
INDIVIDUALISM "bottom–up"	III UNITS AGENTS "rational choices"	IV "Episodes of social action" (MacIntyre) ACTORS members, characters in a narrative history of social action

**Figure 3.1   Approaches to social investigation in international
relations**

(quadrant II of figure 3.1). The English School does not believe
compliance with international rules, norms or laws is what determines the existence of international society. Rather, rules, laws,
and the working of common institutions are intellectual and social
constructs that states accept as part of the idea of belonging to
international society.[31]

Where does this sense of "solidarity" or "commonality" come
from, how does it emerge, or how is it constructed in international
society? It is the notion this sense of commonality is an outcome of
social interaction, and is expressed by developing common practices or institutions, which brings out the similarity between the
English School's early interpretivist understanding, and the social
constructivist approach to international society. The constructivist
approach focuses on the way the interests and identity of states are
not a given feature of the international order (the starting point of
both neorealism and neoliberalism), but are socially constructed
through their interaction.

What is or is not an interest depends on some conception of
individual or collective identity. The identity and interests of states

are mutually constitutive, that is, the collective identity and interests of states are formed by the intersubjective social practices developed by states in the process of their interaction. A normative potential for agency, social action, and global transformation is often part of this approach because it emphasizes the quasianarchical social world of international relations is really what states make of it.[32]

Such an underlying concept of international society may be necessary for the development of common institutions, and for the interests and rationality of states to effectively foment international cooperation. It is for this reason, as we see in chapter 6, the English School emphasized that a common culture or religion often underlies the successful workings of any international society. During the early years of the Cold War, however, with the impact of positivism and behavioralism in political science, what we now call this intersubjective understanding of the social bond between states in international society, gave way to a more objective and mechanistic understanding of the working of the balance of power in what was called an international system (quadrant I of figure 3.1).[33]

For a social constructivist account of social action there is a realm of mutual intelligibility and acceptability of actions within this kind of intersubjective bond or framework of rules, norms, principles, or conventions that constitute the relations between states as an international society. This kind of constructivist account indicates the importance of understanding social action from the inside because it is the constitutive rules, norms, and practices that help to give meaning to the actions of states, and provide the reasons for why states act the way they do in international society.

In some ways this social constructivist account provides a surprisingly accurate description of international society. These rules, norms, or laws—the international trade regime, the nonproliferation regime, the law of the sea, the Geneva Conventions—are real features of international society, and they are not any less real simply because they are socially constructed or acts of the political imagination.[34]

Social constructivists seek to understand state interests and state behavior by investigating the social structure that provides the contested meanings and social values embodied in the norms and identities of the states that make up international society. They are interested in the way the structures of contested meaning embodied in international norms or the identities states influence social action, and in how social interaction can shape, or construct the identities of states or non-state actors, and inform their interests and preferences in international politics.

Individualism

The second way the intersubjective element in the social bond between states (and, increasingly, non-state actors) in international society can be examined is from the perspective of methodological individualism. As we saw in chapter 2 this is a bottom–up approach to social inquiry, and understands the actions of separate actors, units, or agents in terms of simple or discrete components that can influence the larger system or structure (quadrant IV in figure 3.1).

An important part of interpretative theory has been to try to determine an agent or actor's interests and preferences. Social constructivists argue that identities, preferences, and interests of separate or discrete actors are not fixed (quadrant III of figure 3.1) but are shaped or formed through state interaction, and so they are malleable or mutually constituted through social interaction (the purpose of the dashed line separating quadrants II and IV in figure 3.1). In so far as aspects of culture or religion are an important aspect of identity, it can be argued that social constructivism provides a way of taking into account how the identities of states and their national histories, often strongly influenced by culture and religion, help to shape their interests and preferences in international relations.

We now know that we live in a social world. A world of values, beliefs, desires, aspirations, passions, and perceptions as well as a hard world of tangible and observable facts, figures, and calculations. Social constructivism recognizes that knowledge in the social world of international relations must include these aspects of international relations as well. It has brought out what has been neglected in many rationalist accounts of international relations—the way norms and state identities are socially constructed, and how they can influence state interests and preferences. All this is helpful for the study of culture and religion in international relations theory. However, Alasdair MacIntyre's social theory helps us to see more clearly that there is an unbearable lightness to social constructivism.

Narrative Theory:
Can We Learn How to Tell Stories Again?

Some scholars are starting to consider narrative theory as an alternative mode of social inquiry, although they do not all appear to mean the same thing. At least this point is acknowledged within the tenets of explanatory theory by scholars who accept that cultural analysis and interpretative theory can provide new concepts, and ways of looking at the world that are essential if a researcher is to ask the right kind of questions. The point of this exercise, however, is to still formulate theories and hypotheses that can be tested using the explanatory methods of social science.[35]

What has captured the interest of scholars of international relations after September 11 are the research methods interpretative and narrative theorists have already been using to study terrorism, particularly the Red Brigade, although wedded to a social scientific approach to theory, they have been disappointed with the results. These methods have not produced the kind of general explanations about how and why terrorist groups operate or how states can respond to them.[36]

The theory of narrative explanation has made some inroads into the theory of international relations, as John Ruggie, Richard Ashley, Alexander George, and some scholars of critical theory have observed.[37] Quite surprisingly, MacIntyre's social theory has so far been ignored in narrative approaches to international relations, although his conceptual scheme—virtues, practices, tradition, and narrative—has been central to narrative theology.[38] Actually, it is not so surprising, for as we see later, most literary or postmodern approaches to narrative theory in international relations are far more rooted in Western assumptions of liberal modernity— autonomy, progress, and emancipation—than most of their adherents are willing to acknowledge.[39]

Alasdair MacIntyre's narrative theory of social action is used in this book, because his emphasis on identity, narrative, and tradition provides a way of taking culture and religion seriously in the study of international relations. His social theory is rooted in the early virtue-ethics tradition going back to Aristotle in the ancient world and Thomas Aquinas in the Middle Ages. Virtue-ethics is probably the most important development in moral philosophy, Christian ethics, and theological ethics in the late twentieth century.[40] It can be contrasted with Kantian and utilitarian approaches to ethics or normative theory. The story of the revival of virtue-ethics in our day is part of the story of how many people have become disillusioned with some of the things that the Enlightenment has brought us. It appears that it is simply not enough to make appeals to reason, self-interest, or even the common good to produce the good society or a more peaceful world.

MacIntyre's social theory makes clear what is important about culture and religion for understanding social action, which is what has been neglected in many constructivist as well as rationalist accounts of social action. There are two schematic elements of MacIntyre's social theory that are relevant to understanding social action—his tradition-dependent understanding of rationality and his narrative approach to identity and social action.

Rationality, Tradition, and Narrative

The positivist conception of rationality common to neorealism and neoliberalism examined in the last chapter is a rationality independent of social and historical context and independent of any specific understanding of human nature or purpose of human flourishing. We have seen since the end of the Cold War ideas, culture, and ideational factors more generally, have come back into international relations theory. A great deal of effort is now being made to determine how much ideas matter as causes of political outcomes. The question now is how do ideas—even ideas or beliefs in religion—have their causal capacity and influence the decisions of suicide bombers as well as foreign policymakers?

However, as we saw in chapter 2, there is a problem when the "subjectively" held religious ideas or beliefs (as an ideology or belief systems) are separated from the "objectively" determined contexts or environment in which political actors make discrete decisions or policy choices. This is done, so it is argued, to help explain how much ideas matter in specific political outcomes, or why actors, with given preferences, make the rational choices that they do.[41]

MacIntyre's criticism of the modern way of separating ideas or beliefs from rationality and tradition is part of his broader critique of the Enlightenment project's separation of reason and morality from practice and social tradition. In chapter 1, I called attention to the way liberal modernity invented religion as a set of ideas. The various world religions are simply aspects of a universal, pre-linguistic "experience" of the divine in different cultural and religious disguises. What is crucial about how religion is invented in this way is that at first sight it seems consistent with a postmodern concept of religious pluralism. What it is unable to do is take seriously religious beliefs and practices because if we all have a universal experience of the divine than religious ideas or doctrines do not matter.

According to MacIntyre, the moral problem of modern democratic liberal societies is that the moral concepts and ethical conceptions used in ethical discourse, including debates about war and peace, are fragments of conceptual schemes that have been separated from the historical and social contexts that give them meaning and coherence. He argues that values and ethical conceptions about the nature of the good, what is just, what is right, and notions of obligation, and the rationality on which they are based, are socially embodied in particular social traditions and communities. There is no rationality independent of tradition, no "view from nowhere," and no set of rules or principles that commend themselves to all independent of their conception of the good.[42]

This framework leads to a fundamental reinterpretation of the nature of religion. According to MacIntyre, religion is neither a body of ideas or a belief system, nor is it what Max Weber would call a "social ethic," in which the ethics of the religion can be separated from doctrine. Nor is religion what Clifford Geertz has called a "cultural system," that is a set of symbols which locates religion inside the person by establishing certain moods, motivations, conceptions as styles of religiosity. Each of these definitions is part of the "invention of religion" by Western modernity examined in chapter 1.[43]

Instead, MacIntyre holds that religion should be interpreted as a type of social tradition. The practices and virtues in religion are put in their wider social and historical context when religion is interpreted in this way, because for MacIntyre it is a set of practices that constitutes a social tradition. MacIntyre understands a practice to be a systematic form of cooperative activity through which goods (goals) inherent in performing a particular activity are realized in the course of trying to achieve the virtues or the standards of excellence that define and are appropriate to that particular activity.

It is not enough to say obedience or adherence to the rules that define a particular process for that activity to be called a "practice," such as the rules that distinguish chess from moving bits of wood around on a board, or distinguish hitting a ball with a bat one way as cricket and another way as baseball, or the way scholars often discuss rules, norms, and practices such as state sovereignty or diplomatic immunity in the theory of international relations. This confuses practices with rules and they are not the same thing.

In order to define a practice a number of additional questions need to be asked, such as what defines a practice as a craft, that is, as a skill applied to a particular form of systematic activity?; what are the standards of excellence relevant or applicable to this particular systematic form of activity, so what does it mean to be "good" at this particular activity?; and also, what is the good achieved by performing this particular practice, that is, the good internal, specific, or common to that practice? As MacIntyre explains, this is why bricklaying and planting turnips are not practices but architecture and farming are practices, and this is why George Will can understand baseball as a craft or a practice. MacIntyre indicates that this conception of social practices out of which his understanding of morality, tradition, and community emerges also may very well be consistent with the intuitive understanding of social practices and morality still found in most, if not all, parts of the developing world.[44]

Social traditions, as MacIntyre defines this term, can be religious or moral (Catholicism, Islam, or humanism), economic (a particular craft like making single malt whiskey in Scotland, a profession, trade union, or guild), aesthetic (types of literature or portrait painting), or geographical (centered on the history or culture of a house, village, or region). The concept has been ideologically used by conservatives to contrast tradition with reason, and it has been used by liberals—indebted to Max Weber—as well as by modernization theorists, who contrast the concept of bureaucratic authority with traditional authority, and compare the backwardness and stability of traditional society with the social change necessary for modern society.

For MacIntyre, the most important social conflicts take place *within* traditions as well as *between* them. These conflicts are about the various incommensurable goods that members of a particular tradition pursue, and *a viable tradition is one that holds conflicting social, political, and metaphysical claims in a creative way*. Therefore, religion as a type of social tradition is a historically extended, constantly evolving debate about the nature of the good in a particular community. This debate is embodied in, and therefore cannot be separated from, a specific social and cultural context, a view that is increasingly accepted by many scholars of religion.[45]

Over the last 20 years MacIntyre's ideas have been picked up by a variety of theologians, including Hans Frei, George Lindbeck, and Stanley Hauerwas, in developing their schools of narrative theology and "postliberal" theology.[46] What is important about these approaches for scholars of international relations is the way they have extended MacIntyre's social theory to develop a "cultural–linguistic" approach to religion, one which in some respects resembles the linguistic constuctivism of Friedrich Kratochwil and Nicholas Onuf, even though their approaches are not primarily concerned with religion.[47]

Postliberal theologians reject the "cognitive–propositional" approach to religion as a set of ideas, doctrines, or belief systems, in which most rationalist and even some social constructivist research on religion in international relations is clearly embedded. They argue, along the lines of linguistic constructivists, that religious experience and linguistic formulation cannot be separated. This approach to religion recognizes the historical and mediating role of culture in all human thought and experience—so it is communitarian and it is also historicist, in so far as it insists on the importance of cultural and religious traditions and historic faith communities. Therefore, it can provide a richer, narrative conception of human identity since it recognizes how religious traditions shape identity, thought, and experience.

We can now see that what Weber, Geertz, and others miss in their conception of religion is the fact that religious ideas, rules, norms, principles, or moral judgments are dependent on social life. They are not, as liberal modernity assumes, declaratory propositional, moral statements, to which rational (autonomous) individuals give their intellectual consent. What they mean is shaped by the linguistic conventions of a community, connected to the practices of a particular cultural and religious tradition, and are only intelligible because they are recognized types of behavior (what MacIntyre calls social practices) passed on through the narratives that shape the identity of the community.

What does MacIntyre's understanding of religion mean for how religion is interpreted in international relations? Contrary to the assumptions of positivism, MacIntyre argues that rationality, interest, and identity cannot be separated in the way they are in rational choice theory, but also in other rationalist and even some constructivist approaches to international relations. The actual ideas, beliefs, and values—or, even passions—do not seem to matter, for example with an explanatory approach to theory (quadrant III of figure 3.1). Terrorism, for example, is seen only as a particular type of observable activity. Whether the people resorting to this type of collective violence are coal miners or Muslims, or are interested in greater pay or greater purity does not matter if their observable form of collective violence is the same.[48] However, we have already seen how difficult it is to understand Solidarity's actions apart from the Catholic Church, and how important for the future of global terrorism was the CIA's backing of an Islamic movement and not a secular nationalist one.

In other words, it is very difficult to understand terrorism or other forms of collective violence apart from how the people themselves involved understand their goals, values, and passions. It matters that terrorist groups or political movements are religious organizations, or are motivated by how they understand their religion.

Purifying or cleansing your territory from the infidel—getting foreign troops and oil workers to leave Saudi Arabia—may be observed behavior that resembles national liberation, liberating your territory from the foreigners who are occupying it. However, purification and liberation are not the same thing and can have different political consequences. We saw this in Iran and can see it right now in the military and political crisis in Iraq and Afghanistan.

In other words, what makes it "rational" to act in one way and not in another way is the conception of the good embodied in a particular social tradition or community. Individuals, social groups, or even states act not only to gain tangible things—territory or access to resources—but also, as social constructivists point out, they act to gain intangible ones, that is, they act to establish, protect, or defend a certain conception of who they are: an Islamic country (Saudi Arabia), a Christian nation (United States), or a bit less exclusively, a country based on Christian morality (Britain's campaign against the slave trade). States or non-state actors act not only because there are things they want, but also because there is a certain conception of the kind of persons, societies, or communities they want to be in the world. If we are going to understand what states and non-state actors desire or want, and why they act the way they do, we have to ask broader questions. What they are trying to be in the world? What is the purpose of their social life? These are questions of morality, agency and social change, and identity, meaning, and purpose.

If this is the case, then action in defense of identity and authenticity can be more fundamental than action in defense of interests because what is, or is not, an interest depends on some conception of individual or collective identity. This action cannot be redescribed in "rationalistic" terms as a defense of interests because the calculations about interests only makes sense when they are attached to a particular person, social group, community, or state.[49] The "rationality" associated with the construction of the national interest cannot be separated from the matters of culture and religion because they shape, inform, and determine the conception of the good among particular social traditions and communities.

Identity, Narrative, and Social Action

MacIntyre rejects the way social life in the societies of liberal modernity has differentiated the lives of individuals into separate social segments, and so he rejects the idea that individuals can be understood as *separate or autonomous* units, agents, or actors in a larger social system. This is the assumption of methodological individualism that rational choice theories use when they argue that actors make the rational choices or decisions they do based on utility maximization (quadrant III, figure 3.1). MacIntyre does this because he simply contends a human life is more than a sequence of discrete or separate actions. A social action is only an episode in a story or narrative of social action, and so it must be understood in this way.

It is very important to see why this is the case. For MacIntyre the self has a life story, embedded in the story of a larger community from which the self derives a social and a historical identity. The life stories of members of the community are embedded and intermingled with the stories of others in the story of the communities from which they derive their identity. Thus, it follows from MacIntyre's narrative conception of the self, that human action or social action becomes intelligible only when it is interpreted as part of a larger narrative of the collective life of states, individuals, or communities.[50]

In other words, the self in MacIntyre's account is a "situated self" of practice, narrative, and social, cultural, or religious tradition, and this can be distinguished from the "atomistic self" of liberal modernity, and the notions of change, autonomy, and emancipation rooted within it.[51] This is what is missing in the accounts of identity, norms, or social practices in rational choice theory or social constructivism. MacIntyre, like Michael Sandel, argues that any idea that the self is "unencumbered" by culture, religion, or other social "impediments" is an illusion, although it is one of the powerful myths of liberal modernity in this age of postmodernism.[52] Therefore, the reason why liberal modernity gives such a distorted and inaccurate account of identity needs to be explained.

"[W]e are never more (and sometimes less)," MacIntyre says, "than the co-authors of our own narratives. Only in fantasy do we live what story we please. In life, as both Aristotle and Engels noted, we are always under certain constraints. We enter upon a stage which we did not design and we find ourselves part of an action that was not of our making."[53] This was the case with Descartes, sometimes called the father of modern philosophy because of the revolution he effected in the way we think about ourselves and our world.[54] History is so often a fable agreed upon, and in this instance it is the powerful fable of the rise of modern science, which seems to be unquestioned in the mainstream study of international relations.[55]

It is an inaccurate but powerful story because it supports the political mythology of liberalism. It encapsulates all the essential myths of liberal modernity, and is the story we want to tell about ourselves as modern people living in a modern world. It is inaccurate, for as MacIntyre has pointed out, the great medievalist, Etienne Gilson, showed in great detail "how much of what [Descartes] took to be the spontaneous reflections of his own mind was in fact a repetition of sentences and phrases from his school books. Even the Cogito [Descartes' phrase, cogito ergo sum, 'I think, therefore I am'] is to be found in Saint Augustine.[56] What goes unrecognized by Descartes is the presence not only of languages, but of tradition—a tradition that he took himself to have successfully disowned. . . . Thus, Descartes also cannot recognize that he is responding not only to the timeless demands of skepticism, but to a highly specific crisis in one particular social and intellectual tradition."[57]

MacIntyre's example may seem a little outdated. A more up-to-date one comes from the life of Irving Howe, the secular, Jewish, left-wing essayist who founded *Dissent*, the leading magazine of the left in the United States. His secularism and socialism was very much about a search for truth, and the necessity of choosing values and not only internalizing those of the secular, Jewish, and Yiddish world in New York's Lower East Side.[58] Later on, looking back on his life, he made some observations that illustrate MacIntyre's concept of identity and social tradition, and it is a point we return to many times in this book.

Howe states in his reflections on his secular and Jewish upbringing, "it seems unlikely that anyone can . . . simply decide to discard the [tradition] in which he has grown up. Life is not that programmatic; it is rare that the human will can be that imperious; and a *tradition signifies precisely those enveloping forces that shape us before we can even think of choices*" (emphasis added).[59] He even acknowledged, "the whole idea of escaping from Jewishness is itself a crucial part of the Jewish experience," or as MacIntyre put it, a specific crisis in one particular social and intellectual tradition.[60] Indeed, we see in chapter 5 that the very way individuals respond to their social and cultural traditions, as Howe says, to affirm or even to deny them, is itself a part of what Rene Girard has called the triangular structure of desire in identity formation.

The Unbearable Lightness of Social Constructivism?

We have been arguing in this book that the kind of beliefs and practices we have come to call religion are not like other kinds of ideas, beliefs, or practices in international relations, nor is it adequate to describe religion as a belief system or ideology. In chapter 4 we see that a variety of religious non-state actors seek to influence international relations, but what often distinguishes them from secular ones is their local embeddedness as well as their transnationalism.

This means that at times there can be an almost unbearable lightness to social constructivism. In a number of ways social constructivists has not adequately considered the role of culture and religion in their constitutive accounts of cultural norms, social interaction, the identity of states, and how they shape the way actors define their interests or form their preferences through social interaction.

The first question that needs to be examined more thoroughly in constructivist accounts of social interaction in international relations is how the intersubjectivity of the social bond between states that constitute an international society is constructed to begin with (quadrant II of figure 3.1). Where do the rules, norms, and practices in international life come from? What is the origin of the practices that constitute what Wittgenstein might call the games of international life or international orders? Are they simply the result of social interaction? Questions surrounding this area "remain ill-defined, incompletely theorized and understudied."[61]

Many social constructivists seem to think this intersubjectivity, or the sense of belonging and obligation to international society, is just a matter of practicality or social contrivance. This is why applying Wittgenstein's idea of social games or language games in which the rules or norms are constructed to help the players get along in international life—to assure a state's power, wealth, security, and survival—may be a misleading way to understand international relations.[62] When questions about the origins of rules and games are asked the analogy between games and international politics begins to break down, and what becomes more apparent are the unexamined assumptions of liberal modernity behind social constructivism in international relations theory.

The early English School was concerned with answering these kind of questions, and pointed to the role of culture and religion in international society. The English School's answer to this first question—on the origins of the intersubjectivity between states—is that it was not created or constructed to begin with, at least not as social constructivists understand these terms. The intersubjectivity between states *emerged* in the norms, concepts, and principles derived from the cultural and religious contexts of different types of state systems in history.

The intersubjectivity among states emerged in the practices of the ancient Near East state-system, in the early Greek and Italian Renaissance city–state systems, in the Ottoman Empire, and in European international society. Many of the social practices at the foundations of diplomacy including territoriality, treaties, envoys, diplomatic immunity, and, the laws of war began as religious norms and practices in the statecraft of the ancient Near East or in other historic state systems.

This is why the early English School, as we see in chapter 6, emphasized that a common cultural or religious foundation was often necessary for the existence of the different historic states systems or international societies in history. Something more was required than what we now identify as rational choice theories of interests and utility maximization, nor were they constructed by social interaction simply to regulate state interaction or guarantee the rights of mutual recognition claimed by social constructivist theory.

The second question is how the actors or agents are socially constructed in the first place. How does social interaction produce socially constructed actors? How, for example, do states and non-state actors come to embody particular values, rules, norms, or roles that define and channel their behavior? How, to elaborate on a question constructivists ask, do they come to decide or distinguish between what actions are good, appropriate, and necessary from those that are bad, evil, inappropriate, taboo, or forbidden?[63] Questions like these are about what the English School would call society formation, and how or where the boundaries of the international society are drawn.[64]

Some social constructivists have tried to answer these kind of questions by turning to the actor, agent, or individual level of social inquiry (quadrant IV, figure 3.1). Finnemore for example, says social psychology has demonstrated that cognitive scripts help people to internalize values, rules, and roles not out of conscious choice, but as forms of behavior that are considered to be appropriate in ways that can override rational choice or utility-maximizing behavior. Marsh and Olsen point to the rules that agents follow that are associated with particular identities. Therefore, behavior can be governed by notions of duty and obligation as well as considerations of self-interest or costs or benefits. Actors may ask themselves, "What kind of situation is this?" or "What am I supposed to do now?" rather than, "How do I get what I want?"[65]

However, where do such rules or cognitive scripts come from? Why do states or non-state actors follow them or seem obligated to be bound by them? How are they socialized into accepting as scripts these values, rules, and norms to which they are to conform? At issue here is how causal variables of the social structure are conceptualized and function in international society, including those variables related to culture and religion.

The social constructivist answer can at times almost seem tautological since it tends to emphasize social structures or institutions as causal variables—actors become socialized to want or accept certain values, rules, norms, and roles through their social interaction.[66] But why and how does this social process take place? A notion of Wittgenstein's game of nations—to just go on in international life—cannot explain why European states decided to abolished the slave trade, why Britain defeated the slavery of the Barbary pirates, or to use the example at the beginning of this chapter, why European states adopted the Geneva Conventions as new norms governing warfare.[67] It also may not be possible within rationalist theories to fully explain why the foreign aid regime was set up to assist developing countries after World War II.[68]

We can now see that from MacIntyre's perspective, to ask the kind of questions constructivists ask about rationality, identity, and choice cannot be adequately answered without considering another question, "Of what stories or narratives am I a part?" The "good" of a particular cultural or religious tradition is the formation of a particular type of community, one that inculcates those virtues, those qualities acquired through habit and training necessary to sustain a particular social practice, and are necessary for living out an authentic life according to a particular cultural or religious tradition. Such a living tradition, as we have seen, is a historically extended, and socially embodied dialogue about what exactly constitutes such an authentic life—say, Islamic, Christian, or Hindu—that is, what are the goods of that particular religious tradition.

Social constructivists, in a strange way, have not fully acknowledged, as MacIntyre has, the *content* of social interaction. The way religious ideas, rules, norms, principles, or moral judgments are, as we have seen, shaped by the linguistic conventions of a community, and connected to the practices of a particular cultural and religious tradition, and are only intelligible because they are recognized types of social practices passed on through the narratives that shape the identity of the community.

It would seem that if rationalist theories assume that the identities and interests of states are fixed or given—a requirement if actors are to make rational choices—then many social constructivist theories have a conception of the identity of states or non-state actors as entirely malleable and so one that has minimized the importance of culture and religion for identity.

Social constructivists are frustrated by the fact that cultural and religious identities actually matter to people in most parts of the world. The social constructivist emphasis on the mutually constitutive aspects of collective identity from social interaction seems to be based on a rather thin conception of identity, in which the social world is fundamentally a social contrivance.[69] The self in constructivst accounts, for all the emphasis on how identity is socially constructed, is based on an illusion—the choosing, rational, autonomous self of liberal modernity.

CHAPTER 4

THE SOUL OF THE WORLD?
RELIGIOUS NON-STATE
ACTORS AND INTERNATIONAL
RELATIONS THEORY

What the soul is to the body, Christians are to the world. . . . For them, any foreign country is a motherland, and any motherland is a foreign country.

—*The Epistle to Diognetus (A.D. 120–200)*

"How many divisions have the NGOs?" one might ask, echoing Stalin's dismissive question about the Pope.

—*Fred Halliday*

What is the power of religion and how does it operate in the secular world of international relations? The communist leaders in Poland and the Soviet Union discovered that the pope had no army divisions but he had legions of followers. So did Francis of Assisi in his day, and so do the Franciscans and the Sufi orders, and the Dalai Lama and Osama bin Laden, and countless other religious leaders, orders, and movements in our time. How should we understand the meaning and influence of these religious non-state actors or nongovernmental organizations (NGOs) in international relations today?

Much of the study of non-state actors is still dominated by what Fred Halliday has called "the romance of non-state actors." This is the notion that NGO coalitions and new social movements are forming a brave new world made up of a global human rights culture and global civil society.[1] While the role of secular NGOs in promoting global social or political solidarity cannot be discounted, it can be argued that this perspective represents a rather partial vision of the world. It is what David Martin has called "the cultural empire of the liberal establishment of the North Atlantic."[2]

We have already seen that ever since Samuel Huntington popularized the notion of the "clash of civilizations," most accounts of
religion in international relations have followed an analysis of static
and rather well-delineated blocs that make up the main world
religions, which does not reflect the global resurgence of religion.
There is a constantly evolving role of religion in international
relations because of rapid social and religious changes taking place
in all the main world religions. A whole array of new religious
movements and diaspora communities are shaping the contours of
the cultural, religious, and political landscape of world politics.

It is these considerations that lead to the main issues examined
in this chapter. How are religious non-state actors to be conceptualized in international relations? In other words, how do they fit
into the existing literature on non-state actors, transnational actors,
social movements, and global civil society, and how do these
concepts influence our understanding of the role of religious
non-state actors in global security, world peace, or international
order?

In this chapter we will see that what is distinctive about these
religious groups and communities, which the theory of international relations has not been able to incorporate, stems from the
way religion is rooted in and constitutive of particular types of faith
communities in the way that MacIntyre has described, and are also
part of a variety of global religious subcultures or diaspora communities. International relations theory is still trying to grapple with
religion as a global phenomena that is also a local and deeply rooted
one in faith communities around the world.

The global religious subcultures and the new religious
movements facilitated by globalization are as much a part of world
politics as the secular NGOs that are a part of global civil society.
These religious actors will also play an important role in shaping the
contours of world politics in the twenty-first century, and need to
become a part of the study of international relations.

A Place at the Table

It is now widely recognized that a variety of non-state actors
influence international relations, and it is by recognizing religious
groups or organizations as one of the types of non-state actors that
religion has frequently been brought back into the theory of international relations. In this way religious non-state actors fit into the

pluralist image or paradigm.[3] This section briefly examines a variety of types of religious non-state actors.

Substate Actors

The first category is that of substate actors or subnational actors who act as domestic interest groups or pressure groups to influence a state's domestic or foreign policy. The nongovernmental organizations (NGOs), private voluntary organizations (PVOs), or non-profit organizations, as they are called in the United States, occupy a social space in the politics and society of liberal democracies.

This social space is often called the "third sector" between the state (first sector) and the market economy (second sector), and religious organizations have been an important part of civil society, providing health care, education, and a variety of social services.[4] Even though religious substate actors are often a key part of the third sector of civil society in the West, there is a debate about including ethnic or religious groups in civil society in developing countries because of their more exclusive aspects, and this is examined in chapters 8 and 9 on religion, civil society, democracy, and international development.

Even substate actors in liberal democracies can include a variety of ethnic or racial groups, and when these designations are used it is often forgotten that ethnic or racial identity can overlap with religious identity. Greek Americans, for example, form a domestic ethnic constituency, but they are also a part of the larger religious diaspora community made up of the Greek Orthodox Church.[5]

Many religious substate actors belong to larger, formal, multi-purpose umbrella organizations that represent denominations or nationwide religious institutions, and constitute a major type of religious substate actor. In the West this usually refers to the main-line denominations, with a lot of funding and huge bureaucracies, and even state funding, depending on the relationship between church and state as it exists in European countries.[6] There are a variety of examples of umbrella organizations representing the main world religions and the list below includes some of the most well-known religious substate actors in select countries:

- National Conference of Catholic Bishops in the United States
- Catholic Bishops' Conference of England and Wales
- Union of American Hebrew Congregations

- Southern African Bishops' Conference
- Mennonite Central Committee
- National Council of Brazilian Bishops
- French Protestant Federation
- Pentecostal Fellowship of Nigeria
- National Council of Churches in the United States
- South African Council of Churches
- Muslim Council of Great Britain
- Muslim Parliament of Great Britain
- American Hindu Foundation
- Southern Baptist Convention
- National Association of Evangelicals in the United States
- Evangelical Alliance in the United Kingdom
- Jewish Board of Deputies in the United Kingdom.

One thing that should be noticed about this list is that non-Western religious substate actors have adapted their organizational methods and structures to those of Western organizations in a way that has often not occurred in their original country. Many substate religious actors in developing countries are still greatly caught up in the neo-patrimonial politics of religion, ethnicity, and nationalism. In East Africa, for example, the National Muslim Council of Tanzania, or the National Muslim Association of Malawi, are not as independent from the state as similar sounding organizations in the developed world. They were formed mainly as organizations to bolster Muslim support for the existing regimes in these countries.[7] In Buddhist countries segments of the Sangha (the monastic order) often became so dependent on state patronage that the priestly class has turned into another elite sector of society.[8] A similar story can be told about Catholic priests in Rwanda or Croatia and Greek Orthodox priests in the Balkans.

Transnational Actors

A second category of non-state actors are called transnational actors because they operate inside states, or at the national level, and outside states, across state borders in what are called transnational relations. Transnational relations can be defined as the regular contacts, coalitions, and interactions across state boundaries by a variety of non-state actors that are not controlled by states, or by the foreign policy organs of governments, or by an international organization even though they are a part of international relations.[9]

Transnational actors can be distinguished by their motivations and can be divided between those that are "for profit," such as multinational corporations (MNCs), and "non-profit" organizations (NGOs) that are supposed to represent a particular aspect of the public interest or have some conception of the common good for society or for the world. A special category of transnational actors represents those NGOs that mainly operate as international nongovernmental organizations (INGOs).

Religious INGOs come under the nonprofit category. It should be recognized that many NGOs, like many colleges and universities in the United States, which are now entirely secular institutions, were started by religious groups or people of faith, such as Oxfam, founded by a Anglican priest, a Methodist minister, and a Jewish rabbi, and CARE, the largest NGO in the world, which was founded by American Quakers after World War II.

What distinguishes a religious INGO from a secular one is that its mission statement explicitly refers to religious faith as a motivation for its work, its personnel are related to some religious hierarchy or theological tradition, and it hires all or part of its staff on the basis of a creed or statement of faith, although it should be recognized that this definition can be problematic for Hindu or Buddhist organizations.[10]

Religious INGOs can be examined by making reference to some of the standard distinctions made in the NGO literature and according to other distinctions relevant to religious organizations. The first category are advocacy INGOs, which promote particular causes globally—peace, human rights, the environment, and international development—often by forming transnational NGO coalitions or by being loosely organized or federated organizations themselves.

A variety of advocacy religious INGOs can be identified at the level of analysis of the international system. The first type can be called global advocacy religious INGOs that operate at the elite level of ideas and use influential individuals to lobby for global solidarity. This category includes the World Conference of Religion and Peace (www.wcrp.org), the Parliament of the World's Religions, the World Council of Churches, and Hans Kung's Global Ethics Foundation. The main purpose of these religious INGOs, some dating back to the end of the nineteenth century, has been to argue for peace and interfaith dialogue, and, almost like the English School, to indicate the need for a religious order to underlay the international order.[11]

The second type of religious advocacy INGOs are those formed around a specific cause, purpose, or form of solidarity, such as promoting world peace—Pax Christi, and the International Network of Engaged Buddhists (INEB), ending child slavery—Christian Solidarity International, and the International Justice Mission, or support for a broadly based peace in the Middle East—the *Tikkun* community, and the promotion of religious freedom—the Council on Faith and International Affairs.

The second major NGO category is the rapidly growing set of NGO service providers, such as the vast array of humanitarian NGOs that are involved overseas in relief, disaster, and development assistance—CARE, World Vision, or Save the Children. The service provider NGOs, as we see in chapters 8 and 9, benefited from recent trends in ideas about democracy, good governance, and development policy that emerged from the Reagan and Thatcher years, and from the central European intellectuals who revived the concept of the civil society to help bring the collapse of Communism.

A third category of religious NGOs can be called, for the lack of a better term, pastoral INGOs, that is, those religious INGOs that fulfill the more obviously spiritual, evangelistic, or more narrowly conceived functions of religion. Some prominent ones are listed below:

- Sufi brotherhoods
- United Society for the Propagation of the Gospel (USPG)
- Opus Dei
- Focolare, Cursillos, Communion and Liberation
- Inter-Varsity Christian Fellowship
- Campus Crusade for Christ
- Muslim Brotherhood, Jama'at-i-Islami, and Jama'at al Tabligh.

There may be something arbitrary about these distinctions since some religious groups would not want to separate spirituality from the prophetic demands for social justice and world peace, which are also such a key part of a variety of secular advocacy and service provider INGOs.[12] A Buddhist perspective, for example, would argue that the distinction between the individual and the universe is ultimately illusory, and so there is a relationship between working for inner peace, nonviolence, and world peace.[13]

It has to be emphasized that the arbitrary nature of these distinctions among non-state actors is not a special feature of Islam. The West has become suspicious of the kind of links that can exist between Islamic INGOs, terrorist groups, and their networks around the world. It would seem, at least to many people in the West, that it is one thing to provide aid and charity to Muslims in Bosnia, Palestine, Kashmir, Chechnya, and elsewhere, and another thing to send funds that end up assisting terrorist organizations. In the last few years the rules, regulations, and transparency required for charitable giving, financial contributions to nonprofit organizations, and the *hawala* system often used by Muslim migrant workers to remit their earnings to home countries have been tightened.[14]

However, legal and accounting activity such as this has to be put in the larger context of religion and politics. The worlds of the sacred and the secular are not so easily divided in developing countries. It has to be realized that piety and protest, how the flow of grace and the flow of arms are related to each other, is not a new problem regarding non-state actors, and goes back to the colonial era. The Mau Mau in Kenya took sacred oaths, spirit mediums played a part of the armed struggle by the liberation movements in Rhodesia or Zimbabwe, and Islamic resistance groups used the existing transnational network of Sufi brotherhoods to fight the French occupation of North Africa in the nineteenth century.[15]

What is important about transnational Islamic linkages—cultural diplomacy, building schools, medical clinics, and providing Islamic books and pamphlets—is that for quite some time they have helped to revitalize Islamic discourses and reassert an Islamic identity, and this has helped to make political Islam a major force in world politics.

Inter-Governmental Organizations

Another type of non-state actors is international organizations (IOs) or intergovernmental organizations (IGOs) whose members are national governments. The United Nations and its member agencies—like the IMF and the World Bank—are the most well-known IGOs. They have a global membership with a variety of global interests. IGOs may have a regional membership, such as the Arab League, the European Union, and the Organization of

American States, and they may have sector rather than general interests, such as the global economy (WTO) or the security interests of military alliances (NATO). Religious IGOs are a much rarer type of transnational actors in world politics. Most religions, apart from the Islamic world—Pan-Islam—have not used religion as a basis for an international organization. This is why the Organization of the Islamic Conference (OIC) is unique among religious actors in world politics. There is no other international organization whose members are states and the criterion for membership is expressly based on religion. Islamists often consider the British Commonwealth and the European Union to be "Christian clubs," although this seems to be difficult for most Europeans to understand. However, the role of Christianity has emerged as an issue in the EU constitution.

On the one hand, the OIC represents a modern expression of Pan-Islamism, the idea of the *umma*, the unity of the Islamic community that transcends state boundaries. The OIC holds annual high level summits, and tries to mobilize Muslims around the world. It tries to provide a collective official viewpoint on many global issues, such as taking a collective view on Bosnia, the war against terrorism, a war with Iraq, or on diplomatic recognition of Israel as a part of a Middle East peace plan.

It has to be acknowledged, on the other hand, the OIC was created by Saudi Arabia, and pursues Saudi goals in foreign policy, and so it is another example of the problem many non-state actors face regarding political and financial autonomy. The OIC remains a weak and fragmented organization since the ideal of Islamic transnational unity represented in the idea of the *umma* often comes apart over the national interests of Islamic states.[16]

The early literature on non-state actors and transnational relations rightly recognized the Roman Catholic Church as a non-state actor of long standing, and this was the only religious actor considered in the early literature.[17] The problem is that the non-state actor designation does not adequately theorize the actual uniqueness of the legality and sovereignty of the Roman Catholic Church. The Vatican City State is the smallest independent state in international society. It exists only to provide a territorial base for the Holy See, that is, the central government of the Roman Catholic Church, which is made up of the pope and the various offices (or "curia," meaning "court") that constitute this government.

It is the Holy See, led by the pope, which is the formal participant in diplomatic relations, in the same way that diplomatic relations are accredited to the Court of St. James in Britain.[18]

It is unique among religious non-state actors in that it is the only one to have permanent observer status at the United Nations and in its specialized agencies. This is why, after it was perceived by some Western INGOs to play a disruptive role at UN conferences on population, women, and human rights during the 1990s, many of them have tried to get its legal status changed. The Catholic Church is constrained by the Lateran treaties to maintain neutrality in foreign policy, but it has extensive diplomatic relations with 168 countries, and through the UN, its specialized agencies, and missions in New York, Geneva, and Vienna it seems to be far better placed than the OIC to lobby on a range of global issues.[19]

What's in a Name? Conceptualizing Religious Non-State Actors

This section examines the adequacy of the ways in which religious non-state actors have been conceptualized in international relations theory. It goes on to suggest how different concepts may be useful to indicate some of the other ways in which religious non-state actors are becoming a part of international relations.

What may be distinctive about religious groups and communities, which international relations theory is still trying to grapple with using the concepts examined in this section—transnational religion, epistemic communities, social movements, or global civil society, and has so far not been able to fully incorporate, stems from the way liberal modernity has invented religion as a body of ideas, doctrines, or belief systems. When scholars attempt to determine causal beliefs or the causal capacity of religious ideas it is this concept of religion that is assumed.

However, the virtues and practices of particular cultural and religious traditions are constitutive of particular types of faith communities as well as part of their transnationalism. Religion—discourses on doctrine or theology are always and necessarily related to some socially embodied and historically extended religious community and tradition. What was said about the Catholic Church during the age of reason still can be said about Christianity, and—with only slight adjustments—about many of the world religions today.

Dogmas should be regarded not as abstract and isolate propositions, but in relation to the living whole of which they formed a part. They are the fruit of the perpetual effort of the Church to translate into intellectual terms the life of faith. . . . Tradition is not a fixed set of fossilized statements, but the Word of God living in the faithful. It is constantly developing and has constantly to be rethought in the light of the total movement of human culture.[20]

The task before any religious community, which is performed not only by its clerics, priests, pastors, rabbis, or scholars of religious or theological ethics at divinity schools or universities but by its adherents in everyday life—people who are economists, nuclear engineers, biologists, or development practitioners—is to understand the moral and religious significance of their own traditions. They seek not only to clarify the beliefs for the life of the community but also to deploy the resources of the tradition to shed life on the experience and moral challenges that confront the faith community in a global and interdependent world.[21]

Transnational Religion

The force of ideas in international relations is often described by using the concept of transnational ideas or transnational belief systems in international relations. The part transnational ideas play in the drama of international relations seems to have been recognized in the early days of the Cold War, but was lost during the heyday of realism.[22] Ideas or beliefs are transnational when people in many different countries hold to a similar worldview, belief system, conception of morality, or believe in particular international laws or norms. Transnational ideas include ideologies such as feminism or Marxism, and laws and norms, such as anti-slavery, human rights, or humanitarian intervention.

Transnational ideas are usually thought to be at odds with nationalism became as an ideology nationalism brings together a particular territory, state, and people, or nation; however, this is not always the case. The aim of some transnational ideas is the creation of multiethnic or multinational states, such as Pan-Islam, Pan-Arabism, or Zionism. Transnational ideas often also have a coherent set of symbols and texts, such as the Cross, the Crescent, the star of David, or the red flag and *The Communist Manifesto*. Transnational ideas also have leading prophets: Marx, Theodore Hertzel, or Muhammad, or in the case of modern Islamists, Sayyid Qutb, Abdul Ala Mawdudi, and Ayatollah Ruhollah Khomeini.[23]

Transnational ideas often give rise to transnational actors or institutions, which are meant to monitor, facilitate, or implement these ideas in international relations. Ttransnational ideas, in some of the above examples, have given rise to the Socialist International, the Anti-Slavery Society, the Arab League, the World Zionist Organization, and the Muslim Brotherhood.

Religious transnational actors have given rise to the concept of transnational religion, and so this concept is considered to be a variant of the notion that religion is a set of ideas, a type of ideology, or belief system.[24] When religion is conceptualized as one of the types of transnational ideas in international relations this category can include Islamic fundamentalism, Pentecostalism, evangelicalism, and engaged Buddhism, which can be seen as part of a global discourse on nonviolence in world politics.[25]

Religious ideas or beliefs, like other ideas and beliefs, have been categorized in three different ways in the literature on international relations: as worldviews, principled beliefs, and as causal beliefs.[26] *Worldviews* are embedded in cultural symbolism, and deeply affect thought and discourse involving views on ethics, cosmology, and ontology. The world religions provide worldviews as well as the scientific rationality characteristic of liberal modernity. Clearly, one aspect of the global resurgence of religion is the way each of the main world religions have engaged with the beliefs and values of liberal modernity, producing various types of political theologies, liberal theologies, and fundamentalist theologies that are embodied in a variety of religious groups, denominations, or new religious movements.

Religious ideas are also often categorized as one of the types of *principled beliefs* in world politics because these beliefs and values are often a part of larger worldviews that are frequently framed by religious traditions. Indeed, what makes them what Alasdair MacIntyre would call living traditions, which is not captured by such static concepts as world views or belief systems, is the dialogue within them about what are the goods of that tradition. This is why there are ongoing debates within these religious traditions about slavery, women, abortion, contraception, homosexuality, just war theory, pacifism, and so on.

The third category is causal beliefs, which are beliefs about *causal relationships*; a category that is not often linked to religion. However, in so far as causal beliefs are derived from a shared consensus by elites about the kind of beliefs that inform strategies to achieve particular goals—which themselves are valued because they reflect more widely held worldviews than beliefs about human rights, nonviolence, or even faith-based diplomacy—they can be considered causal beliefs.

Epistemic Communities

Religious transnationalism has been conceptualized is as one of the types of epistemic communities in world politics. It is increasingly recognized that a variety of state and non-state actors occupy a kind of global public square in international relations. This global public square is occupied by communities of experts, scientists, and policymakers from various countries working, with recognized expertise and competence, on a variety of global issues. The concept of epistemic communities refers to such knowledge-based communities, and examines the overlap between experts and policymakers that help to organize the way states manage these global issues. It is argued epistemic communities can have a major impact on the global diffusion of values, norms, and ideas on a variety of issue-areas, including human rights, the environment, international security, or international development.[27]

Until recently religious movements have been omitted from the category of epistemic communities. It now has been used by some scholars to theorize about the role of religion in a conception of world politics as a global public space, a densely packed, cross-cutting arena of key individuals, states, and non-state actors that form various types of transnational solidarities and transnational communities as part of a global or transnational civil society. In other words, the solidarity of religious transnationalism is only one of the types of transnational solidarity in world politics.[28]

While it is important to find a space for religious groups in the theory of international relations, it is unclear how helpful the concept is for theorizing about religion in international relations. The kind of knowledge categorized by epistemic communities has been strongly influenced by Max Weber's legacy, and is based on his definition of the different forms of rationality. This is why it is usually argued that it is hard to fit the idea of religious knowledge into the category of causal beliefs, or the type of consensual knowledge that is characteristic of epistemic communities.

In other words, the concept is rooted in a logo-centered, may be even a Western, conception of power and knowledge. The kind of knowledge epistemic communities deal with is procedural knowledge, what Max Weber called "formal rationality," action based on the kind of "goal-oriented," rational calculation that provides policy guidance on how best to achieve preferred objectives, while religion was supposed to be a form of value rationality, action taken for some ethical, aesthetic, or religious purpose.[29]

The kind of consensual scientific knowledge, embodied in epistemic communities, however, has been criticized for being too rational, "objective," technocratic, and apolitical. It is now argued — almost like the gospel parable — that the kind of policy and knowledge claims epistemic communities make must be framed in a way that is compatible with the prevailing discourse in society if it is to be received, or it will fall by the wayside on stony ground.[30]

However, a dialogue between religious knowledge and this kind of knowledge is a fundamental part of the ongoing debates over modernity taking place in the developing world, and needs to be made a part of the dialogue on the forms of knowledge in international relations theory.[31] It can be argued that in many issue-areas religious groups and institutions do not possess what Weber described as formal rationality, although it may be the case that this point should not be pressed too far.

We are now learning, as we see in chapter 7, that in many developing societies there are indigenous remedies and medicines and even ritual practices for healing and conflict transformation that are a type of elite or specialist knowledge by individuals and religious practitioners. This type of knowledge might be classified as religious forms of an epistemic community, although not of the logo-centered, formal rationality familiar to most practitioners of international relations. In most cultures over the millennia there has been a complimentary relationship between healing and religion, and it was their separation that became characteristic of modernity, which is only now being over come as a part of peacebuilding and conflict resolution.[32]

It is because of the Weberian legacy that religious knowledge, as a body of ideas or beliefs, has not been considered to be another form of consensual knowledge embodied in epistemic communities. Religious knowledge is categorized as moral or ethical knowledge — the notion of a separate religious social ethic mentioned in chapter 3, and this kind of knowledge is based on what Weber called "value rationality," which he applied to the "criteria of ultimate ends."[33]

It is for this reason that religion is primarily thought to be what Joseph Nye has called the "soft power" of moral authority, the power of persuasion, or the power of attractive ideas or culture. In contrast to hard power (mainly military, or sometimes economic power), religion can become a form of soft power when it informs the attitudinal capabilities that make up the intangible elements of power for states or non-state actors in international relations.[34]

It is these kind of distinctions about rationality and knowledge that is at least one of the reasons for the notion that ethics and morality is the only proper place of religion in foreign policymaking. As we see in chapters 8 and 9, religious values have often been an important part of value rationality, the motivations behind the field of conflict resolution or international development, but the substantive concepts and approaches to these issue-areas are based on the consensual knowledge that emerges out of the secular rationality of the Enlightenment.

Thus, many religious leaders, politicians, and the public at large seem to have accepted the implications of the Weberian legacy. As the noted Christian ethicist, Paul Ramsey, bluntly stated during the moral hiatus of the Vietnam War, "The church's business is not policy formation."[35] This is why the impact of religious knowledge on foreign policy making, at least in the developed world, is most often considered to be a form of indirect influence. Religious ideas, embodied in religious NGOs, transnational advocacy networks, or religious institutions are useful to develop the kind of values, moral norms, and inspiration needed to guide a country's moral or political conscience.

Religious groups and institutions have little direct influence on foreign policy making because it is broadly accepted that unlike the area of personal morality—abortion, women, or homosexuality—formulating foreign policy is an arena of public life beyond their expertise and technical competence.[36] The real difficulty with the concept of epistemic communities is when it is given its narrowest definition the concept hardly seems relevant to religious transnational actors.

However, even if a more restricted definition of epistemic communities is adopted, the distinction between religious knowledge and knowledge about international relations is breaking down. This is reconfiguring, especially since September 11, what the relevant epistemic communities are in the study of religion and international relations. There are now, for example, a variety of masters programs in the United States on religion and international affairs.[37]

If more inclusive concepts of epistemic communities, diplomacy, and foreign policy making are adopted, then there are a variety of religious organizations with knowledge relevant to the study of international relations. There are a growing variety of institutes and organizations that are part of religious epistemic communities with policy-relevant knowledge regarding religion and conflict resolution, peacemaking, faith-based diplomacy, and international development. Some of these new possibilities are explored in part two of this book.

Another difficulty in applying the concept of epistemic communities to the study of religion is the way the concept is often linked to strategies for promoting collective goods in international relations. It is easy to see how the concept of epistemic communities can be used to help experts, policymakers, and politicians to overcome the free riding problem, in which the costs and benefits of states participating in or defecting from collective decisions, need to be clear to all if some global problems are to be solved, such as global warming or pollution in the Mediterranean Sea.[38]

What are the types of collective goods promoted by religious non-state actors? It is easier to see how the Vatican's Pontifical Council on Inter-religious Dialogue, or the peacemaking activities of the Iona Community, Scotland or the Sant'Egidio Community are a part of epistemic communities helping to provide a collective good—world peace or conflict resolution. What kind of collective good does the Muslim Brotherhood or Campus Crusade for Christ provide?

How religious transnational actors might assist in providing different types of collective goods and limit free riding seems one way of bringing the debates in international relations over the problems of interdependence, cooperation, and international order together with the debates in theology and religious studies over interreligious dialogue. At the popular level in a small, but funny way, this is starting to happen in parts of the evangelical community. During the second Gulf War the connection was made between faith, gas-guzzling automobiles, oil in the Middle East, and U.S. foreign policy—in the popular question, what kind of car *would* Jesus drive? The mimicry of Christ is not the same thing as the imitation of Christ, but at least some of the global dimensions of faith and life are being acknowledged. The idea that religious groups, institutions, or communities *constitute* epistemic communities on their own, the idea that the church, for example, embodies a Christian ethic, rather than merely has an ethic, raises complex issues of modernity and ecclesiology beyond the scope of this book.

Some religious transnational actors are often a part of wider epistemic communities that seek to provide collective goods in world politics—world peace, deterrence, arms reduction, nonproliferation, conflict resolution, and the protection of the environment. Religious NGOs involved in religious environmentalism, for example, can be seen to be a part of epistemic communities dealing with global environmental issues. Some of these linkages are listed here. It should be recognized that behind these religious coalitions and transnational networks are wide-ranging debates over religion, theology, ecology, and spirituality.[39] Chapter 1 discussed this type of religious or spiritual awareness and the environment as a part of the global resurgence of religion.

- UN Conference on Environment and Development (UNCED)
- "Justice, Peace, and the Integrity of Creation" (World Council of Churches)
- International Conservation and Religious Network (World Wildlife Fund)
- International Coordinating Committee for Religion and the Earth
- Alliance of Religions and Conservation (ARC)
- Christian Ecology Link
- European Christian Environment Network.

Social Movements

Religious non-state actors have also been identified as one of the forms of global social movements in world politics. When religious non-state actors are labeled in this way, how does this contribute to our understanding of their impact in international relations? What does it say about why religious non-state actors emerge in domestic politics, and how they become a part of international relations?

A social movement can be defined as a set of beliefs and opinions in a segment of the population that seeks to bring about in a conscious, collective, and organized manner some kind of social change in society. Social movements differ from state elites because they do not possess the coercive apparatus of the state, and they differ from business interests, which rely on the movement of capital to achieve their objectives. Arguably, they also differ from interests groups or pressure groups that fit the pluralist conception of political liberalism since they have a broader vision of social transformation. Thus, they often rely on mass mobilization and are not a part of existing political institutions in a liberal democracy. What this definition emphasizes is that social movements are anti-systemic, disruptive, and are involved in contentious politics, and so they adopt the methods of noninstitutionalized political action.[40] A global social movement refers to people in different countries working consciously in the global public square for far-reaching social change in their own societies, and who see the prospect for social change at the local or national level to be a part of social change globally.

The notion that religious groups can be characterized as global social movements is to identify religious global social movements as a part of the global resurgence of religion. They are a type of social movement that also seek fundamental social and personal transformation by mixing together in complex ways piety, religious observance, personal morality, social justice, and political action.

In many ways the purpose of social movements is similar to that of prophetic religion—to afflict the comfortable, and to comfort the afflicted. This is why religious groups have often been *a part* of social movements, or have been the *crucible* of social movements out of which protest is formed.[41] In this sense prophetic religion has emerged at the grass roots—in bases communities through liberation theology, as part of the nationalist struggles for political freedom from colonial rule—the role of Buddhist monks in Burma's national movement, or the Association of Algerian Ulama who opposed French colonialism, and the church struggle against apartheid in South Africa, and in the civil rights struggle in the United States.[42]

Social movements can be characterized by what Martin Wight has called the Kantian or the Revolutionist tradition of international theory. Wight considered theological—instead, he used the word, religious—premises about salvation and theodicy to be at the root of the Revolutionist tradition. The Revolutionist tradition, as Wight expounds it, has many characteristics that scholars identify with the new social movements—with the emphasis on moral solidarity, the community of humankind, or cosmopolitanism. Wight makes two important claims about the Revolutionist tradition, and few scholars of international relations have remarked on the fact that he considered both of them to be based on theological assumptions: first, it regards the existing arrangements of international relations to be invalid and illegitimate; and second, it holds that these existing arrangements are going to be radically modified, or even swept away, by the coming course of events.[43]

The first assumption he said expresses the impulse for salvation—to eradicate the sin and suffering of the world. The Revolutionist declares, "This ought not to be," and so Wight says, "the facts are so horrible that one must make a wild leap of faith and believe that progress is going to transform them."[44] "At the heart of Kantianism," he wrote, "is a religious element: the desire to convert the world, to save mankind from the wrath to come"—Aids, nuclear holocaust, world poverty, or ecological destruction—and so the objective of Greenpeace is no longer to save the whales but to save the world. Social movements share what Kierkegaard called "the passion of the infinite."

Wight says the supreme test of religious emotion is how it responds to a situation where it is clear that a large proportion of mankind is obstinately uninterested in being converted. Here religious emotion easily swings over from the yearning to convert the world into the impulse to condemn the world. This is the root of the Kantian or Revolutionist ideological division of the world into the saved and the damned, the orthodox and the heretic, the virtuous and corrupt.[45]

Wight claimed it was this "theological" perspective which is behind the diplomatic principle, "He who is not with us is against us."[46] Anita Brockner, the founder of the Body Shop, at the time of Seattle anti-globalization protests, called the World Trade Organization the incarnation of evil in the world. John Foster Dulles and Ronald Reagan said pretty much the same thing about the Soviet Union, and President George W. Bush has divided the world into the same categories for the war against terrorism.

The second assumption shows a desire for a theodicy, to "justify the ways of God to man," and this is for the course of events to bring about the desired change. "Every age," Wight says, "has wanted to vindicate the justice of the universe in view of the existence of evil, but it is a peculiar modern manifestation of this desire, to believe that this vindication will be accomplished by the historical process itself."[47] It is the doctrine of progress that brings about the abolition of evil and the vindication of justice as part of history. Realists, Wight said, "believe that the sinful nature of politics is unchangeable, Kantians believe it can be changed."[48] It is in relation to the doctrine of progress, even if it is not explicitly stated, which determines the variety of secular as well as religious ideas about sin, redemption, and eschatology that influences the kind of social action, social movements, and transnational NGO coalitions activists are willing to form or participate in.

On the one hand, as explained in the next section, religious NGOs and institutions are creating transnational advocacy linkages and coalitions with new social movements on a variety of global issues that can be interpreted as a part of a growing cosmopolitan ethos that might underlay a global civil society. There are still a variety of theological liberalisms out there, which accept the appeal to universal rationality based on the Enlightenment, the immediacy of a religious experience common to all humanity, and interpret the task of ethics and theology to formulate ways to come to terms with modernity.

What these forms of religious liberalism recognize is that religion can be decisive as a unifying force and a universally human reality that gives rise to common ethical insights—Hans Kung's Global Ethics Foundation, the InterAction Council, or the Parliament of the World's Religions. They can help to reinforce secularly rooted approaches to global ethics, global governance, and global political community.[49]

On the other hand, many new religious movements, particularly global evangelicalism or Pentecostalism, have not prospered by blending into this allegedly global ethos of liberal modernity, but have criticized it, and have produced alternatives to it.[50] Globalization has helped create alternative transnational religious subcultures or communities that are revitalizing Islam and Christianity in the global South. They are open to people as they move from city to city or from one country to another one, promoting closer links, and solidarity between people of similar religious, cultural, or ethnic backgrounds. How these transnational religious subcultures are as much a part of the global public square as the global human rights culture is the task of the next section.

Global Civil Society

The concept of global or transnational civil society are terms that are trying to describe the emerging global social sphere of states and non-state actors as an existing social reality in world politics, a global reality that is above and beyond national, regional, or local societies. The concept of global civil society is used in place of terms that still emphasize the state-centered nature of international relations, such as international society or global international society. What the concept of a global civil society emphasizes is that the connectedness among states, non-state actors, and individuals is creating a sense of global solidarity with the poor and the oppressed, and so global civil society is becoming thicker, with emerging values shared over the entire world.

For other scholars the notion of transnational civil society is preferable to global civil society. Transnational coalitions and networks of NGOs do constitute the international dimensions of the so-called "third sector" in domestic politics, and so now a third force in world politics. However, these links are not global, but are transnational in form. Even though they may cross state borders they are rarely truly global, in the sense of involving people from all over the world. It has been argued, for example, that Africa and the Middle East are underrepresented in transnational NGO coalitions, and tend to be more restricted to regional and developmental concerns.[51]

Conclusion

How should we understand the role of religion in a global or transnational civil society? One of the main issues carrying on from the earlier debates on interdependence and transnationalism is whether the global public square brought about through globalization constitutes an entirely new kind of social space, with new kinds of solidarities—made up of states and non-state actors; or, whether this global or transnational civil society is really a partial, more limited understanding of the global public square, one that fits within the framework provided by the states that make up the international system or global international society.[52]

The issue is how this global social space is characterized, that is, what is the nature of the social bond between the states and non-state actors in international relations? An earlier version of this question has already been examined in chapter 3 regarding the nature of international society. We see in chapter 6 that the English School was concerned about the cultural and religious foundations of international order. It was only with such a foundation that transnational relations flourished. In other words, non-state actors can only operate in a relatively stable, if not always peaceful, international system, one built on an underlying consensus about the rules of the international order. Non-state actors cannot provide international order on their own.

Therefore, the expansion and contraction of non-state actors has accompanied the growth and decline of international society.[53]

What is the basis of the shared beliefs and understandings underlying the relations between states and non-state actors today? Some specialists in religious studies or the sociology of religion seem to almost accept the English School's perspective regarding the cultural or religious foundations of international order. They have considered various prospects for a new global religion or "world theology" to underlay the coming world civilization. Thus, the debates about the global religion of a global civilization or what the religion of globalization will be are similar to some of the debates about normative theory in international relations.[54]

The alternative to this brave new world of a global civil society is the perspective that it is really part of the hegemony of Western modernity.[55] A clear example of this was the Lambeth Conference in 1998, the meeting of Anglican or Episcopal bishops from around the world, which for the first time was no longer dominated by white men from the rich West, but by nonwhite bishops from the developing world. A minority of mainly white, liberal bishops from the rich countries were pitted against the majority of nonwhite and non-Western bishops on a whole host of issues—Islam, sexual morality, social policy, and evangelism.[56]

Globalization may not mean the world is being swept up by the unrelenting and unstoppable homogenizing forces of a blandly uniform globalization. What is taking place has more accurately, if awkwardly, been called "global localization" or "glocalization." What is taking place is that worldwide processes are being adapted to *local* circumstances, and so globalization may be a self-limiting process insofar as it incorporates locality. Many of the forces that appear to be homogenizing the global market involve subtle, but important cultural differences, and so what is actually taking place is the universalization of particularism and the particularization of universalism.[57]

If religious traditions are being enhanced by globalization in this way, then it may be better to describe religious groups as a part of wider transnational religious subcultures. This notion focuses on the way religious power and knowledge are not only ideas or belief systems that are free-floating in the ether of some kind of global public sphere. They are rooted or embodied in the virtues and practices of particular religious traditions, embedded in actual faith communities in ways that bring together forms of piety and cultural and religious identity as a basis for political action.

It is very important to recognize this. One of the lessons of transnational NGO coalitions is that they must be firmly connected to a local constituency, and are more likely to be effective when they are helped by the strength of domestic civil society in countries targeted for global action.[58] Certainly, as we see in chapters 8 and 9, mosques, churches, and temples are a key part of those real existing communities in which civil society must be grounded. Therefore, transnational religious subcultures are powerfully embedded in faith communities around the world, and this is what helps to make religion so effective in both positive and negative ways. Transnational religious subcultures promote closer links and solidarity between people of similar religious, cultural, or ethnic backgrounds, and this is helping them to revitalize marginalized communities, and to assert their identities in world politics.

PART TWO

THE SUBSTANTIVE ISSUES IN INTERNATIONAL RELATIONS

CHAPTER 5

WARS AND RUMORS OF WAR? RELIGION AND INTERNATIONAL CONFLICT

Religious and political leaders of all stripes claimed in the aftermath of September 11 that religion had nothing, or almost nothing, to do with the terrorist attacks on the Pentagon and the World Trade Center. They rejected the notion that religion—or, Islam in particular—was responsible for international conflict. All of the world's great religious traditions—"rightly understood"—so their adherents say, almost in the form of a postmodern cliché, preach a message of peace and goodwill.

The members of religious traditions have had to deal more than ever before with what R. Scott Appleby has called the "ambivalence of the sacred."[1] This is the often-painful dichotomy between the best and noblest sentiments of religious traditions, and the way they have been associated with the most horrible forms of violence.[2] We have to reckon with the fact that Islam, as an empire of faith, first conquered by the sword (and only later on through trade). Jesus may have told Peter, "Put your sword back in its place for all who draw the sword will die by the sword" (Matt. 26:52), but for St. Clovis, as for St. Olaf, and countless other Christian soldiers, the Cross was also a sword.[3]

Buddhism is often thought of in the West as a religion of peace and nonviolence, and so a kindly alternative to the war-making of religious monotheism. In Hinduism and Buddhism there may be varieties of gods (or a variety of forms of the divine), but countries with these religious traditions still have their fair share of violence and intolerance. Recall that a Hindu nationalist assassinated Gandhi, and Hindu–Muslim communalism has been a constant feature of South Asia. Sri Lanka has had its share of Buddhist-inspired violence and terrorism. Thus, religion has been about war-making as much as it has been about peacemaking. It has always had the capacity to reduce violence and to produce it.

How are we to make sense of the ambivalence of the sacred in international relations in a way that is helpful to foreign policy, national security policy, and the war against terrorism? We have to begin with an understanding of how culture, religion, and violence are related. One of the most significant approaches to examining these relationships is the theory of culture and religion developed by the French philosopher, anthropologist, and literary theorist Rene Girard, who was the Andre B. Hammond Professor of French Language, Literature, and Civilization at Stanford University.

The first part of this chapter introduces his theory of culture, religion, and violence. Over the last thirty years, his ideas on culture and religion have been very influential in the humanities and in anthropology, comparative literature, theology, religious studies, and the sociology of religion.[4] Unfortunately, Girard's ideas are not as widely known as they ought to be in political science and international relations. His theory of culture and religion, as Girard has recognized, offers a way of overcoming the way culture and religion have been marginalized in the humanities and social sciences.[5]

The second part of the chapter examines Girard's ideas in relation to terrorism, ethnic conflict, and international conflict. During the Cold War most political scientists looked at the level of analysis of the international system, the great powers, the changing nature of military power, and alliance configurations to explain international conflict. Now, after decades of neglect, with the end of the Cold War, they have more widely recognized the state and society levels of analysis and the domestic sources of international conflict.

The rise of religious militancy is located at these domestic levels of analysis, and is part of what scholars have come to call the politics of identity in international relations.[6] Identity politics draws its strength from bonds of culture, religion, history, and memory, and not entirely from material or functional sources. In these kinds of conflicts, ethnic, religious, or national criteria are used to make claims against the state or against other social or political groups.[7] In a number of countries around the world bloody battles are taking place over the boundaries between the sacred and the profane in public life.[8] There is a growing concern these new forms of religious nationalism, and the battles between religious groups and the secular state have the potential to turn into a "new Cold War" against the hegemony of the secular West.[9]

What is breaking down in domestic and international politics are the precise boundaries we have inherited from Max Weber to interpret violence, ones that distinguish the more vague, larger, category of violence from the state's legitimate use of force. If this is the case, then Girard's theory of culture, religion, and violence may be relevant to ethnic and internal conflicts in international relations since his ideas were developed with this larger concept of violence in mind, and are located mainly at the state and society levels of analysis.

Taking Religious Conflict Seriously

Girard's theory of culture and religion has to be located within the existing literature on violence and conflict in the social sciences. Charles Tilly has argued that broadly speaking there are three approaches to explaining violence. First are what he calls ideas people, who stress that the ideas and beliefs are the basis of human action as people act out their socially acquired ideas. Ideas people examine how different cultures, states or non-state actors incorporate the kind of ideas and beliefs that promote violence.

Therefore, variations in the forms of violence is attributed to the changes in the type of ideas acquired by states or non-state actors. The debates over whether religion in general, or religious monotheism fosters war or violence, whether Islamic fundamentalism foster terrorism, or whether religious terrorists use certain concepts, like holy war or cosmic war to demonize their enemies are examples of the ideas approach to violence. Not surprisingly, this approach is common among theologians and sociologists of religion since it takes the beliefs and doctrines they study seriously. We return to this approach in the final section of this chapter on Girardian theory and terrorism.

Second are what Tilly calls the behavior people, who stress the autonomy of motives, impulses, choices, and opportunities for human action. This category includes the rational choice and economic approaches, which sees civil wars to be a result of greed, rather than "ancient hatreds" or long-held grievances rooted in culture, religion, or historical memory. We return to this approach in the section on rational choice theory and ethnic conflict.

Third are what Tilly calls the relations people, scholars who emphasize the role of social interaction in influencing human practices, personalities, and the outlook toward others in society. This approach focuses on the social processes or mechanisms that can inhibit or promote collective violence, or that can connect it with nonviolent politics or forms of passive resistance.[10]

Rene Girard is one whom Tilly would call a relations person, and his theory of culture and religion broadly fits into this approach to explaining violence. According to Girard, the key to understanding the roots or foundation of violence in culture and religion is to be found in a basic insight from anthropology, the way human beings learn. He argues that how human beings learn is why they are prone to the kind of rivalry that can lead to collective violence.

Fundamentally, Girard has observed, through his study of human behavior in literature and anthropology, that human beings are social beings, and the way they learn is by imitating other people in society. Girard does not only mean that people copy a style or pattern in the actions, speech, appearance, or mannerisms of others, but more importantly, what human beings copy or imitate is connected to *acquisitive desire*. It is because of the strong connection between desire and imitation that he uses the word, *mimesis*, the Greek word for imitation, which includes the idea of borrowed desire. In other words, as social creatures, human beings are also mimetic, that is, they are the kind of creatures that acquisitively imitate other people.

Thus, from a Girardian perspective, the desires of human beings do not aim at a definite good or object (contrary to economic notions of scarcity or Tilly's behavior people), but what is desired is socially constructed. How desire is socially constructed occurs through what Girard has called the *triangular structure of desire*, and it is with this concept that Girard comes closest to Tilly's ideas people, particularly in relation to ideas in culture and religion. Triangular desire is made up of three parts: the self, "the Other" as mediator or model of desire, and the object that the self or subject desires because the person knows, imagines, or suspects that the model or mediator desires it as well. Therefore, the goods or objects people desire, and their ideas about what to desire, are based on the ideas and desires they learn from others.[11]

How does the concept of mimetic desire or mimetic learning operate? If, at the most basic, individual level of analysis, I cut a cardboard sword out of cereal box for my friend's five year old son to play with, I can be sure that his three year old brother will want me to make one for him too. Rich people, like other kinds of animals, lord it over their inferiors, wallow in their status, and love exaggerated displays. The rest of us fear the rich but mimic them in what we buy or consume, even as we say we loath them and deny that we are imitating them.[12]

The concept of mimetic desire is also an inevitable part of the rough and tumble of politics. "Politics," says Mark Shields, one of the leading syndicated columnists in the United States, "is a very imitative art, probably almost as imitative as political journalism." "The thing about it," he says, "is you can always tell if somebody is doing well by whether his opponents imitate him" in their ideas, concepts, and strategy.[13]

Shields was talking about the contenders for the democratic presidential nomination in 2004. A more serious example of the politics of mimetic desire comes from Kashmir, where Kashmiri rebels have killed their American and European hostages, or from the Punjab, where Sikhs felt obliged to kill Hindu and government officials, partly because they were not only imitating their rivals, but also because they wanted to show their superiority in a way that their rivals would respect and understand.

Girard recognizes mimetic desire as an inevitable part of the human condition, and is a good in itself for this reason. Mimetic desire can be the imitation of positive models, such as St. Paul's admonition, "follow me," as I am imitating Christ, or the Muslim's desire to imitate the life of Mohammed, and as a positive desire for "the Other," mimetic desire is the basis of love.[14] Later on we see that one of the problems in some of the most devastated parts of the developing world is the silence or absence of positive models of mimetic desire.

Mimetic desire, however, can, and usually has in history, taken on competitive and destructive forms. There can be negative mimetic desire, in which rivalry and competition lead to violence or anti-social behavior with the imitation of negative models, and this is the concern of parents everywhere. They don't want their kids "hanging around with the wrong sort of crowd," picking up through mimetic desire the wrong kind of values or habits. Mimetic desire can be seen more ominously in Israel and Palestine where young people learn how to be suicide bombers—as one dark cartoon on the Internet put it, of a young boy in Gaza holding the hand and looking admiringly at an older suicide bomber, "I want to be like you when I blow up," or the conflicts in the Congo and West Africa, where young people learn to kill their parents, siblings, and neighbors by following the negative imitation of child soldiers in their society.

Girard argues that the whole process of mimetic desire in culture and society is prone to violence and conflict. Why is this the case?

If the models for what human beings desire—the ideas and the objects of desire—are based on the desires and ideas they have learned from others, then the rivalry and competition with other human beings for the same objects of desire has the potential to cause violence and conflict.

An important corollary to Girard's theory has to do with the type of goods or objects mimetic desire is oriented toward. If mimetic desire is oriented toward nonexclusive goods, such as learning a language or how to milk a cow, or plant maize, then imitation is peaceful and productive. If mimetic desire is oriented toward what are called exclusive goods or objects, whether they are intangible, such as status or prestige, great power, or hyper power status, or tangible goods like territory, the West Bank or Kosovo, or sexual objects, Helen of Troy, Marilyn Monroe, or Brad Pitt, then the inevitable result of imitation is rivalry, violence, and conflict, as we know so well from the reality underlying the myth of the Trojan War.

A Girardian perspective indicates that it is the mimetic rivalry for exclusive goods or objects that produces what political scientists call the anarchy problematique, the Hobbesian condition, in which life without a ruling authority would be as Hobbes indicated long ago, a constant war of all against all. "If any two men *desire* the same thing," he says in *Leviathan* (1651), "which nevertheless they cannot both enjoy, they become enemies, and in the way to their End . . . endeavor to destroy, or subdue one another."[15] Thus, Girard's theory may help to explain the root cause of the kind of anarchy, violence, and lawlessness Hobbes believed threaten society.[16]

It can be objected that people don't live in a Hobbesian world most of the time, at least in the West. Mimetic desire, however, along the lines of Hegel's notion of the desire for recognition, can lead to violence because it leads to desires through the mediator or model of desire that by their very nature can never be satisfied. The German poet and essayist, Hans Magnus Enzensberger states, "Every community, even the richest and most peaceful, continually creates inequalities, slights, injustices, unreasonable demands, and frustrations of all kinds. The more freedom and equality people gain, the more they expect. If these expectations are not fulfilled, then almost anyone can feel humiliated. The longing for recognition is never satisfied."[17]

It might also be argued that people in the Balkans or Rwanda lived in relative peace and stability until recently, or that Hindus and Muslims got along in South India before the mass agitation of the early twentieth century. Quite so, violent conflicts have broken out in some places—riots in Los Angeles and Birmingham—and in some countries and not other ones. Among ethnic and religious communities, historical grievances also do not always lead to violence and conflict—the Czechs and Slovaks, the Russians and Ukrainians, and French-speaking and English-speaking Canadians.[18]

Therefore, a key question for Girardians is why do some societies manage to limit their proclivity for mimetic rivalry and violence and others do not? How is it possible to stop collective violence and the kind of vengeful reciprocity that appears to break out in some places and not other ones? Violence does seem to breed more violence in a (seemingly) unending cycle of tit-for-tat violence, but not everywhere nor all the time. Therefore, what social scientists want to know is can Girardian theory help explain the variation in ethnic or internal conflicts?

Girard's answer to the first question, what is the way in which societies get out of this Hobbesian cycle of mimetic rivalry and violence, begins to provide an answer to the second question regarding the variation in violence. This leads to the second part of his theory of culture and religion. According to Girard, culture and religion originate in the need for societies or civilizations to keep mimetic rivalry in check so the kind of general crisis of order and collective violence that Hobbes described as man's natural condition in the state of nature does not happen.

The way societies keep mimetic rivalry in check is by finding an outlet, a replacement for the cycle of reciprocal violence, or potential violence between antagonists that mimetic desire has produced. The outlet or replacement is through what Girard calls the scapegoat mechanism. It is the age-old way—what social scientists would identify as a common type or pattern of event, found in the literature and anthropology of cultures and around the world. A society gains release from the collective violence that mimetic desire and rivalry produces by finding and blaming a scapegoat—a single victim or social group—to replace the violence between the antagonists in society. It is the scapegoat that helps save society from the devastating effects of collective violence.[19]

It is through the scapegoat mechanism that Girard's theory brings out the disturbing relationship between violence and the sacred, how ritual, sacrifice, and violence are an inherent part of the construction of culture and religion. Durkheim, of course, in his famous distinction between the "sacred" and the "profane," recognized long ago the social function religion could play in promoting order and social cohesion. Girard goes beyond his descriptions and analogies between religious ideas and social order by examining the social mechanism from which arise the rites of sacrifice and the projections of the sacred. He shows that the sacred is essential to the functioning of society because it alone can protect society from the destructive consequences of mimetic rivalry and violence. It is for this reason that all societies do not break out into violence or conflict all the time.[20]

Girard argues that the purpose of rites or rituals of sacrifice is to give (profane) violence in society a substitute object or victim. Religious sacrifice—sacred violence—is in the first instance the ritual through which a scapegoat or surrogate victim—animal or human—is a substitute for the real victim. What is the relationship between the actual and the surrogate victim? Girard argues it is not in relation to the guilt of the actual victim or innocence of the surrogate victim. Rather society is seeking to deflect or divert on to another object the (profane) violence in society that would otherwise be vented on the whole of the community. Therefore, the scapegoat becomes a "sacrificial" victim—which is what from the Latin this word means, "to make sacred," the one upon whom the violence can be vented, or redirected, without unleashing a further cycle of reciprocal violence in society. What links the notion of sacrifice to the scapegoat mechanism is the recognition that the scapegoat is part of a theory of sacrificial substitution.[21]

Now, the notion of a victim that is a substitute may be hard to grasp for many of us who claim to be modern people. We come back to the notion of the victim in a moment. An example of how ordinary people can accept a person as a substitute, even in a non-sacrificial way, can be seen during the war in Yugoslavia. The independent radio station in Belgrade, B-92, sponsored what was supposed to be a slightly humorous film in 1994 called *Tito: For the Second Time among the Serbs*, but it turned out to be far more serious instead. An actor was dressed up as Marshal Tito (who had died in 1980), and he was filmed wandering around the streets of Belgrade. What was meant to be a funny prank turned darker, as people started to react as if the actor *really was* Tito, and they started to explain to him all their gripes and grievances of the present day.[22]

According to Girardian theory the fatal penchant for internal violence in society—its dissentions, rivalries, jealousies, and quarrels, needs a sacrificial outlet, and it can only be diverted by the intervention of a third party—the sacrificial victim or victims. The purpose of the scapegoat or sacrificial mechanism is to protect society from its own violence, to stem the rising tide of indiscriminate substitutions, and redirect the violence into proper, acceptable channels—determined by culture and religion, and provided by the scapegoat and the practice of the sacrificial mechanism.

Girard's theory of sacrificial substitution shows that the underlying purpose of culture and religion is to accomplish what political scientists argue Hobbes's *Leviathan* was meant to accomplish—to help maintain order, restore harmony, and reinforce social cohesion. It is the scapegoat mechanism—sacred awe—that holds the dangerous desires in society in check; whereas, for Hobbes it is political awe—fear of the Leviathan—which accomplishes the same purpose, the title, coming of course, from the book of Job in the Old Testament. The scapegoat mechanism turns Hobbes's war of all against all into a war of all against one—the victim or scapegoat. It is in this way that the problem of order and violence is resolved in domestic society and social cohesion is maintained.

Can those of us from the developed world, with stable governments, and a smoothly functioning judiciary imagine a world in which society is threatened by internal violence because of the absence of any social or political mechanisms or institutions to restrain or regulate violence and aggression? Ask anyone from any of the failed states in Africa—Chad, Uganda, Somalia, Liberia, Mozambique, Ethiopia, Angola, Algeria, Rwanda, Liberia, and Sierra Leone, if what Girard is saying is not true. The rites of sacrifice, the sacrificial system, as Heraclitus foresaw long ago in ancient Greece, served exactly this purpose—to control, channel, or deflect the violence in society on to a scapegoat to maintain stability and social cohesion. "War [strife] is the father and king of all things," Heraclitus declared, "Everything originates in strife. . . . All things both come to pass and perish through strife." Thus, the key point in Gerard's theory is that what Heraclitus called strife or violence can be culture-founding as well as culture-destroying.[23]

Girard's theory has provided an answer to the disturbing question posed at the beginning of this chapter, why is there such a paradox regarding religion and violence? The good clerics are wrong. The ambivalence of the sacred is rooted in the very nature of culture and religion. Culture and religion from the beginning have controlled violence through violence. Religion contains violence by effectively applying "good" violence—the sacrificial mechanism—in order to control "bad" (or profane) violence, the indiscriminate, reciprocal, or collective violence of society.

Thus, from a Girardian perspective, the paradox of religion and violence that we see in war, ethnic conflict, and terrorism is caused by far more than what Charles Tilly's ideas people or what political or religious liberals often seem to suggest—religious militants who are simply misguided, and have misinterpreted religious texts in violent ways. The ambivalence of the sacred is rooted in the very complicity of the institutions of culture and religion with political power in the underlying violence on which any society's social cohesion, political order, and social stability are based.

Identity and Difference: The Myth of Spontaneous Desire

Ethnocentrism is a strong feeling about the superiority of one's own ethnic group. It is the result of describing an insider—"us" versus an outsider—"them" dichotomy, an in-group bias, which sees one's own group in favorable terms and constructs an out-group in the form of enemy images or stereotypes. The human need for identity is the reason social psychologists and other social scientists give to explain why such social constructions are a part of identity formation. It is when the in-group begins to see the out-group only in dehumanizing ways—as vermin, barbarians, degenerates, or—as, is more commonly the case now, as infidels or heretics, that various forms of collective violence can occur.

A sense of identity seems to come from denigrating some set of others as outsiders even in the absence of any solid evidence confirming a group's hostile intentions. Among scholars there seems to be surprise or puzzlement, perhaps betraying their materialist bent, over the fact that social differentiation takes place even in the absence of scarcity or any material or economic basis for conflict.[24] However, this is what Girardian theory indicates is a common pattern of action found in any society—victims, outsiders, or scapegoats promote social cohesion.

Girardian theory is not at odds with many of the insights from psychology and social psychology, but what it calls attention to is the cultural mechanism that produces in-group bias, and the sense of "us versus them" in society to begin with. In Girardian language it calls attention to the disturbing way, as the Greek philosopher Heraclitus could foresee, *violence is what inevitably constructs social cohesion and political stability.* This does not mean Girardians endorse a realist or Hobbesian conception of a world of violence, insecurity, and conflict, only that they take more seriously how pervasive violence really is in the world. What ethnic, religious, or national groups may affirm as the difference between them, Girardians, as well as many other types of scholars, now recognize as a narrative of social identity, which itself is socially constructed.

What are the social mechanisms that encourage or generate such narratives of identity and difference, and how do such narratives become a part of cultural and religious traditions?[25] A Girardian perspective emphasizes that mimetic desire, as a social mechanism, is an inevitable part of the social construction of identity. Both Girard and Alasdair MacIntyre, as was explained in chapter 3, have a narrative conception of how identity is constructed. MacIntyre emphasizes the role of virtues, practices, and cultural or religious traditions in the construction of identity. Girard emphasizes mimetic desire as the social mechanism through which identity is constructed. However, Girard and MacIntyre both agree that liberal modernity has exaggerated the extent of individual autonomy in the social construction of identity.

The notion of agency or autonomy, the idea that identity is "freely chosen," so dear to the conceptions of liberal modernity or liberal individualism that underlay the social construction of identity, is premised on what Girard calls the myth or illusion of spontaneous desire. It is the illusion that individuals choose the objects of their own desire. Liberal modernity, with its abstract conception of the self, "overplays the role of the will in the construction of persons."[26] Dostoevsky's narrator, for example, in *Notes from Underground*, describes St. Petersburg as the "most abstract city in the world," as if among its citizens there is "the anonymity of desires circulating in its streets and byways, *unmoored from history and traditions*."[27] Social constructivists are right to point out that people do not have readymade identities, they are socially constructed. They are wrong, however, or Girard would say, they are misled by the liberal assumptions of what he calls "the reigning ideology of the age," regarding the autonomy of desire in the way identity is constructed.

Girard says this because the triangular structure of desire is important for understanding the social construction of identity. The assumptions of liberal modernity shifts desire from the object to the subject, that is, to the individual, but this ignores the triangular structure of desire—a point we return to when we examine religious terrorism. Girardians, by pointing to the imitative nature of desire, emphasize that individuals or social groups learn what to desire through others as a model or mediator of what to desire.

What a person becomes, and what they are, is worked out in a process of mimetic learning involving who or what they are *attracted* to or *repelled* from (recall Descartes and his Catholicism and Irving Howe and his Yiddish background in the discussion of MacIntyre's narrative structure of identity). This is the case even as a person denies the extent to which their desires are mediated through the desires of others in order to make a social space for their own identity and authenticity. It is in this way that mimetic desire or what can be called "deep learning" is part of the social mechanism through which identity is socially constructed.[28]

Ethnic and Internal Conflict:
Failed States, the Sacrificial Crisis, and Violence

Rene Girard has not really engaged in debates over ethnicity, religion, and violence in the social sciences. There are, however, in Girard's theory, concepts—mimesis, mimetic rivalry, the scapegoat mechanism, and the sacred—and propositions about how these concepts are related: sacred violence, the scapegoat, sacrificial mechanism, the sacrificial crisis, apocalyptic violence, and contagious violence, which are relevant to the debates on international conflict.

Political scientists have tried to explain the scapegoat mechanism at work in war and ethnic conflict by referring to it as mostly a conscious plot of crafty and cynical rulers who stir up nationalist passions, and manipulate the masses to mask or conceal what are really political or economic purposes. The kind of conscious ethnic scapegoating in the political science literature, to the extent that it is conscious, is a modern parody of the scapegoat mechanism, rather than a Girardian recognition that it underlies politics, culture, and society.[29] The scapegoat mechanism, from a Girardian perspective, is *not* the kind of aberrant phenomena political scientists have argued that it is. It is part of the social order of any society, although the actual violence of the scapegoat mechanism becomes "unveiled," and is more apparent at times of what Girardians call a "sacrificial crisis" in society.

Girardians argue that what many of us call "political stability" is when the violence of society is "veiled violence," veiled by those institutions of culture and religion that provide an aura of moral legitimacy and respectability for violence. Max Weber recognized this as the legal, official, and authoritative use of force or "good violence" by the state (which is why we refer to it as the use of force). Charles Tilly, in his concept of "violence as politics," like the French sociologist Jacques Ellul, as well as many Girardians, reminds us that the precise boundaries of legitimate force is fiercely contested in all political systems—proper police behavior, capital punishment, peaceful demonstrations, or the legitimacy of torture in interrogation by the French in Algeria, by the British during the Mau Mau uprising in Kenya in the 1950s, as well as by U.S. armed forces in Iraq or Guantanamo Bay.[30]

What Girardians call apocalyptic violence is "unveiled violence," that is, violence that has been shorn of its cultural, religious, or political boundaries and legitimations. It is increasingly difficult to tell the difference between the—allegedly—"good violence" or official violence of the state, and "bad violence" of those individuals or social groups that oppose it. In this kind of world the boundary between force and violence is blurred. It becomes difficult to tell the difference between the police, thugs, comrades, warlords, criminals, or neighborhood gangs. In this kind of world, warlords have seats in the Serbian parliament or the United States supports paramilitary forces in Guatemala or El Salvador, and it is at the heart of the confusion between groups that seek violent leverage in international relations through holy wars and terrorism, through guerrilla warfare, or wars of national liberation.[31]

Once these kind of violent distinctions begin to break down, Girardians argue, unveiled violence does what it always does—it incites more violence, into a contagion of violence.[32] It is the contagious rage of the mob or the crowd that we have seen so often—the genocide in Rwanda, ethnic cleansing under the watchful eye of UN peacekeeping troops, "Blackhawk Down"—the attack on the U.S. Rangers in Mogadishu by a Somali mob—the riots in Los Angeles after the beating of Rodney King by the LAPD, or "necklacing," the burning of town councilors in the black townships during the anti-apartheid struggle in South Africa. We also have seen it in history, most famously, in the role of the crowd during the French Revolution.

The regional spread of internal conflicts has been called a contagion problem.[33] It refers to the way we often talk about conflicts like a fire or a disease, and so they are said to "spread like poison" throughout a region, or if peace negotiations fail "a war will reignite and spread."[34] This kind of popular language to describe internal conflicts is simplistic and mechanistic. It is simplistic because it assumes the conflict is not a two-way interactive process between states and their regional environment, and so neighboring states become passive victims of epidemics, firestorms, floods, and rivers of refugees. It is also mechanistic because it sees internal conflicts happening in an uncontrollable way, leading to a kind of "no-fault" history of a conflict, as if there is no one to blame except the "gods of war."[35]

Girardians need to be careful that they also do not talk carelessly about the violence and the crowd contagion in this way. Tilly warns us that the mob has a role to play in violence even when it is the form of violence he calls coordinated destruction. The mob or the general public is often linked to elites, rulers, warlords, militias, or armies in training, advance planning, and logistical preparation.

Girard reminds us that the scapegoat mechanism is a social or collective phenomenon—it is a two-way phenomenon, and it would not work if this was not the case, which is why it is a relational theory of collective violence. What Girard calls the "mimetic behavior of crowds" is when rationality vanishes, and "ordinary reasoning loops back on its own premises"—the role of the crowd, or what we might politely call public opinion. We can see this if we examine historical scapegoats like Jesus Christ, Alfred Dreyfus, or St. Joan of Arc.[36]

Rulers and elites can manipulate the scapegoat mechanism, but there must be *something* there in the first place to manipulate, to stir up the masses, and that is the belief of the crowd. Rulers and elites cannot accomplish their goals without stirring up the crowd. Recall that Girard's concept of mimetic desire, and the illusion of spontaneous desire is contrary to the assumptions of liberal modernity, which sees agency, individuality, and spontaneity as the essence of society.

Girard argues that these concepts or human attributes are a part of mimetic desire, as something less consciously intentional than a deliberate act of imitation, but, nevertheless, they are a part of mimetic desire. The human predilection for falling under the influence of the desires, positive or negative, adulating or accusatory, of others—Lenin, Hitler, Mussolini, Slobodan Milosevic, Nasser, the Ayatollah Khomeini, or Muqtada al-Sadr—is the underlying dynamic of what Girardians call the crowd contagion, crowd violence as a form of coordinated destruction.

The question is why does ethnic or religious scapegoating work so convincingly to promote ethnic conflict? Why do ordinary people—and yes, clergy and intellectuals as well—respond to the way rulers and elites manipulate appeals to ethnicity, religion, or nationalism? Why do the followers follow, and why does the scapegoat mechanism work in some places or countries and not other ones?

The Girardian answer is that ethnic scapegoating works so well and some situations are more prone to violence than others because it is symptomatic of a wider, underlying sacrificial crisis in culture and society. This occurs in what are called failed or collapsed states. The primary characteristic of failed or collapsed states is political or Hobbesian—it is states that lack political legitimacy, sensible borders, and political institutions, or are capable of exercising meaningful control over their territory. It is a deeper form of political crisis than a riot, a rebellion, military coup d'etat, or even a civil war. The concept refers to states in which the structure, authority, and political order have fallen apart and must be reconstituted.[37]

Recall that for Girardians the political crisis of authority and governance—political awe, as important as it is—is only symptomatic of the underlying cultural crisis in society. There is an erosion, or decline in sacred awe, the rituals, taboos, and mores that kept in check the violence of society. The suppressed violence begins to spread like a contagious disease throughout society (acknowledging the limits of this kind of language).

Certainly, there are social or economic factors leading to failed states. A state's economy is in shambles, with run-away inflation or unemployment, there is competition over resources, or a population explosion, and environmental degradation, and people may be discriminated against on a racial, ethnic, or religious basis. What a Girardian perspective may recognize, and this is also what has interested Robert Kaplan on his journeys, is how various cultures respond to these factors by redefining themselves along ethnic, cultural, or religious lines. In other words, the ways these cultural, political, and economic problems become a part of the ambivalence of the sacred.[38]

For Girardians this cultural and political crisis is what they call a sacrificial crisis. The wars in Bosnia, Kosovo, Rwanda, and Iraq have shown a lot of hatred, bloodshed, and violence, but they have not shown any sacrifices or burnt offerings—or, have they? What is the concept of a sacrificial crisis with regard to the relationship between the sacred, culture, and violence?

The first characteristic of a sacrificial crisis is the decay or erosion of sacrificial rites or practices, or the sacrificial system has been reduced to relative insignificance. It is their inability to purify what is impure, and so religious beliefs are compromised by the decadent state of the ritual. For Girardians it is this underlying cultural crisis that results in political breakdown, and the emergence of reciprocal and collective violence. The *political crisis* observed by political scientists is about how people respond, and the *cultural* or *religious crisis* is about why they respond the way they do—by seeking out scapegoats—and not in some other way, a way arguably more deeply consistent with their religious traditions.[39]

Girard also understands the concept of a sacrificial crisis in a broader sense. There is a deeper cultural and religious breakdown in society because the purpose of law, ritual, and sacrifice should be the love of one's neighbor, and the maintenance of harmonious relationships in society. It might be said that rooted in Girard's concepts is a rather high expectation of what religious authenticity means for treating those who are outcasts or marginalized in society.[40]

There is a paradox of religion in the ethnic conflicts in the cynicism, shallowness, and insincerity that seem to accompany their appeals to religion. Religion is often an important part of the value system in a society or community, but differences over religion—ideas, doctrines, or practices—hardly seems to be the source of ethnic conflict. People seem to be defending their families and not the doctrines of their religion.

However, this paradox over religion and violence is what is to be expected with the erosion of the sacrificial system. A shared "Balkan mentality," at least among the Orthodox Christians, for example, existed in the pre-nationalist Balkan society of the eighteenth century. This was turned into a perverse mythology by the appeal to Orthodoxy as a common symbolic banner, "as if Balkan Orthodoxy today is what it used to be in the eighteenth century, before its inner unity was subverted and its soul perverted by nationalism."[41] People may no longer think of themselves as performing the rituals of religion, that is they are participating in rational historical events, and yet their rituals still consume a lot of victims.[42]

The second characteristic of a sacrificial crisis is the breakdown or collapse in civic and moral order, and the disintegration of moral and psychological coherence. This dimension of the sacrificial crisis is part of what political scientists refer to as the structural factors that can cause ethnic and internal conflicts. Tim Judah, for example, constantly uses the words, terror, insanity, madness, and collective insanity to describe the war in Croatia and the Serbian-held parts of Bosnia in 1992. He cannot explain how the Serbs simply suspended all critical faculties.[43] The rational accounts of ethnic or internal conflict hardly recognize this dimension of hatred and violence.

What takes place in a sacrificial crisis are attacks on social groups and individuals, but the blows really fall on social and political institutions. "[T]he combatants finally assist in the downfall of the very order they strove to maintain . . . the general decadence that pervades the religion of the community—are surely part of the same phenomenon that works away at the undermining of family relationships, as well as of religious and social hierarchies."[44]

Physical violence, acts of reprisal, the cycle of vengeance—all imitative acts of violence—set off what was described earlier as a contagion of violence, a chain reaction of reciprocal violence that starts to be characterized in confusing ways—as a riot, an uprising, an insurrection, civil war, revolution, or simply as anarchy. The army can sometimes collapse, as did the Czarist army during the Russian civil war of 1919–1920.

A related characteristic is the kind of lawlessness that took place during the war in Bosnia, where criminal gangs or individuals looked for loot or revenge or angry refugees looked for housing. Stories circulated about who was allegedly killing whom, and the fear and ignorance helped to spread the contagion of violence. Under these kind of circumstance it is not surprising that transnational crime has been identified as a crucial aspect of ethnic conflict. The rise of warlords, drug lords, and criminal gangs are part of the collapse of the civic and moral order, as is the spread of the contagion of violence.

One of the puzzling aspects of ethnic conflicts for outsiders to understand was how very much alike the people killing each other often are in culture, ethnicity, and language. How is it that brothers and neighbors, people who lived cheek by jowl for years or centuries, were transformed into enemies, or that no hatreds are more intractable than those between the closest kin? How is it that ordinary people become mass murderers and torture their neighbors before killing them? How could people in Rwanda pray all night and then pick up machetes to kill their neighbors in the morning?

The answer to this question might be found in the third characteristic of a sacrificial crisis. It is a crisis of distinctions, a breakdown in the separation of the scapegoat from those in society for whom the victim is a substitute. When the sacrificial mechanism is in a state of decay or is reduced to relative insignificance there has been either too much or too little contact between the victim and the scapegoat. Violence is no longer eliminated and conflicts take place within the community.

Michael Ignatieff argues that the myth of Cain and Abel is about these troubling questions. They are troubling because we often regard fraternal relationships with affection, but Girard reminds us that in mythology and history rivalry, jealousy, and violence is the more usual part of the story.[45]

One of things the myth of Cain and Abel could be about is the paradox that brothers can hate each other more passionately than strangers can. Girard offers a more disturbing interpretation. It is that violence and difference are at the very foundation of culture, religion, and society. There is a "fatal penchant for violence [in society] that can only be diverted by the intervention of a third party, the sacrificial victim or victims. Cain's jealousy of his brother is only another term for his one characteristic trait: his lack of a sacrificial outlet." Sadly, what we learn from literature and history is that "[v]iolence is not to be denied, but it can be diverted to another object, something it can sink its teeth into," and that something is a scapegoat, a sacrificial victim.[46]

Girardians point to the universal antagonism of doubles in mythology and literature, Romulus and Remus, and Cain and Abel, and so it is the killing of a brother, an enemy twin, that provides the reappearance of difference, or a differential system, which serves to discourage mimetic rivalry and collective violence, and so allow the founding of a cultural order—Rome or the Cainite community.[47]

Therefore, it is not the existence of differences but the uncertainty surrounding the collapse of differences that leads to violence and conflict. Is this what we can see in the cycle of killings between Azeris and Armenians, Abkhazi and Georgians, and so on? When *differences are more certain* communities can participate in a kind of syncretism, in which Hindus might attend the celebrations of Moharram and Muslims would attend Dussehra feasts. The more recent riots in Gujarat show that the danger comes when elites—not the poor or uneducated—seek to purify and reform their religious traditions.

Where does the impetus for such purity, reform, and violence come from? In order to answer this question scholars have reached back to the Greek myth of Narcissus to find a link between narcissism and nationalist intolerance. Nationalism is considered to be a kind of narcissism, when a nationalist takes what are (by the outside observer) the neutral, minor facts about people—language, religion, culture, tradition, and history—and constructs a narrative in which they become major differences between them. Rulers and elites—political entrepreneurs—now fortify the boundaries, they empty the middle ground, and increase the uncertainty between friends and neighbors, and people that are fundamentally the same—Serbs and Croats or Hutu and Tutsi.[48]

The narcissism of minor differences is what Girardians would expect as one of the indicators of a sacrificial crisis in culture and society, but they reject the notion that the differences themselves are responsible for ethnic or religious conflict. It is not the existence of these differences in some primordial sense, but the loss, or the threat of the loss, of them that can lead to violence and conflict. "[I]t is not the differences but the loss of them that gives rise to violence and chaos. . . . This loss forces men into perpetual confrontation, one that strips them of all their distinctive characteristics—in short, of their 'identities'."[49]

The Girardian importance on maintaining ethnic and religious differences for stability and social cohesion is borne out in the literature on civil wars and post-conflict transformation. For many scholars the surprising result of this literature is that ethnic and religious divisions significantly reduce the risk of conflict. It is more difficult to mobilize and organize rebellions across ethnic groups in the same country. Therefore, strengthening and maintaining ethnic and religious diversity can actually make states and societies safer rather than more dangerous.[50] Globalization, like modernization, can pose a threat to this kind of stability, and so there are, as we see in the next few chapters, cultural and religious resources necessary for sustainable globalization.

Mimetic Rivalry and the Rational Choice
Theory of Violence and Conflict

The literature on civil wars and post-conflict transitions appears to be at odds with a theory of mimetic rivalry and violence because it discounts culture and religion. It would seem that poverty and inequality, contrary to what many people seem to believe, is not the cause of violence or rebellion. Civil wars or internal wars are about greed and not the purported grievances social groups use to justify their conflicts or rebellions. It is economic agendas, the economically motivated actions by individuals and social groups rather than ancient hatreds, or long-suppressed ethnic or religious grievances that are the cause of civil wars or internal conflicts.[51]

What is to be made of these arguments from a Girardian perspective? The first thing a Girardian perspective might question about the economic motives for violence is how economists determine the motives of people involved in civil conflicts. Economists, following the methods of social science, infer or explain human motivations from observed patterns of human behavior. What this allows them to do is ignore the realm of ideas or culture as the reasons people give for their actions as relevant for explaining human actions because they can conceal the true motives for action. What is important for economists, as well as for other social scientists, is what people do that can be observed, and not what they say are the reasons for their action (this is the approach adopted in quadrant III of figure 2.1 in chapter 2).

Thus, "if someone says, 'I don't like chocolates,' but keeps on eating them, we infer that she really likes them, and the question of why she says the opposite is then relegated to being of secondary importance."[52] Well, if someone in Poland in the 1970s had said "I don't like communism," but could be observed at all the local communist party functions, would we infer that person really liked communism? I don't think so. We would probably argue there were hidden aspects of power at the time that influenced her decision.

This narrowly focused approach to human motivation is based on the illusion of autonomous desire, and Girardians might even deplore the notion that human behavior can be reduced in this way.[53] Recall human motivation is based on the triangular structure of desire so the goods or objects people desire, and their ideas about what to desire, are based on what they learn to want or desire from other people in society.

Girard recognizes mimetic desire as an inevitable part of the human condition. The issue is where do the models or mediators come from—the gun-toting fourteen year old in Liberia or Sierra Leone, Serbia's lieutenant who shows his troops what it means to be a man, and spreads Serbian seed by raping Bosnian Muslim women, or is it more positive models?

Girardians argue a person copies, mainly unconsciously, who or what they are attracted to or repelled from ("I hate chocolates"), even as they deny the extent to which their desires are mediated through the desires of others in order to make a social space for their own, seemingly original identity. I very much doubt economists think child soldiers in Africa "really liked" killing their parents or siblings even though they said they did or could even be observed killing them.

The second thing Girardians might say about this explanatory approach is that it is based on a social scientist's conception of human motivation, what Irving Kristol once called the elephantiasis of reason. The notion that economic factors are the main drivers of conflict, along with demographics, natural resources, and the environment explain conflict without the passions, religious ideals, dreams, urges, altruism, and malevolence of human beings. Where in this kind of analysis are people who believe things and feel passions, who have visions of a future world that they are often willing to take risks for, and which they are even willing to sacrifice themselves?[54]

The third thing a Girardian perspective might emphasize is that what is important is the type of good rather than the supply of good that is the object of rivalry and conflict. Girard argues that with nonexclusive or collective goods, like renewable resources, or learning the appropriate way to milk a cow, mimetic desire can be peaceful and productive, but with the mimetic desire toward exclusive goods or objects (social positions, territory, or nonrenewable resources) the inevitable result is mimetic rivalry that often spills over into a contagion of conflict and violence.

Is Terror in the Mind of God?
Mimetic Rivalry and Religiously Motivated Terrorism

Religious terrorism is a type of collective violence. It can be called terrorism because the acts of violence are aimed deliberately and indiscriminately at the civilian population. It is religious in so far as its ideology, motivation, and organizational structure can be identified with those of the main world religions. Many scholars point out that terrorism as a form of collective violence is a strategy of a political movement, and is not a creed, doctrine, or ideology. The saying goes, "one person's terrorist is another person's freedom fighter," and while this may be true, a holy martyr is not the same thing as a freedom fighter. What the subjectivism of this common phrase hides is that there can be different types of motivation and legitimacy for what social scientists seek to identify as a certain type of collective violence.[55]

Religious ideas—including here, beliefs, virtues, and practices—matter, and they have consequences for terrorism or political action because ideas and the social or religious groups that espouse them provide the mimetic model for what it is that is desired in society. Therefore, religious ideas—including holy war, cosmic, or religious warfare—and the triangular structure of desire need to be brought together if we are going to fully understand global rise of religious violence.[56]

It has already been pointed out that the social construction of identity involves forces of attraction and repulsion that are part of the triangular structure of desire. It is now possible to argue that some of the analysis of religious militancy or fundamentalism is based on what Girard would call the illusion of spontaneous desire. Girardian theory suggests that resentment arising from the triangular structure of desire is one of the underlying sources of Islamic militancy or fundamentalism. Girard, in the immediate aftermath of September 11 argued, "what is occurring today is a mimetic rivalry on a planetary scale," but something more is required as a part of this explanation.[57] There are nonethnic origins of nationalism in Asia or the Middle East, in which anti-Western nationalism is an expression of a deeper sense of humiliation by the secular West.

What took place on September 11 was an Islamic phenomenon as well as a terrorist phenomenon. It is widely regarded that the nature of the object, Islam, the object inspiring such passion or militancy, is not sufficient to account for such desire, and so analysis shifts from the object, Islam, and to the subject, the Islamic militant, and so the person's agency, liberty, or psychology are what is examined. We, in the West, ask questions such as, "Why do men rebel?" or "Why do Muslims rebel?"[58] What is not done is critically evaluate the assumptions about modernity behind why these questions are framed in this way.

What needs to be examined as part of the triangular structure of desire is how the West—or, really, the United States—is the model or mediator of Islamic desire, and so the source of Islamic militancy. Sheik Yusuf al-Qaradawi offers a good example of the way the triangular structure of desire influences the social construction of identity. Sheik al-Qaradawi is arguably Sunni Islam's most influential cleric, with an immensely popular television program on al-Jazeera broadcast throughout the Islamic world.

The mimetic model for his religious mission is provided by the United States, the most modern country in the world, and the "tele-evangelists" that are part of American culture. The country is "acting like a god on earth" he says, and yet even as he "rails against the United States" in his sermons, and is repelled by the United States, he and his followers embrace "its protection, its gossip, and its hipness." The mimetic model for the al-Jazeera reporter in the "flak jacket, irreverent and cool against the Kabul or Baghdad background, barrows a form—a mimetic model—perfected in the country [the United States] whose sins and follies that the reporter has come to chronicle."[59]

Hisham Sharabi, a noted Palestinian nationalist who studied at the American University of Beirut in the 1940s, provides an older example of triangular structure of desire. Sharabi recalls from his student days, "Our leaders and teachers hated the West but loved it at the same time; the West was the source of everything they despised and the source of their misery and contempt. It was thus that they implanted in us an inferiority complex toward the West combined with a deification of it."[60]

The United States as mimetic model mediates reality about life-settings to the object, in this case the Islamic world. The United States, as the world's mimetic model of modernity—and only superpower—is inevitably in this kind of mimetic relationship toward the Islamic world; indeed, as it is toward the entire world. According to Girard this is what mimetic desire is, a form of barrowed desire, in this case the fast-paced, hip culture of the United States, which bears the mimetic model of modernity, democracy, and globalization, and so those who want it, and who are attracted to it, also rail against it, and are repelled by it at the same time.

The mimetic rage against the United States "is oddly derived from that very same attraction," a process that can also be seen in modern Saudi Arabia, the source of so many of the highjackers, and the key members of al-Qaeda. The United States helped to invent modern Saudi Arabia, and the mimetic model of the country can be seen in Saudi suburbs, in its urban sprawl, shopping malls, and in the education of its elite at American universities. It should not be surprising that this is also where anti-Americanism is fierce. "A culture [like that of the United States] that casts so long a shadow is fated to be emulated and resented at the same time."[61]

Islamic civilization, like other non-Western civilizations, has had to respond to the conquering West. The wounds to the Islamic world's self-esteem, which itself had once been a conquering civilization—let us not forget, has stimulated Islamist reformist or revivalist movements for years. However, the way the United States is resented and emulated as a mimetic model will be a result of the impact of triangular structure of desire in world politics.

Girard argues in relation to the September 11 terrorists, "By their effectiveness, by the sophistication of the means employed, by the knowledge that they had of the United States, by the training, were not the authors of the attack at least somewhat American? Here we are in the middle of mimetic contagion." It is through the triangular structure of desire that Islamists are in many ways the most modern—dare I say most "American"—when they think they are being most true to the Islamic tradition.[62]

The triangular structure of desire does not fully explain the rise or the legitimacy of religious violence in the Arab world or the Islamic world. The mimetic rivalry, the attraction and resentment of the United States, is also widely found among Europe's elites and young people for whom "America is both menace and seducer, both monster and model."[63] But it wasn't Germans, the French, or other Europeans, nor was it Chileans or even the Vietnamese who carried out the September 11 attacks. The acts were carried out by Islamists, and not people who shared with the European Left its reading of U.S. foreign policy. This explanation, as popular as it is in some circles, provides no insight into the grievances of radical Muslims or their fantasies of a U.S. war against Islam.[64]

Something more was required, and that something is a particular form of Islamic resentment, and terrorism as a form of behavior that had to be desired and learned through the mimetic models of Islamic militancy. Religious violence has sources quite apart from, or in addition to, the political dynamics of collective violence. Large-scale religious change in world politics or shifts in the popularity and distribution of the main world religions are not the result of individual conversion or the spread of global missions. It is a result of shifts in the power of the religions or civilisations in which they are embedded.

The primary issue between the West and the Islamic world is the shift in world power since the sixteenth century. At its root is cultural and religious resentment, which cannot be resolved by greater economic development or modernization. What is resented—Arab, Ottoman, or Islamic—is their inferiority, and the gradual fall of Islam, and the object of desire—the rise of the West, which is the model of modernity.[65] Western modernity, which is a form of borrowed desire, has been going on in the Islamic world for over two centuries. Muslims have wrestled with the questions about what ideas and institutions they could barrow from the West and still remain Arabs or Muslims.[66] The struggle in the Islamic world has always been for authenticity as well as development.[67]

The point of departure, as I argued in an earlier chapter, was the modernizing mythology of the West. The modern Islamic revival, like the rise of modern evangelicalism, begins with a rejection of this modernizing mythology as the only point of departure, and is a turn toward a revitalization of the religious tradition. These projects of religious renewal do not necessarily lead to violence or terrorism, but why they sometimes have done so is because of a sacrificial crisis in world politics.

A Sacrificial Crisis in World Politics?

The motif of sacrifice is clearly apparent in the Islamic violence in Algeria, Lebanon, Israel, Egypt, Iraq, Chechnya, Russia, Indonesia, and elsewhere in the Islamic world, but it can also be found among Sikh militants in India and Sinhalese militants in Sri Lanka. A Girardian understanding of religious violence is that it is one of the results of the erosion of the sacrificial system. The decay of religious practices is linked to the deterioration of behavior in society, and so inevitably the eroding of the sacrificial system results in the emergence of reciprocal violence. The civil war in Lebanon, the Israeli occupation of Gaza and the West Bank, and the U.S. occupation of Iraq provide examples of how neighbors who once discharged their mutual aggressions on a third party—scapegoat, who joined together in promoting social solidarity by the sacrifice of an "outside" victim: the American troops in Lebanon, the Israelis in southern Lebanon, the Israelis in the occupied territories, and now the American and British troops in Iraq—are now turning to sacrificing one another.[68]

The erosion of the sacrificial system is what was behind the Islamic violence and terrorism: the "self-martyring" or sacrificing of young people in Amal and Hizbollah in Lebanon during the civil war, and it is behind the conflict between Hamas, Islamic Jihad, and the PLO's al-Aqsa Martyrs' Brigade in Israel and Palestine since the second Intifada began in 2000. The young people resemble the sacrificial victims of many religions, although they are agents of self-sacrifice or self-martyrdom, and are in fact chosen by society, or at least by social pressure from their communities, and are then trained by terrorist organizations.

Greed or grievance is not what determines how people respond in different economic, cultural, or political situations. What determines how they respond is the social construction of mimetic desire, the goods or objects people desire based on the desires and ideas they learn from the others in the culture of violence or the terrorist groups around them. They provide the models or are the mediator for their ideas about what to desire in society.

The young people are victims in the sacrificial competition between Hamas, Islamic Jihad, and the al-Aqsa Martyrs' Brigade in Gaza and the West Bank in the same way as there was sacrificial competition between the rival Shi'ite terrorist groups Amal and Hizbollah in Lebanon during the civil war. The same thing could be said about Muqtada al-Sadr, accused of having murdered Abdel-Majid al-Khoei, a rival shiite cleric in Iraq. Islamic terrorism is caused by mimetic rivalry, as each group attempted to outdo the other one in acts of self-sacrifice or martyrdom.

The difficulty with the terrorist organizations in Lebanon was that while they were conceived of largely as "acts of war," and therefore, fulfilled functions that were useful politically, the very structure of their operations suggested a religious rite was taking place. The perpetrators went deliberately to their deaths, and these acts of self-sacrifice were designed not only to maximize their political impact as acts of war, but they functioned the way Girard has indicated the sacrificial mechanism should function. They were a diversion and dissipation of violence born of an inner feud, that is, they helped to forestall fratricidal violence from within the Shi'ite community, as the suicide bombers are now doing within the Palestinian community. In other words, the competitive cycle of violence, done in the name of Islam, helped to avert a cycle of violence among the adherents of Islam. It was when this sacrificial cycle collapsed that violence turned inward upon the Shi'ites of Lebanon.[69]

Among Shi'ite groups in Iraq, who are all ostensibly opposed to the American occupation, the same kind of mimetic rivalry and failure of the sacrificial system may have started to spill over into collective violence. One of the indications of this failure may be the murder of the young, prominent, cleric, Abdel Majid al-Khoei, inside Najaf's most holy shrine, and the bomb attack on Mohammed Said al-Hakim, the conservative ayatollah, as part of the conflict between those Shi'ites clustered around Ali al-Sistani, the Grand Ayatollah, who supports a democratic Shi'ite state, and those backing Muqtada al-Sadr, who has more aggressively pursued an Islamic state modeled on Iran's clerical rule.[70]

Religious ideas matter and we now know only too well that they can have deadly and horrific consequences. While the triangular structure of desire and the failure of the sacrificial crisis may be crucial for understanding the cultural, religious, and political dynamics of religious violence, the mediator or model of desire is important for understanding the ideology, motivation, passions, and vision that are learned by those involved in religious violence. Hamas, for example, rejects the idea that what they call holy martyrs are suicide-bombers because this seems to convey the idea that their acts were done idiosyncratically or thoughtlessly. Like all "true believers," whether they believe in Hitler, and the triumph of a greater Germany, Lenin and the class struggle, or Mohammed and Islam's final triumph, the power of the suicide bombers' belief comes from the fact that they have learned from others to interpret the meaning and significance of their lives beyond any immediate context of history.[71]

Religious terrorism seeks a cosmic or transcendent justification rather than only political, social, or economic objectives. The would be martyrs or suicide bombers have to learn that "terror is in the mind of God," that is, they have to learn from others in their community and in the terrorist organization to place their lives within a mimetic model of martydom and cosmic war that sees martyrdom as a religious obligation.[72]

The life of a martyr or suicide bomber is intelligible when it is interpreted within a model of sacrifice, martyrdom, and victimization. Young people learn how to become suicide bombers by the mimetic model of other suicide bombers, and their familiarity with organizations whose identity as cultural, religious, political, social welfare, and terrorist organizations is inherently blurred, which helps recruits in the training, planning, and carrying out of their deadly operations.[73]

Chapter 6

"Creating a Just and Durable Peace": Rethinking Religion and International Cooperation

So in the name of Christian principles and the prophetic tradition I have argued the necessity of destroying the moralistic arrogance of the concept of a just and durable peace in a situation in which tragedy and possible grace are the only categories that can be applied to the present disrupted world.[1]

—*Paul Tillich*
Response to John Foster Dulles, Secretary of State (1953–1959), Head of the Commission on a Just and Durable Peace (1943)

Conflict and cooperation have always been a key part of the study of international relations since the discipline started after World War I. The role of religious non-state actors has been most noticeable in activity to promote international cooperation through peacebuilding, conflict resolution, faith-based diplomacy, interfaith dialogue, and economic development; some of these issues are examined in the next few chapters.

The focus of this chapter is on the role of religion in promoting those forms of international cooperation that have become organized or institutionalized, that is, it refers to the cooperative activity between states that reflects the rules, laws, norms, or practices of international society. International regimes such as the financial institutions set up after the World War II known as the Bretton Woods system, and regional or international organizations like the European Union or the United Nations are examples of this form of organized cooperation in international relations.

One of the reasons for the blind spots in U.S. national security policy, as we saw in chapter 2, was the way culture and religion have been ignored or marginalized in international relations. There may be blind spots regarding the role of culture and religion in theories of international cooperation as well. The mainstream rationalist theories argue that realism and power politics—states, national interests, alliances, and interstate bargaining, or liberalism, with its emphasis on economic interdependence and the role of international institutions—can adequately explain international cooperation. However, in this chapter we will see that the English School argues that a prior or deeper agreement among states may be necessary to develop the rules, laws, norms, or institutions of international society. In other words, a deeper understanding may be necessary for the rational interests of states to foment international cooperation.

The importance of religion can be seen in the role of Protestantism in shaping the nature of American hegemony in the Bretton Woods postwar international order, and in the way European integration was, and for many Europeans still is, a political project of Christian Democracy and Catholic social thought. This remains the case even though secularists recently won the day, and eliminated any mention of Christianity in the new European Constitution. What both of these case studies illustrate is that, in the future, we may have to take more seriously the role of culture and religion in promoting international cooperation on a whole range of global issues.

Rationalist Theories of International Cooperation

We have already seen that rationalist theories share many of the same assumptions, which tend to marginalize the role of culture and religion in international affairs, so it should not be surprising that there is very little place for culture or religion in the theories of international cooperation. First, both neorealism and neoliberalism emphasize an objective or functional conception of the social bond between the states in international society. If states cooperate, according to neorealists, if they form regimes or alliances, or join international organizations, international cooperation is explained as a rational response to threats to national security.

Neoliberals effectively concede one of the neorealists' main explanations for international cooperation. States do pursue their national interests but added to one of those interests is efficiency, a desire to put their relations on a stable basis by providing predicable and enforceable rules, norms, or laws to govern their relations.

Therefore, quite apart from hegemonic stability or "idealist" appeals to morality, it is in the rational interest of states to cooperate with each other in international relations.[2]

Second, and most important, both rationalist approaches assume what I have called the "Westphalian presumption" in international relations. Recall, this is the notion, going back to the mythology of political liberalism surrounding the Treaty of Westphalia, which says religious and cultural pluralism cannot be accommodated in a global multicultural international society, and so must be privatized or nationalized if there is going to be domestic or international order. Thus, both of these rationalist perspectives marginalize the impact of culture and religion in their explanation of international cooperation. In their objective or functional understanding of international society states cooperate without a shared sense of identity, belonging, or obligation.

Some scholars have tried to use Ferdinand Tonnies's concepts of community and society to bring together neorealism and the English School's concept of international society. They have described a *gemeinschaft* understanding of international society as something that grows organically from a shared culture, involving bonds of common sentiment, experience and identity, such as the ancient Greek international society of city-states. This can be distinguished from a *gesellschaft* understanding of international society, as something that is contractual and constructed. A *gesellschaft* understanding sees international society as a rational and functional response to the interdependence among states that are part of an international system.

Therefore, whether or not states share a common culture, at some point the scope, intensity, and regularity of their interactions will force the development of a degree of recognition and accommodation, and they will work out common rules, norms, or laws among themselves. An international society can evolve functionally from the rational "logic of anarchy," that is, the situation of states without any overarching sovereign or world authority and without any preexisting cultural bonds between them.[3]

One of the main flaws with this approach is that it is really based on an unstated Western hegemony of the international order. We know—in the IMF, the World Bank, and the United Nations—who makes the rules of the game of nations. The rise of key, non-Western, powers in the twenty-first century, such as Japan, India, China, Brazil, and Russia, and the global resurgence of religion may require a better understanding of international cooperation. What is the basis of the international order in a global and multicultural international society?

The English School and the Cultural Foundations of International Society

We have already seen that the English School and social constructivism raise a question about the nature of the social bond in international society and how it should be characterized. They argue rationalist approaches leaves out a crucial part of the story, the intersubjective element of the social bond in international society. Should we forget about culture and geography for the meaning of Europe? Are nationality, democracy and free markets the only factors that constitute the identity of Europe today?[4] For the new European Constitution, for example, to ignore that Europe is primarily a cultural and historical concept, with Christianity as its cultural foundation, is another stark reminder of how culture and religion are marginalized in international relations.[5]

In fact, a prior or deeper agreement—an organic or intersubjective understanding among states—may be necessary for the development of rules, norms, or institutions that govern the social structure of any regional or international society. A deeper agreement also may be necessary for the rationality and interests of states to foment international cooperation effectively.

According to the early English School, the intersubjective sense of belonging between states *emerged* through a common culture, which underpinned different states-systems in history. This contention was mainly developed by Martin Wight, Herbert Butterfield, and Michael Donelan, who recognized the role of religious doctrines in different cultures and civilizations, and examined their consequences for international society.

The notion that religion and culture underpin international society was one of the main reasons for an organic conception of international society (quadrant II in figure 3.1, chapter 3). It was Wight who believed that a common culture, a degree of cultural unity among states, was necessary for the existence of international society. Why was this the case? What was important to Wight was the degree of intersubjectivity, or sense of belonging and obligation, which a common culture provides for any meaningful conception of international society. Wight argued a common culture or civilization was one of the most important foundations for past international societies.[6] This was the case even if a prior political hegemony, caused mainly by colonialism or imperialism, was responsible for the spread of the common culture which formed the foundation of international society.[7]

Wight recognized that "the greater the cultural unity of a states-system, the greater its sense of distinctness from the surrounding world is likely to be."[8] This led to two interrelated problems, which have become accentuated by the global resurgence of religion. The first problem is the relation with "the Other," the outsider, what Wight called "the barbarian problem" in international relations. Wight, although this was less appreciated at the time, was clearly on the side of the "barbarians," and vehemently criticized the moral pretensions of European colonialism, or the view that developing countries were outside the moral parameters of international society.

Although the English School was concerned from the beginning with the incorporation of "the Other" as international society expanded, in the first instance this concern was expressed over the resiliency of the existing institutions of international society. The English School exhibited a conservative concern for international order, and this is why it accepted a partial accommodation to the demands of developing countries. However, the way the English School accepted some of these demands fits uneasily with their assumptions, made during the heyday of modernization theory, that the Western-educated elites in developing countries represented the will of their populations.[9]

We have already seen how tenuous this assumption was. The global spread of democracy has been accompanied by the global resurgence of religion and demand for cultural authenticity and development, which are at odds with the modernizing mythology espoused by developing countries. What was less appreciated at the time was the extent to which the revolt against the West took place within the discourse of Western modernity. This explains why the English School at this time was relatively sanguine about accommodating some of the demands of developing countries within the existing international order.[10]

The second problem Wight raised was concerning religion, and this was the concept of "holy war" or jihad, since political communities outside the states-system were subject to different rules of war than those within international society. Wight asked, "have all states-systems entertained some notion of Holy War in their external relations? Or is it a product of the Judeo–Christian–Islamic tradition?"[11] He did not think the evidence was clear. Given the global resurgence of religion and the rise of ethno-national conflicts and terrorism, Wight's question is an increasingly important one. Contemporary scholars, as we saw in chapter 5, have reformulated it as a question about the relationship between war, religion, and monotheism.

The later English School has marginalized the study of religion and the kind of questions Martin Wight and Herbert Butterfield asked about religions and civilizations, even as it has accepted the need for a common cultural foundation for international society. It was the "solidarist" interpreters of the English School—John Vincent, Andrew Linklater, and even Hedley Bull in his later writings—who were most interested in a cultural underpinning of international society.

As a foundation for international society they turned to the common culture of liberal modernity. The solidarist interpreters were rightly concerned that the neorealist and neoliberal accounts of international society overlooked the deeper structure on which it rests. In other words, the pluralism of international society rests on a deeper solidarity. However, they accepted the English School's early arguments about the cultural foundations of international society, but only if they could be transformed into support for the cosmopolitan culture of liberal modernity as the common culture of a global international society.[12]

Non-Western countries have reacted to the way the culture of liberal modernity is being imposed on other societies, and this can be seen in the way religion and culture strongly influence social policy. In some instances social policy has become foreign policy. We could see this in the often angry debates at UN conferences on human rights, women, and population, where the Vatican, often in alliance with delegations from developing countries, opposed the secular liberal views of the mainly rich and white delegations from North America and Western Europe on a whole range of social policy issues.[13]

At these conferences the "cosmopolitan" culture of Western modernity confronted the new assertiveness of elites from developing countries who, in response to the cultural and religious response of their own populations, want the United Nations to show a greater sensitivity to their cultural and religious values in social policy. This was also the case regarding human rights, where there was a call for a greater appreciation that one dialect of human rights, the dialect of a rights-based liberalism of a highly individualistic culture—the United States—was being globalized without due regard for the cultural and religious traditions of human rights in other countries.[14]

Thus, the global resurgence of religion challenges the English School's complacency about the kind of challenges that face the international order. The global expansion of international society, the incorporation of non-Western cultures and societies into a global international society, and global resurgence of religion have brought into prominence the role of religion and culture in international cooperation.

Protestantism and Hegemonic Stability in the Postwar Era

One of the most important forms of cooperation between states is through international regimes. Regimes are arrangements based on agreed rules, norms, or practices to govern the conduct of states on specific functional aspects of international relations that have become global issues, such as trade, foreign aid, monetary stability, the environment, or nonproliferation, and so cooperation is organized around these issue areas.[15] Regimes often depend on states for their rules to be enforced, and so they are most effective when a single power or hegemon holds a disproportionate or preponderance of military and economic power to enforce or dominate the rules and arrangements that maintain the international order.

What is called the theory of hegemonic stability holds that a stable world and a stable world economy need a "stabilizer," leadership exercised by one state in the international system. Some degree of hegemony helps to maintain international stability by reducing anarchy, deterring aggression, promoting free trade, and providing a hard currency that can be used as a world standard. One of the most important examples is Britain's role in international relations in the nineteenth century. It was the absence of British leadership or hegemony because of its weakened position after World War I that led to the chaos and instability of the 1930s, and ultimately to World War II.[16] The most recent example is the United States after World War II, and its role in constructing the postwar Bretton Woods international order.[17]

We have seen that both the English School and social constructivists emphasize the intersubjective bond between states that
make up international society while rationalist theories emphasize
the objective and material interests that lead to international
cooperation. What this section probes is the adequacy of the existing
theory of regimes and hegemonic stability to explain America's
postwar role, and the particular form of hegemony that developed
under American leadership.

The United States has shown considerable ambivalence regarding
its role as a single power or hegemon maintaining the postwar international order. Its foreign policy stance toward the rest of the world
has oscillated between isolationism and internationalism, unilateri-
alism and multilateralism, and between moralism and realism. The
moralism in U.S. foreign policy has oscillated between seeing itself
as too good for the world or too evil for the world.[18] The cultural and
religious dimensions of these debates, in this case the debate over
hegemony or hegemonic stability in the postwar era, have not had
much of a place in regime theory or the study of U.S. foreign policy.

How is the shift from American isolationism to internationalism
after the World War II to be explained, or how is the nature of
both *American* hegemony and internationalism to be explained?
Most studies of U.S. foreign policy now recognize that the standard
dichotomy between isolationism and internationalism going
back to the U.S. refusal to join the League of Nations paints far too
stark a contrast in American foreign policy. What was at issue
in Wilson's day, as well as in our own time, are different types of
internationalism.[19]

Therefore, what needs to be explained is the type of internationalism being promoted by American hegemony in the early postwar international order. The United States became committed to
multilateralism and internationalism in the early years of the Cold
War. It established the principle of foreign aid with the Truman
Doctrine and the Marshall Plan, and it was instrumental in forming
the United Nations and the Bretton Woods system as a type of
international regime.

The usual explanation is the need for security, prosperity, and the
rebuilding of Europe following the beginning of the Cold War.
It is the structural features of international relations, the existing
distribution of power (i.e., the rise or decline of British or American
dominance), or the interdependence of states that are said to
account for developments in international cooperation.

Scholars now recognize that in their study of regimes they need to look beyond the holistic level of analysis of the international system. A single power or hegemon tries to persuade other states to conform to its vision of the world, but where does that vision and the motivation to support the regime come from? Questions like these are examined at the state or society levels of analysis. The role of domestic politics, institutions, and leadership are all factors that influence a state's actions in international relations. It turns out that these factors are important for the way regimes are constructed, and for the maintaining of hegemony because they influence the political willingness of the hegemon to make and enforce the rules or to let regimes breakdown.

Therefore, domestic attitudes, belief systems, religious beliefs, civil religion, and political ideologies all help form the kind of political culture that influences how regimes are formed, what maintains them, and how they operate in international relations. This means that it is also important to examine the formation of political coalitions, political structures, and the processes of decisionmaking that are important for understanding the construction and breakdown of regimes.[20]

There are two key areas in which these factors affect regimes and hegemonic stability. The first area relates to the social bond between states and is about the problems of regime compliance and the hegemon's regime commitment. Vision and vigilance are a part of the maintenance of regimes and hegemonic stability. "Any strategy of hegemonic leadership must . . . seek to maintain the national base of resources upon which governmental influence and leadership rest. From this perspective, the failure of U.S. foreign policy lay not in American leaders' attitudes toward international cooperation, but in their inability to implement their preferred policies in the face of domestic political constraints."[21]

The second area relates to the impact of interest group politics on regimes. It needs to be recognized that hegemons do not face the same kind of constraints in the international system that prevents small countries from succumbing to domestic special interest groups. Therefore, hegemons are prone to the sclerotic tendencies of some of these pressure groups.[22]

What do these factors have to do with the U.S. shift from isolationism to internationalism, and for what regime compliance and commitment mean for our understanding of the postwar international order? If the shift in U.S. foreign policy toward multilateralism and internationalism are to be explained during the early years of the Cold War—support for the United Nations and the Bretton Woods system—then this may require looking for changes in the political culture inside the United States as well as at the security situation in the wider world. It requires looking at the content of the ideas, values, and motivations for American hegemony, and the interest groups that supported this type of American hegemony, as well as the kind of principles they supported for the postwar international order.

When we do this what we may find is that Protestantism was related to hegemonic stability during the early years of the Cold War. Culture and religion may not be as detached from regime theory or theories of hegemonic stability as many scholars have imagined. Reinhold Niebuhr and an influential coalition of Christian realists and Christian liberals became what Heather Warren has called, the "theologians of a new world order" after the World War II. They helped to articulate and implement a type of ecumenical Protestantism that shaped the goals and nature of the support for U.S. hegemonic leadership and U.S. foreign policy in the early years of the Cold War.[23]

The idea that Protestantism may have had a role in providing the cultural and ideological foundation for hegemonic stability brings out important aspects of rationalist and social constructivist theories of international relations. The first aspect is the way the rationality of states as actors in neorealism and neoliberalism is detached from the larger considerations of culture and religion in which states are socially and historically embedded.

Because of the spread of modernization, of which secularization is considered to be an inherent part, the importance of culture and religion to political culture and to the formation of "national culture," and how these factors influence styles of diplomacy or the substance of foreign policy are no longer considered to be relevant to foreign policy analysis (as states make the inevitable transition from traditional to modern society).[24] However, as we see in the next chapter on diplomacy, scholars are rediscovering the impact of culture and religion in these areas of international relations as well.

The second aspect is the way social constructivism has influenced our understanding of the impact of culture on *the form of hegemony* shaping the postwar international order. John Ruggie claims that at the unit, state, or individual level of analysis social constructivism seeks to examine the full array of ideational factors, such as beliefs, principled beliefs, aspirations, and ideology that shape the actor's outlook and behavior on a whole series of policy problems.[25]

Ruggie has argued that it was not only hegemony but also the cultural and political form of *American* hegemony that led to the shaping of the postwar international order. The fact that the United States as a hegemon acted in its interests after the World War II does not explain the choices its leaders made, or why the country acted the way it did since other single powers could or would have acted differently. It was also possible, as George Kennan had predicted, that multipolarity would remerge after the World War II as the power configuration of international relations. President Roosevelt believed that the isolationist tendencies in the country had to be neutralized and the only way of doing this was by binding the Unites States to a more permanent framework of multilateral institutions.[26]

The role of Protestantism in shaping U.S. foreign policy during the early years of the Cold War is an example of the way, as social constructivists indicate, ideational factors can influence the nature of hegemony and hegemonic stability. The notion that it was *a type of ecumenical Protestantism* that helped to shape the political form of *American* hegemony in the early days of the Cold War is meant to restore a sense of balance to the accounts of hegemony and stability that have ignored or marginalized the impact of culture or religion on U.S. foreign policy.

There is both a biblical and a republican strand to American political culture or American civil religion. This biblical or Protestant strand of American political culture goes back to the impact of the Puritans on the founding of the country. What was central to this heritage was a combination of personal faith, calling or vocation, and public engagement with the world.[27] It was a dominant part of its political identity until the late twentieth century when a more pluralistic religious culture has dominated American life, which is one of the factors that has lead to the culture wars in American politics.

There is another strand of American political culture variously called civic nationalism or the republican tradition. It is this tradition that recognizes the Enlightenment origins of the United States, the rule of law, democracy, and civic engagement, and has looked back to the early Roman republic for inspiration. Robert

Bellah has argued that both the biblical and the republican strands are deeply interrelated in American history.

John Ikenberry, contrary to this view, has argued in relation to American multilateralism, "Ethnic and religious identities and disputes are pushed downward into civil society and removed from the political arena."[28] This seems like a remarkable distortion of American politics and the diplomatic record. It is an indication of the way culture and religion are still marginalized in the study of American foreign relations to acknowledge only the republican strand as important for American support for multilateralism and international cooperation.

Why is it so important to study Protestantism as an important part of American hegemony? Henry Luce, the publisher of *Time, Life*, and *Fortune* magazines, foresaw an American Century at the beginning of the twentieth century, but we may have to be reminded in our time that this was still very much a *Protestant* American Century. It was the Protestantism of American political culture at this time that provided the cultural foundation of U.S. foreign policy. The term "post-Protestant" was only popularly applied in the 1960s after John F. Kennedy was elected as the first Roman Catholic president of the United States.[29]

Robert Keohane argues that the American Century began in 1947 with the Truman Doctrine and the Marshall Plan, and it was already beginning to fade in 1963 with the Interest Equalization Tax, which was the first attempt by the United States to protect the status of the dollar against the consequences of the open world economy. Thus, it might be said that the end of the American Century and the end of ecumenical Protestantism that determined the moral and political vision as well as the culture of the American Century roughly occurred at the same time.

Who were the theologians of the new world order? Key members, such as Reinhold Niebuhr, John Bennett, Henry P. Van Dusen, Francis P. Miller, George Harkness, and Samuel McCrea Cavert, were public intellectuals as well as part of the Protestant establishment, at a time when Protestantism was a key component of American political culture. In some ways another person should be included in this group, more as a political heavyweight than as a public intellectual, and that is John Foster Dulles. Dulles was on the governing board of the Presbyterian Church in the United States, he was an influential voice in ecumenical circles, as well as Secretary of State in the Eisenhower Administration. It might be argued that the moral and religious vision behind his ideas has been lost in many accounts of U.S. foreign policy.[30]

It was this group that helped to shape and change America's political culture so it was willing to accept the hegemonic responsibilities of global leadership after the World War II. Many of these members played a key role in forming as well as supporting the Marshall Plan, the United Nations, and the Bretton Woods system. The secularism of our political analysis has distorted our understanding of what took place during these years. At least during the early years of the Cold War, Christian ecumenism, multilateralism, and internationalism should be seen as a set of interlinked political and cultural narratives that led to the founding of the United Nations, the Bretton Woods system, and the World Council of Churches at the same time.

The interlinked nature of these narratives helps us to understand a lot of other events during the early years of the Cold War. It should not be surprising that some of the theologians of the new world order influenced the drafting of the United Nations Charter, or that the Methodist Central Hall in Westminster, London, was the venue for the first meeting of the UN General Assembly, or that across the road, the first meeting of the Security Council took place in Church House, the main administrative building of the Church of England. Later on, staff members of the Church Commission on International Affairs helped in drafting key sections of the Universal Declaration of Human Rights.[31]

What was the theology of world order proposed by Protestant theologians and public intellectuals during the early years of the Cold War? During the high point of their engagement in world affairs they explained the importance of world events in religious or theological terms that the laity could understand. Remarkably, they made no triumphal reference to the end times schemas of earlier Protestant leaders (pre-millennial dispensationalism), did not emphasize Christ's Second Coming, and did not emphasize America's destiny or American exceptionalism.

What they formed was a "realist" theology meant for the here and now, the "time in between" creation and the end times. They were not on a crusade, to right every wrong in the world and to hasten the Second Coming, nor did not try to achieve heaven on earth, the absolute renewal of the world, nor were they about to build the "New Jerusalem," as the Christian Socialists in the Labor Party were trying to do in Britain.[32] The goal was to mitigate international hostility with the onset of the Cold War by a thoughtful Christian engagement in politics and interchurch relations, and later on in relation to deterrence in a nuclear age.[33]

In general this public theology held that the nations of the world were interlinked under God's sovereign control, and theology had a sovereign remedy for international discord. First, as Christian realists they did not shrink from the realities of power politics in international relations. In the late 1930s and 1940s this was expressed by a break with Norman Thomas, the leader of the Socialist Party in the United States, and with other pacifist liberals and socialists. There was a belief that Christianity was the one ideology that could challenge fascism, and the church could check the decline of the kind of secular politics that plunged the world into violent barbarism. In the late 1940s and 1950s, the church could do this again with the fight against the spread of communism.[34]

Second, the public theology of world order involved a self-critical ecclesiology, one that fostered a self-critical internationalism, one which, as Jefferson phrased it in the Declaration of Independence, had "a decent respect for the opinions of mankind." This ecclesiology was Christ-centered, with a realist bent to it, which meant that in Christ's light all people were shown to be sinful and in need of salvation. However, this perspective also led them to challenge the pride of nations and the fickleness of alliances, a perspective, which as David Brooks has recently said, is woefully missing from the debates on U.S. foreign policy today.[35]

The theologians of the new world order repudiated the simple dichotomy between the Soviet Union's evil empire and the virtue of American democracy, even as they vehemently escalated the rhetoric against the Soviet Union. They implicitly came to accept the postwar division of the world into spheres of influence, and recognized the value as well as the limits of the United Nations. It was not a world government nor did they expect it to become one.[36]

Third, the public theology of world order recognized that there was to sin and to God's grace a sense of universalism, which had been discarded and needed to be restored. It was this theological combination that led them to strike a balance between Christian humility and determined moral action in world politics. "To this end they spoke of the church being instrumental first in pronouncing which international arrangements accorded with Christian order and in establishing them through institutions, the United Nations in the secular form and the World Council of Churches in the religious."[37]

Now, it can be acknowledged, the global perspective and the views of the theologians of the new world order in these areas was probably beyond the levels of commitment found by the average, church-going population. Their public stature, or even the misperception of their public stature, still meant that they could shape public discourse at a time when Protestantism was a key part of the political culture in the United States. Recall that in chapter 3 one of the criticisms that explanatory theorists make regarding interpretive theory is its lack of law-like generalizations or general conclusions that can inform policy. It was pointed out there that one of the possible ways of overcoming this criticism is to locate key decision points in which different actions might have produced a different ending.

This is what happened during the 1940s. What we see is that given the public stature of the theologians of the new world order at crucial times, unlike during the debate in the 1920s over the League of Nations, such as the campaign in 1944 to promote UN membership, they had an important role in shaping public debate on this issue; and, even at times, in influencing the proposals at the conference at Dumbarton Oaks, which drafted the UN Charter.[38]

The theologians of the new world order helped to provide a moral optic with which to interpret international affairs, and believed that the postwar international order needed a spiritual foundation. In the first instance, leading to World War II, this led to a criticism of racist nationalism, and they established a reputation for themselves as a "prophetic" band of Protestant critics of the then reigning, optimistic, liberal theological tradition as it was applied to the social order. They rejected its chief emphasis on God's immanence and a weakened view of the impact of sin—personal and corporate—as the root of society's ills. This is what distinguished them from the "Social Gospel," liberal reformers in the United States, and from many of the Christian Socialists in Britain.[39] It is for this reason they opposed the pacifism of the liberals and socialists who advocated isolationism during World War II.[40]

Unlike many liberals or socialists who wanted to create opportunities for progress, for this group sin—individual and corporate— was part of the reality of the world. They believed Christians should take political action to prevent society's backsliding into moral barbarism, whether that meant fascism or communism. What was to prevent this from happening was the democratic states and the United Nations.[41]

The theologians of the new world order were concerned about communism but kept a distance from conservatives, and throughout the 1950s and 1960s they articulated a " 'mainstream' internationalist ideology" for American Protestantism, which combined "liberal transnationalism with a sobering emphasis on sin, God's transcendence, and revealed religion."⁴² It was the heyday of Protestantism's influence on American public life, and they unabashedly presumed they rightfully had the leadership to determine America's moral code, its national ideas, and its foreign policy.

What did this group of Protestant theologians and public intellectuals do to help create the postwar international order? John Foster Dulles was one of the people behind the Commission on a Just and Durable Peace set up by church leaders after the bombing of Pearl Harbor in 1942. Its purpose was to get the churches to support the war on the grounds of national defense, and at the same time to consider preparations for a just and durable peace after the war (this American vision is all the more remarkable given Britain's dire situation at the time). The church leaders did not presume that the churches would be the *source* of truth at the center of the postwar international order, but they did believe the churches would be *instrumental* in building it. Therefore, they set out to determine what principles of the postwar order would in some sense be consistent with a Christian international order.

What took place is a case study of social constructivism: it shows how ideas can shape the meanings states attach to their power and security in ways that help to explain their behavior. Even if it is difficult to determine exactly how important such ideas are, it does show that they do have consequences for foreign policy and how interest groups can shape the moral and political discourse and the political culture in which foreign policy is made. Cordall Hull, the secretary of state, had been cut out of the policymaking for the wartime alliance, and so he devoted his time and his staff at the State Department to devise schemes for the postwar international order. Therefore, he was greatly interested in the proposals set out by the Commission on a Just and Durable Peace.

Dulles reduced these proposals to what were called "Six Pillars of Peace," six short bullet points or what we call sound bites today, which summarized the proposals. A copy was sent to every Protestant chaplain in the armed forces, commentaries on them were written by public personalities and appeared in *Christianity and Crisis*, the leading magazine of Christian realism, study packs were produced to be used in Sunday schools and by church groups, articles on them appeared in over one hundred American newspapers, and they were even published on the front page of *The Times* in London. All the main Protestant denominations had top–down campaigns under way in a matter of weeks to mobilize support for the creation of an international organization—the United Nations. By the fall of 1943 there was an unprecedented volume of mails, mostly handwritten notes and post cards, "simple, heartfelt declarations. Most said isolationism was unchristian and a policy of international cooperation was needed."[43]

It is in this cultural and religious context that the debate over the forming of the United Nations took place in the United States. It is not sufficient to argue that Cordell Hull was the principle apostle of free trade after the World War II or that this was the heyday of Cobdenite liberalism, with the belief that free trade was an essential ingredient of world peace.[44] The Commission on a Just and Durable Peace responded to the proposals for the UN set out at the Prevention of War Conference at the Dumbarton Oaks estate in 1944 in light of the Six Pillars of Peace. The State Department surveyed its response, along with the response of other religious leaders, and a series of meetings was set up with these religious leaders as part of the educational campaign to swing public opinion behind the idea of a United Nations, what Cordell Hall called, a "Town Meeting of the World," an allusion to the town meetings in colonial New England. A further conference was held by the Commission on a Just and Durable Peace to evaluate the Dumbarton Oaks proposals and to make amendments.[45]

The influence of interest groups or non-state actors can in some ways be evaluated by political outcomes. At the San Francisco Conference of the United Nations amendments to the Dumbarton Oaks proposals were made, and came from many sources, but "those from the American religious organizations were particularly successful. Four of the nine submitted by the Commission on a Just and Durable Peace entered the final document"—a preamble on the moral aims of the United Nations, a commitment to develop a body of customary international law, a Trusteeship Council to promote self-government among the colonies, and a declaration of human rights.[46]

"While it is impossible to say that public opinion shifted toward international organization because more Americans now considered it a religious matter, it was certainly sold as such, coming through the churches' educational programs and campaigns," and informed by the theologians of the new world order.[47] Christian realism's theological analysis of the causes of the world crisis, the ideas of corporate sinfulness, and the rejection of the doctrine of progress, translated into a public theology that supported political measures to check government's that violated basic human rights or the sovereignty of weaker nations.

The United Nations did not satisfy the requirements of the theologians of a new world order in this respect, but it did put together a structure to thwart "sinful" aggression through collective security. It was this collective security requirement, and the social and economic concerns for developing countries that made the United Nations "acceptable to Protestant Americans as a means for fighting evil" in international relations at a time when the secular establishment regarded it as the triumph of reason and hope for the future of mankind.[48]

The theologians of the new world order argued the United States had to uphold its responsibilities—what we now would call hegemony—and had to become permanently involved in the United Nations and other international institutions. They were also concerned about the religious foundations of the postwar international order, and so they believed the United States should be actively involved in the World Council of Churches.

Christian Democracy and European Integration

European integration is another area of international cooperation where there are blind spots regarding culture and religion. Christian Democracy may not be as detached from the relations between states as theories of international cooperation suggest is the case, and this has also led to empirical blind spots as well.[49] What is striking is the way Christian Democracy has been ignored, marginalized or explained away in the theories scholars have developed to explain European integration. Nelson Gonzalez argues that many of the main theories, such as functionalism, neo-functionalism, and intergovernmentalism have discounted the fact that in the early years European integration was very much a project of Christian Democracy.[50] In fact, it is only the over whelming secularism of social theory that has made it necessary to try to demonstrate within the nostrums of social science Christian Democracy's key role in European integration rather than the opposite proposition—that it did not have such a role.

What has to be explained satisfactorily, as John Ruggie has pointed out in relation to American hegemony and I have argued is the case of Protestantism and hegemonic stability, is not only why international cooperation took place—regional European integration—but why it took place the way it did and not in some other way. Even when the problem is formulated in this way culture and religion can be marginalized.[51] Why was it, as Gonzalez has argued, a particular set of normative understandings concerning European federalism took the form they did? How and why did this particular set of moral understandings become institutionalized in the early framework for European integration?[52] Questions like these as we have seen are about ideas and political vision, as well as domestic politics, institutions, and leadership, and require an analysis of state and society as well as the level of analysis of the regional European society of states.

Many of the accepted theories of regional integration marginalized the impact of culture and religion. "For intergovernmental or 'state-centric' analysts, the European Union is merely a forum for interstate bargaining. Integration is about the 'practice of ordinary diplomacy under conditions creating unusual opportunities for providing collective goods through international exchange' " between the states in the region.[53]

Some scholars see the EU as simply another kind of international regime. "They are not convinced by evidence of increasing power in supranational institutions or by the internationalist preferences of some European actors. For them, the sovereignty of the nation state remains the central force in European Union politics, since 'the unique institutional structure of the EC is acceptable to national governments only insofar as it strengthens, rather than weakens their control over domestic affairs.' "[54]

However, the same criticisms made of rationalist theories of hegemonic stability also apply to these theories of European integration. The idea of European integration was a practice of the political imagination, but it can be argued that it was much more than this. It was also an act of the theopolitical imagination of Christian Democracy. European integration, like Protestantism and American hegemony, required states to conform to a vision of the world, which in this case was a particular vision of a united and federal Europe. It was a vision, as Romano Prodi, the president of the European Commission, has recently stressed at a conference of European charismatic and evangelical Christians, that was at once a political and a spiritual vision.[55]

"Christian Democracy was, arguably, the single most *influential* political tradition in the construction of the European Union. Not to understand Christian Democracy is not to understand a determining input into the integration process. Christian Democrats not only dominated the institutional agenda setting frameworks of early integration, but also contributed a good deal of the normative *content* that helped to legitimate the political entrepreneurship of the early post-war era."[56]

Almost all the fathers of the European project were Christian Democrats—Robert Schuman, Alcide de Gasperi, Konrad Adenauer, and Jean Monnet. Christian Democratic parties were in power in almost all of the founding member states during the early stages of the European federation. "Christian Democracy's commitment to the creation of a continental supranational polity has always been taken for granted. Christian Democrats have been the most coherently and consistently pro-federalist national and supranational set of political actors in Europe."[57]

Therefore, not to understand Christian Democracy is not to understand the main ideological and political force in European integration. What is it, as Gonzalez argues, that explains why the Christian Democrats pursued a federal vision of Europe, and why did that federal vision take the form that it did, and not some other form? Any adequate explanation for the role of Christian Democracy in European integration has to combine actors, institutions, and ideas. What has to be shown is that they had a key political role in creating the institutions of European integration, and it was the ideas of Christian Democrats that both motivated the actors, and led them to create European institutions in the form that they did.[58]

However, as Daniel Philpott has pointed out, the paradox is that the national Christian Democratic parties, which until recently has ruled longer than any other political parties in Europe in the postwar era, were seemingly committed to the undermining of the nation-state, the very institution that has sustained them in power for so long. In other words, it is a very particular kind of political imagination to envision a world with a supranational institution that takes Christian Democrats and the states they grew up in beyond themselves, to envision their world in a new way.

Recall from chapter 2 that the Catholic Church condemned the diplomatic settlement at Westphalia, and to many secular liberals at that time and in our own day this was simply little more than the politics of the medieval Church's reactionary conservatism. However, after the World War II, Christian Democrats, under the influence of the Catholic Church's social teaching, strongly and powerfully promoted a vision of a united and federal Europe, governed by liberal democratic principles and held together by European institutions that transcended national loyalties.

For many people this change is simply a matter of the political mythology of liberalism. It is a matter of the Catholic Church changing its mind, and catching up with the more liberal politics of the twentieth century. Catholic doctrine has no doubt developed, and this has certainly happened in many areas. There is another possibility, however, one that sees a continuity between Pope Innocent X's condemnation of the Treaty of Westphalia and Christian Democracy's vision of European integration. "All along, the Church has condemned the absolutely sovereign state as an idolatrous claimant to godlike status, an affront to a moral order and to a natural law, whose authority lies ultimately far outside the borders of the state." This moral order calls the state to account, and its claim to sovereignty and human loyalty, which should not be made by any earthly secular political power or institution. In other words, Christian Democracy from the beginning has been motivated by a different vision of faith, life, and politics.[59]

Gonzalez argues Christian Democrats dominated the postwar governments of key European states, and this allowed them to influence the agenda setting for the framework of European integration. This was helped by the strong cohesion among Christian Democrats, and their deep socialization in Catholic social thought and Christian Democratic civic organizations—women's and youth movements, trade unions, professional associations, mutual insurance societies, credit unions, and sport and recreational associations. Christian Democrats also had the common experience of living through the resistance during World War II.[60]

It was this dominance that allowed them to institutionalize many of the normative ideas they had developed during the interwar years as part of their political and military resistance to Nazism. In other words, according to Gonzalez, it was not simply a matter of states deciding to cooperate to achieve common ends. It was Christian Democratic ideas and culture, the common normative framework of Catholic social teaching, which influenced the form of European institutions after these leaders came to power in the postwar era.[61]

What were the ideas of Christian Democracy that were so crucial to European integration? The Christian Democrats contributed to the realm of ideas and morality for European integration through the concepts of modern Catholic social teaching. It was this normative content that helped to legitimate the politics and vision of the early postwar era. The Christian Democratic political tradition is critical to understanding the founders' vision and motivations, and it still animates many politicians who today play a role in the European Union.

What Gonzalez has called "normative basis of Christian Democratic federalism," which animated the founders vision, consisted of the following elements: (a) "the principles relating to national sovereignty and federalism of subsidiarity and sphere sovereignty, which in turn were rooted in," (b) the concepts of pluralism and Christian personalism, "which were used to criticize the notion of absolute national sovereignty as demeaning to the social and political implications of 'personhood.' " How were these principles related?[62]

Christian Democrats, in the aftermath of the two world wars, were forced to examine the causes of such a horrific breakdown in European civilization. What they "quickly fixed their attention on" was what Philpott has identified as the main continuity in Catholic teaching over the centuries—the idolatry of the state—nationalism, and its roots in absolute national sovereignty.[63] However, how they arrived at this diagnosis is not as obvious as it may seem. They got there by invoking an understanding of the relatedness of "personhood" (rather than individual autonomy within liberal political thought). In other words, their diagnosis of nationalism was based on what Gonzalez has called a particular "normative anthropology" rooted in Catholic social teaching, at least in relation to the nation-state and nationalism, going back to the Church's opposition to the Westphalian settlement.[64]

The theories of social constructivism and the new institutionalism may provide a new way of examining the early motives behind European integration. They are concerned with how ideas interact with institutions, and the way ideas can shape the interests, preferences, strategies, and the identity of actors. These approaches may be better able than rational theories to account for the impact of ideas, values, aspirations, and intentions, although as Gonzalez has shown, culture and religion are often still underplayed in their accounts of European integration.[65] Recall, in part one, I also challenged the way scholars have tinkered with some of the existing concepts of international relations, such as transnational ideas or epistemic communities, to try to account for religion. Scholars pointing to the role ideas in the formation of the European Union have emphasized rights, aspirations, and legitimacy, but surprisingly, given the central role of Christian Democracy, they have said remarkably little about culture or religion. John Ruggie, for example, uses the EU to explain how ideas can provide key reasons for action in international relations. "[T]he aspiration for a united Europe," he explains, "has not caused European integration, but it is the reason the direct causal factors have had their causal capacity."[66]

Surprisingly little is said about the deeper origins of the aspiration for a united Europe that Gonzalez has explained, nor as he has also emphasized, is anything mentioned about the particular form these aspirations have taken. A lot more can be said here. Why not add piety, sacredness, or public theology to Ruggie's list of reasons for ideational causation? In fact, we can say a particular type of moral conviction and the ideas of Christian Democracy, informed by the principles of Catholic social thought, contributed to making the aspiration for European integration take the form that it did.

Conclusion

We have begun to see in this chapter that culture and religion can matter for international cooperation. This is part of the early English School's understanding of international society as well as social constructivism today. International cooperation is embedded in broader normative frameworks, and so ideas, norms, values—sometimes associated with religious traditions—can be important for the ways institutions are formed. We have seen how a public theology of world order influenced the nature of American hegemony in the postwar international order, and how the concepts of Catholic social teaching that informed Christian Democracy helped to shape the particular form of European integration.

Ecumenical Protestantism and its moral–practical quest for stability in the postwar era is all the more striking because of the relative absence of any substantive public theology of world order among the churches today, or any public theology supporting the active engagement of the United States in international affairs. Hopefully, this may be beginning to change.[67]

The Christian Democrats' vision of a united and federal Europe has remained since the concepts from Catholic social teaching used to shape and promote European integration have become part of European institutions. What may not be as important today, given the secularism of European society, is the theopolitical vision behind Christian Democracy.

We can see how the changing fortunes of American religious groups and their theological ideas about America's role in the world—mainline Protestants and evangelicals, for example—informed the political culture in ways that contributed to isolationist, nationalistic, or internationalist forms of American foreign policy.[68] However, it should be remembered that the ecumenical Protestants who tried to establish a new world order after World War II, also wanted to provide, in a way the early English School would have understood, a spiritual or religious foundation for this new order as well. The calls today for a global ethic and for a dialogue between civilizations are in some respects a return to this early postwar vision of the religious or spiritual foundations of international order.

CHAPTER 7

SOULCRAFT AS STATECRAFT? DIPLOMACY, CONFLICT RESOLUTION, AND PEACEBUILDING

There have always been people of good will belonging to different faith communities—or none, who in the past have devised peace plans, promoted interfaith dialogue, and in a variety of ways worked for a world without war. A variety of religious groups or religious traditions, Buddhists as well as Quakers and Mennonites, for example, have been committed to peace and conflict resolution as an integral part of their religious tradition.

These religious traditions have strongly influenced the areas of peace studies and conflict resolution in the study of international relations. They broadly fit into the liberal tradition of international theory, or as we see, what Martin Wight has called the "inverted revolutionist" tradition of international thought.[1] Therefore, there is no need in this chapter to survey the ways religion has been a part of conflict resolution and peacemaking.[2] However, as a result of the global resurgence of religion something else is happening in international relations. Globalization and the global resurgence of religion are changing the nature of diplomacy, peacemaking, and international conflict. New approaches and possibilities have opened up for a variety of non-state actors in various forms of diplomacy and peacemaking.

Certainly, with the rise of religious or ethnic conflict the historic traditions of religious peacemaking have come back into fashion, and are no longer at the margins of international relations theory.[3] The global resurgence of religion has meant that the virtues and practices of particular religious traditions embodied in faith communities are becoming a more central part of diplomacy and peacebuilding. It is this new situation that is examined in this chapter, and the way the modern virtue–ethics tradition developed in the aftermath of Alasdair MacIntyre's social theory more clearly indicates what it means to take religious pluralism seriously in diplomacy and peacebuilding.

The Limits of Track-One Diplomacy: Diplomacy and Conflict in a Global Era

During the Cold War, the superpowers suppressed many of the latent conflicts within their spheres of influence, particularly in central Europe and Central Asia (e.g., Armenia, Azerbaijan, and the Balkans), even though the Cold War intensified conflicts in Vietnam, the Horn of Africa, Southern Africa, and Central America. From the vantage point of many developing countries— rather than the Kremlin or the White House—the concept of the Cold War was from the beginning a very American or Eurocentric one, which did not recognize how really hot the Cold War was for most people in the world.

Now, in the aftermath of the Cold War, the new domestic sources of conflict are intersecting with globalization in ways that influence the conduct, motives, and goals of civil wars and internal conflicts, changing the way violence between individuals and ethnic or social groups is organized in a global era. Ethnicity and religion have intermixed with other class or regional factors contributing to a variety of identity conflicts within countries as well as between them.[4]

The first way globalization has contributed to changes in diplomacy is related to the kinds of actors involved in diplomacy. Most conflicts today take place within states rather than between them, and so states are only one of several types of actors, groups, or factions involved in conflicts. Diplomacy today needs to take into account the changing actors as well as the changing location of international conflict.

States have had the legitimate and authoritative control over war and violence in international relations since the Westphalian era. What is called interstate or track-one diplomacy operated with an assumed hierarchy of power and violence in which states—really, the great powers—were the key to war or peace. They maintained the international order through the mechanisms of the balance of power—making alliances, demarcating spheres of influence, holding multilateral conferences, and so forth. It was also assumed that it was mainly military power rather than other kinds of power, such as political, economic, or cultural power, which determined war and peace, and so these other sources of power were subservient to military force in any conflict situation.[5]

A more positive way of interpreting this situation is to say that non-state actors should not simply be seen as the competitors of states in international relations. Non-state actors can create problems for traditional diplomacy as well as provide new opportunities for statecraft. States no longer have to bear the burden alone of the tensions and antagonisms that characterize international relations. The activity of many non-state actors, for example, the Carter Center, the National Endowment for Democracy, or the U.S. Institute for Peace, have goals that coincide with states in so far as they promote human rights, democracy, or economic development.[6]

A second way globalization has contributed to changes in diplomacy relates to the nature and purpose of international conflict. Interstate diplomacy assumed that the purpose of armed conflict was to defend the national interest, and so diplomacy was about the dialogue, bargaining, and compromise associated with security and defending the tangible or objective national interests of the states that make up international society.[7]

Many conflicts today as we saw in chapter 5 are identity conflicts, often driven by long-standing animosities rooted in a perceived threat to identity and survival of ethnic, religious, or social groups or communities, or they are new animosities that have developed as a result of the way ethnic or religious differences have been exacerbated by globalization. It is not the existence of these differences that have led to conflict, rather it is the ways global social forces have created greater uncertainty with the breakdown of these differences. Along side the problems of promoting civil society, democracy, and development in post-conflict situations are a host of interrelated issues, including the treatment of ethnic or religious minorities, conflicting interpretations of religious freedom, force and nonviolence, religion and human rights, the role of religion in public life, and the problems of how to promote peace, justice, and reconciliation.[8]

Thus, diplomacy is no longer, or is no longer only, concerned—if it ever was—with the rational calculation of the tangible interests of states. Cultural factors have always had a role in international negotiations even if diplomats have not always been aware of it.[9]

Diplomacy now takes place in a cultural and religious context, which as we saw in chapter 3, social constructivists argue is concerned with the way identities are constructed as well as challenged by the interplay of factors in both domestic and international politics. This makes the struggle for authenticity and development a part of diplomacy and international conflict. An individual, social group, or community has to have a secure sense of the social or national self before the social or national group can rationally calculate or determine what is in its interests.

Diplomacy is also now concerned with the subjective and experiential realities that shape the interests, objectives, and perspectives of diverse groups in society. The issues that are seemingly tangible or objective (as such as territory or governance), and are open to rational calculation are now intimately rooted or connected to the cultural and psychological factors that are driving and sustaining the conflict.[10]

Unfortunately, track-one diplomacy—involving states, diplomats, or top-level governmental actors, or international organizations such as the United Nations or regional organizations like the Organization of African Unity (OAU), Organization for Security and Cooperation in Europe (OSCE), the Arab League, or the Organization of American States (OAS)—have not been very adept at stopping these new kinds of wars or forms of intrastate violence, civil wars, guerrilla wars, secessionist struggles, and religious or ethnic conflicts, which have engulfed entire societies since the end of the Cold War—Bosnia, the Sudan, Ethiopia, Rwanda, Somalia, Sierra Leone, Liberia, Chechnya, or Afghanistan.

The Rise of Multitrack Diplomacy

The changing nature of diplomacy and international conflict has led to what is called multitrack diplomacy to describe the variety of methods of diplomacy that are outside the formal diplomatic or governmental system. Multitrack diplomacy refers to the informal, nongovernmental contacts that take place at the individual, state, and society levels of analysis below the level of analysis of the international system. It includes private citizens, social groups, religious groups, and a wide range of non-state actors.

At first the term track-two diplomacy was used to describe the activity of a variety of people other than diplomats—social scientists, conflict resolution professionals, and so on—involved in diplomacy and peacemaking.[11] The role of non-state actors in diplomacy has now been extended more formally. These various tracks of diplomacy are given below.[12]

Track 1 — Governments
Track 2 — NGOs and professional organizations
Track 3 — Business community
Track 4 — Private citizens
Track 5 — Research, training and educational institutes
Track 6 — Activists
Track 7 — Religion
Track 8 — Funding organizations
Track 9 — Media and communications

A number of factors have contributed to the emergence of multitrack diplomacy. The first factor has been briefly mentioned already. It is the changing nature of international conflict. Most conflicts in developing countries are now within states rather than between them, and the state has become only one actor among several involved in violence. Informal or multitrack diplomacy explores the role of civil society in diplomacy, conflict resolution, and peacebuilding. In other words, it examines the role of non-state actors — NGOs, religious leaders or groups, private citizens, and even the business community — and the capacities in local communities for peace and conflict resolution.[13]

The rise of multitrack diplomacy is a recognition that civil or internal wars require civil or internal action by societies or communities as a whole if a conflict is to be ended. It is part of a growing recognition that diplomacy now has to cope with situations where there is greater complexity in the causes of conflict, in the forms of conflict, and in the actors that participate in it. The expertise for dealing with these kind of conflicts does not only reside with officials, or government personnel, but also active citizens with a wide variety of backgrounds who can play a role in diplomacy and peacemaking. Multitrack diplomacy in this sense is part of a growing movement in civil society for citizen diplomacy.

A second factor that has led to multitrack diplomacy is global interdependence. This is the recognition the effects of states, individuals, and communities now reach across national boundaries, although the decisions people in the developed world make no doubt have a much greater impact than any peasant in Bangladesh or Mozambique. We can now see wars, famines, and natural disasters around the world because of global telecommunications, and many people want to respond to them in some way. It is for these reasons multitrack diplomacy fits within a concept of world politics and global civil society, or at least it fits into a broadly liberal or pluralist conception of international relations.

However, Hedley Bull reminded us a long time ago that although changing technology can facilitate global awareness, it is unclear to what extent this can be transformed into a sense of global responsibility. "[T]he interdependence of one society's decisions and another's, even where it genuinely exists and there is awareness of it, does not in itself generate a sense of common interest, let alone of common values."[14]

At times it sounds as if multitrack diplomacy is based on some of the same liberal assumptions that E. H. Carr criticized during the interwar period, that is, the idea that all good things go together, and so each of the tracks of multitrack diplomacy are considered to be complimentary rather than contradictory.[15] From Alasdair MacIntyre's viewpoint multitrack diplomacy seems to be based on Enlightenment assumptions regarding universal rationality, without any regard for the way rationality may be dependent on different cultural or religious traditions, nor the possibility that different tracks may use different forms of moral reasoning.

A third factor that has contributed to multitrack diplomacy is the political and legal constraints built into the United Nations. The permanent five members—the United States, the United Kingdom, Russia, France, and China—have a veto power on matters of peace and security in the Security Council. This means any serious response to a conflict can be sidelined by them—the Arab-Israeli situation, Rhodesia and South Africa, Northern Ireland, Kashmir, Chechnya, the civil wars in Central America during the 1980s, not to mention Iraq, Bosnia, Kosovo, and Afghanistan. The inability of the United Nations to resolve many of these conflicts has led to a greater impetus for civil society in diplomacy and peacemaking.

The second problem is the domestic jurisdiction clause—Article 2(7)—hinders UN action on international conflicts. This clause says that states may not interfere in the domestic affairs of other states, and so this legal provision can hinder effective action on peace and security since most conflicts today are within states rather than between them. It is this problem that has led to the debate over national sovereignty and humanitarian intervention.[16]

These nine tracks of diplomacy are recognized in the literature on diplomacy and peacemaking. It is track-seven, on "religion, or peacemaking through faith in action," that is covered in this chapter. Diamond and McDonald consider religion to be the heart of the system of multitrack diplomacy. "It provides the spiritual impulse, the idealism, and the ethical foundation that, though perhaps present elsewhere in the system, are most publicly and acceptably articulated here." "Without an open heart," they explain, "the system could not manage its ultimate aim: to relieve the suffering of humanity by bringing about a world of peace."[17] When religion is described in this way it is not surprising its role in multi-track diplomacy is more narrowly linked to pacifism, sanctuary, and non-violence. We will see that the rise of faith-based diplomacy requires a broader frame of reference for religious or track-seven diplomacy.

Religion and Conflict Resolution

Conflict resolution is a comprehensive term referring to the peaceful resolution of disputes between states or non-state actors. It can include negotiation, mediation, arbitration, or it can be the formal adjudication by the International Court of Justice at the Hague, in the Netherlands. These activities—brokering a cease-fire, negotiating a peace agreement, or implementing a peace accord—are used to resolve a specific issue that has led to a dispute or a disagreement that has turned into a violent conflict, and so in the first instance what is sought is to resolve the problem that caused the conflict.

Conflict resolution has also become a specialist field within the study of international relations. It started during the Cold War when the development of nuclear weapons and the rivalry between the superpowers seemed to threaten the survival of humanity. Almost from the beginning certain religious traditions have been more closely associated with this field than almost any other one. The practices and traditions of pacifism such as those within the Quaker, Mennonite, and Franciscan traditions, the ideas of Gandhi, and the teaching of Buddha have significantly influenced the field of conflict resolution.[18]

One of the most important questions facing the field today is whether it is a truly global effort by scholars from around the world; or if its concepts, theories, and discourses are really based on Western assumptions regarding peace, stability, and conflict resolution. What has made this question so important has been the rise of ethnic and ethno-national conflicts since the end of the Cold War, the global resurgence of religion, and the unexpected expansion in peacemaking, peacekeeping, and peacebuilding activity in the 1990s.[19]

Although the religious traditions noted above have had a significant influence on the field, it can also be argued that the concepts, theories, and principles derived from them have been translated into a secular discourse as part of programs in Peace Studies or Conflict Resolution, and so they are based on Western assumptions of rationality and liberal modernity.[20] A similar point was made in chapter 2 regarding the theories of international relations and it is picked up again in chapter 9, regarding the concepts and theories of development.

The expansion of conflict resolution activity in the Islamic world and in the developing world more generally has called into question what are essentially Western approaches to conflict resolution, peacemaking, and peacebuilding.[21] A tension, if not always a contradiction, exists between Western notions of minority rights and individualism given the priorities of nation building in developing countries.[22]

The assumptions many Western governments, the United Nations, and development practitioners make about peacebuilding also seem to involve Western liberal assumptions regarding civil society, democracy, and what MacIntyre has called the expressive individualism of liberal modernity. Indeed, as we see in chapters 8 and 9, the NGO discourse in development on grass-roots participation is rooted in such Western concepts, which may not be appropriate for non-Western cultures, or are at least contested as part of the struggle for authenticity and development.

Clearly, what is now being faced are the liberal dilemmas of multiculturalism in the field of peacebuilding and conflict resolution, issues which challenge the liberal or optimistic assumptions that all tracks in multitrack diplomacy are complimentary. On the one hand, the field of conflict resolution wants to help strengthen the local capacity for conflict resolution in societies and communities; but, on the other hand, a part of the way outside experts try to do this is by promoting an understanding of social change and development rooted in the ideas, values, concepts belonging to Western modernity.

"Faithful Realism"
The Rise of Faith-based Diplomacy

We have seen how the changing nature of diplomacy and international conflict has led political leaders, governments, and NGOs, to recognize there is a role for non-state actors in diplomacy and conflict resolution. What is also more greatly recognized is that there may be indigenous knowledge and resources, that is, cultural and religious resources, for diplomacy, peacemaking, and conflict resolution, and this has given rise to faith-based diplomacy.[23]

There is also a recognition, given the global resurgence of religion in the Islamic world, and a new generation of politicians and theologians, such as Iran's President Muhammad Khatami and Tunisia's Rached Ghannouchi, that faith-based diplomacy may help promote the kind of dialogue that is needed within a religious tradition, as MacIntyre has indicated, on what are the main values or goods of the tradition. It is a dialogue that takes place between states and non-state actors within a religious tradition, and is what needs to take place in the Middle East.[24]

Although this type of multitrack diplomacy is rather new, it is already a part of training of diplomats in the United States. The U.S. Foreign Service Institute—the training arm of the Department of State—now requires its students to study religion and international affairs. In Britain the Foreign and Commonwealth Office offers a training program in diversity awareness and multiculturalism, and the Department for International Development has conducted research on faith-based organizations, but there is no comparable UK program on religion in the training of diplomats.

Faith-based diplomacy is more directly and clearly identified with matters of faith and religion than the more indirect way religious traditions have influenced the fields of conflict resolution and peace studies. In contrast to these fields, faith-based diplomacy should not be identified with the realist tradition of international theory, nor should it be identified with the pacifist perspective within the main religious traditions.[25]

Faith-based diplomacy is not a part of *realpolitik*, at least it is not a part of the hard, tough-mind, dogmatic secularism of the realist tradition.[26] Faith-based diplomats, however, might find some encouragement from the earlier generation of Christian realists mentioned in chapter 2 who were more influenced by history and philosophy than social science.

Rather, faith-based diplomacy can be more easily identified with what the early English School called the Rationalist tradition of international theory. Martin Wight called this the "broad middle road" in international relations. In so far as this tradition recognized some of the realities of power politics and yet saw that there is an element of interstate intercourse and cooperation, diplomacy was conceived as a dialogue between states that comprise an international society.[27] Faith-based diplomacy might more aptly be described by what Paul Tillich called "faithful realism"—a type of realism that refuses to ignore the realities of the brokenness of the world nor the reality of the world's divine purposes.[28]

Faith-based diplomacy should also not be identified with what Wight called "inverted Revolutionism" of the Anabaptists, Quakers, Mennonites, and other pacifist religious traditions that have influenced the fields of peace studies and conflict resolution.[29] Faith-based diplomacy recognizes that religion has been a *missing* dimension of statecraft.[30] It seeks to *expand* the role of faith, of religion into the existing tools of statecraft, and it seeks to incorporate the realm of faith and religion into U.S. foreign policy and, by implication, the foreign policy of other countries as well.[31]

In other words, faith-based diplomacy, in the first instance, still operates from within a problem-solving approach to international theory. It focuses on integrating faith into the existing frameworks of diplomatic or political institutions, social relations, and social meaning, and does not, as in critical theory or the Revolutionist tradition, challenge the existing framework of social order in international relations, nor does it consider how it may be fundamentally transformed.[32]

This does not mean that faith-based diplomacy is only about dispute settlement or conflict amelioration, and is opposed to a more far reaching or deeper social and political transformation. Faith-based diplomats, at least many of them, reject the secular rationalism upon which the project of progressive notions of emancipation are often predicated—Marxism, critical theory, postmodernism, and so on—since from a faith-based perspective they are often not radical enough in their criticisms of liberal modernity.

Faith-based diplomacy is only beginning, and it may be sowing the seeds for deeper, more lasting forms of social transformation. Like Pentecostal Christianity or liberation theology, the whole basis of multitrack diplomacy and the growing role of religious groups in diplomacy establishes over the long term a less exclusive and hierarchical approach to politics and diplomacy. Faith-based diplomacy, like multitrack diplomacy more generally, largely involves a variety of new actors, including religious groups and organizations, as a key part of civil society who are now involved in diplomacy and international relations.

Faith-based diplomacy relies on, and is actually based on, a more fundamental transformation than what is expected by critical or postmodern theory in international relations, or by what may be accepted by the nostrums and methods of secular social science. It is the way people in conflict can be transformed by their relationship with God and so transform their relationships with others in their community.[33] Is it at all possible to make an idea like this one intelligible in international relations theory? If it is to happen at all, then faith-based diplomacy has to be studied and evaluated, as I indicated in chapter 3, by methods and approaches that extend beyond what John Milbank has called the secular reason of social theory. It is for this reason it has been an uphill struggle to bring faith-based diplomacy and its research program into the mainstream study of international relations.

What may distinguish faith-based diplomacy from other aspects of religion and diplomacy examined in track-seven and from other types of multitrack diplomacy is not only the fact that it makes use of religious actors in diplomacy. It is that it is "faith-based," and it is not only "religion-based" in so far as faith can be separated from religious institutions (the main aspect of track-seven).

Faith-based diplomacy is rooted in a "two-vectored spiritual orientation" that is common to types of religious believers with a "this-worldly," less separatist orientation: first, politics—like all of life, is properly oriented and ordered in a teleological sense toward the transcendent; and second, there is a real recognition of the active role of the divine in human affairs.[34] In other words, faith-based diplomacy is rooted in an active, integration of faith and life, and does not only involve what Max Weber called a "religious ethic," in which the accepted realm of religion is limited to private religious "motives" for public goals or social action, but in which the goals themselves are articulated within a discourse of secular reason and instrumental rationality.[35] It is this aspect of faith-based diplomacy that makes it different from the activity of other religious NGOs involved in track-seven diplomacy or from secular NGOs involved in peacemaking.

Faith-based diplomacy is based on more than fuzzy, idealistic, religious motives for peace, reconciliation, and brotherhood. It is itself a specific *mode* of dialogue and diplomacy between states and non-state actors, with what I identify below as a set of social *practices* rooted in particular religious traditions. As this book has argued, this is not to deny the role of religious motives, passion, and convictions in promoting social or political change—civil rights, world peace, the anti-apartheid movement, ending world poverty or promoting fair trade. It is to acknowledge that there are deeper motives that originate from a religious identity and sensibility that distinguish faith-based diplomacy from secular diplomacy.

How is faith-based diplomacy based on more than deeply held religious or idealistic motives regarding peace, brotherhood, and reconciliation? It is a way of bringing religion—really, more than this, an active or living faith—back into diplomacy and international relations, in a way that has been marginalized since the principles and practices of the Westphalian international order were established in the seventeenth century. In some ways it might even be said that faith-based diplomacy begins to envision an alternative form of world order to one predicated on secular rationality. At this level it can be seen as part of a more grass roots approach to the dialogue between civilizations.

Faith-based diplomacy does draw upon secular expertise in conflict resolution, political science, philosophy, and experience in diplomacy and national security. It is not, however, wedded to or even embedded in the widely held assumptions of secularism and rationalism on which these disciplines are based.

Faith-based diplomacy can be distinguished, however, from the traditional models of peacemaking and conflict resolution by its holistic approach to the sociopolitical healing of a conflict that has taken place.[36] In other words, the objective of faith-based diplomacy is not only conflict resolution (the resolving of the issue or dispute in question). The objective of faith-based diplomacy is also the restoration of the political order that has suffered from war and injustice, and the reconciliation of individuals and social groups. Faith-based diplomacy is rooted in the transformation of individual lives and over time the social and political transformation of communities.[37]

What do religious actors and faith-based diplomats bring that is different to the negotiating table? First, the motives for peace and reconciliation are rooted in a deep sense of religious identity and a religious sensibility. Unfortunately, this can also include the sad legacy of historical events, whether it is the collective memory of Muslims regarding the crusades or that of Greek Orthodox Christians who recall the fall of Constantinople and the Ottoman empire's legacy. It is for this reason, as we see below, one of the practices of faith-based diplomacy is truthfulness.

A second aspect of faith-based diplomacy is related to multitrack diplomacy more generally. Political and religious leaders, NGOs, and governments increasingly recognize that religious leaders and institutions, given their familiarity with local situations and close contacts with grass roots movements are particularly well placed to play a role in multitrack diplomacy.

Religious leaders and organizations are particularly well placed to (a) act as mediators, and (b) provide a "neutral" space for negotiations. They are, or can be (this is not always the case), well placed to act as mediators partly because of their apolitical reputation in support of constructive social change and reconciliation, and because they represent a widely respected set of values in the community. They act at the grass roots level, involving local religious leaders, indigenous NGOs, and community groups to bring people together in a neutral space from different religious communities for mediation and cross-community dialogue in ways that nurture reconciliation and peacebuilding.

At this level faith-based diplomacy can be seen as a part of the social practice of community formation. The participants come from different religious traditions and most likely different communities. The participants, in so far as religion has been a main component of ethnic or communal identity, may not have a deep knowledge of the theology or history of their religious tradition.

Conflict situations like this may be part of what I identified in chapter 5 with Rene Girard's concept of a sacrificial crisis in failed or collapsed states. They may carry a deep baggage of prejudices, preconceptions, and stereotypes associated with their religious tradition, as well as having anger, hatred, guilt, and animosities toward those of other communities.[38] It is for this reason that faith-based diplomacy and peacebuilding are about healing, forgiveness, and repentance. These activities, however, do not happen as free-standing acts for they are a part of community formation. The social transformation peacebuilding requires means rebuilding communities in ways that are consistent with their life of faith for there is no future without forgiveness.[39]

A third aspect of faith-based diplomacy is the active use of rituals, symbols, practices, prayer, and sacred texts rooted in their religious traditions. A wide range of religious sensibilities recognize the role of ritual and symbol as an outward expression of an inward reality. It is this dual recognition that becomes a more formal aspect of the faith-based mode of diplomacy.[40] It is in this context that rituals and prayers for victims on both sides of a violent conflict, for example, become political acts in which participating in what is called the social practice of remembering can be the beginning of healing, forgiveness, and reconciliation. The use of religious precepts and rituals in mediation and conciliation, for example, were used to reach peace agreements, such as those promoted by the interreligious council in Uganda, Sierra Leone, and Bosnia-Herzegovina.[41]

A fourth aspect of faith-based diplomacy is that religious actors simply have a unique leverage, given who they are, and what they represent—a deep spiritual or a transcendent authority—to reconcile conflicting groups and rehumanize relationships. It is also for this reason they have a unique capacity to mobilize a local community in support of a peace process, and gain national and international support for it. The All Africa Council of Churches, the World Council of Churches, Buddhist peacemakers in Cambodia, the role of the Community Sant'Egidio in mediating the civil war in Mozambique, and the role of the Catholic Church in mediating the conflict between the Zapatista rebels and the Mexican government are only a few of the examples of faith-based NGOs in diplomacy and conflict resolution.

The Practices of Faith-Based Diplomacy

We have seen that the purpose of faith-based diplomacy goes beyond an action-oriented or problem-solving approach to conflict resolution. It goes beyond what should be done to resolve a dispute that has led to violent conflict to include sustainable reconciliation and peacebuilding. I have already identified the practice of community formation with the main objectives of faith-based diplomacy and peacebuilding. It also goes beyond resolving disputes, and is primarily concerned with persons and communities, and is about establishing the conditions necessary for a viable polity in a community. It so happens, going back to Aristotle, this is the original setting of the virtue–ethics tradition, with its concept of human flourishing that involves active citizens in the life of the community. Therefore, the rest of this chapter explores how faith-based diplomacy fits within the concepts of MacIntyre's social theory and the virtue–ethics tradition because it takes seriously the virtues and practices of religious traditions.

The basic concepts of MacIntyre's approach—virtues, practices, narrative, and tradition—have been explained already. Recall that MacIntyre's understanding of practices as socially established cooperative activities is missing from the interchangeable way scholars often discuss rules, norms, and practices in the theory of international relations. In the same way that farming is a practice while planting turnips is not, or that building a house or architecture are practices while taking long showers or laying bricks are not, diplomacy, peacebuilding, and reconciliation can be defined as social practices in a way that shaking hands (like the famous Arafat–Rabin handshake as part of the Oslo Accords in 1993), or disarmament or the laying down weapons as part of a peace accord (as in Rhodesia, Namibia, South Africa, or Mozambique) are not practices according to MacIntyre's understanding of these terms.

Faith-based diplomacy harks back to an older diplomatic tradition, or even ancient understanding of diplomacy before the modern era. We have already seen how the early English School recognized that many of the diplomatic practices of ancient state-systems emerged from different cultural or religious traditions. What can be identified as the practices of faith-based diplomacy?

A few preliminary observations can be made. The first thing to say is that faith-based diplomacy recognizes the value of multiple forms of rationality. Most faith-based diplomats recognize that political order is teleologically ordered by a divinely grounded vision of the good life, and what is required for human flourishing. What MacIntyre's account of tradition-dependent rationality indicates is that if faith-based diplomacy is to take cultural and religious pluralism seriously, then it must recognize, as many practitioners do, that the rationality behind such a political vision is not independent of social and historical context, nor independent of any specific understanding of human flourishing. The nature of the good, what is just, what is right, and notions of obligation and the rationality on which they are based are socially embodied in a particular moral tradition, most often embedded in the cultural and religious traditions of faith communities in most parts of the world.

The second thing to say is that faith-based diplomacy recognizes the narrative structure of community formation. Faith-based diplomacy is about over coming the effects of community deformation— the faith of the communities in discord or conflict. Faith-based diplomacy actively recognizes the ambivalence of the sacred. I pointed out in chapter 5 that Rene Girard's social theory helps us to see more clearly how deeply rooted this ambivalence is since many ethnic and religious groups have constructed their identity and social cohesion through scapegoating, religion, and violence. It is a recognition that what Girard has called the sacrificial crisis in divided societies results "at least in part from too little religion rather than too much, from spirituality that has been enfeebled by such forces as communist rule in Yugoslavia."[42]

Peacebuilding seminars often use the method of story telling, getting people to share their suffering across racial, ethnic, or religious divisions as part of the practice of forgiveness.[43] The method has also been institutionalized as in the Truth and Reconciliation Commission in South Africa.[44] What faith-based diplomacy requires is what MacIntyre would identify as an alternative reading or narrative from *within* religious traditions regarding the proper ordering of social, political, and economic life. What is distinctive about this type of diplomacy's two-vectored spiritual orientation from a virtue–ethics perspective is that the prior question in diplomacy is, "What kind of people ought we to be or to become?" MacIntyre's answer to this question depends on the kind of story or narrative communities tell themselves, and what narratives they see themselves to be a part of in their lives.

What is the meaning of faith and life lived out within the religious traditions in which these communities are embedded? What are the diplomatic implications, for example, for the leading of Islamic lives, Hindu lives, or Christian lives, and for the corporate life of their communities, that is, for those whose identity is shaped by the texts, rituals, and practices of their religious traditions?

The deeply divergent narratives of the communities in Yugoslavia can be seen in the identities and narratives of two of its prominent Catholic prelates. Bishop Josip Strossmayer, a Croatian Catholic patriot and intellectual and founder of the University of Zagreb, was increasingly drawn toward Christian unity among the South ("Yugo") Slavs in reaction to the iniquities of the Austro-Hungarian Empire. Alojzije Stepinac, who became the Archbishop of Zabreb, was a purely Croatian nationalist, who backed the struggle of the Vatican and the Austrians against the Serbs, their fellow South Slavs.[45]

A third aspect of faith-based diplomacy from a virtue–ethics perspective is that it takes seriously the distinctive identities of communities grounded in particular cultural and religious traditions. Key religious individuals or groups retain their distinctive identity even as they explore what it now means to be friends and neighbors with those who were once their enemies.

What this means is that in the discourse of faith-based diplomacy, the meaning of moral concepts or practices such as mercy, justice, goodness, and peace is removed from the kind of post-Enlightenment discourse that has dominated debates about ethics or human rights in international relations. Faith-based diplomacy rightly locates these practices within particular religious traditions.

Practices adopted by the International Center for Religion and Diplomacy, such as prayer and fasting, forgiveness, and spiritual conversation, are first located within the participant's own religious tradition. What the virtue–ethics approach recognizes is that for the members of these communities moral or ethical reflection begins with the practices that are internal to particular religious traditions. Only then does the dialogue between similar social practices in different traditions take place, and offer a way forward in faith-based diplomacy. In other words, the similarity between social practices in different religious traditions becomes the bridge for a deeper dialogue between those religious communities. A commonality between social practices and religious traditions emerges, but it is not predicated on the rationalism of the Enlightenment. It is a "rooted cosmopolitanism," predicated on practices in different religious traditions and the virtues or qualities necessary to sustain them in the community.[46]

A final aspect of a virtue–ethics perspective on what is distinctive about faith-based diplomacy is a recognition that the particular issues or problems that have led to discord and conflict need to be dealt with corporately, that is, as the church, as the mosque, or as the temple. This is the case not only in a general sense because good practice in conflict resolution shows that all the elements of the communities in a conflict need to be involved if genuine peace and reconciliation is to take place. It is also the case that there is a distinctive identity and integrity to each faith community, and the diplomatic response must be fashioned according to virtues and practices of its particular religious tradition.

MacIntyre argues that one of the central mistakes of the Enlightenment project is the idea that the goal of society should be to create and preserve individual autonomy as the greatest good of a liberal society. This idea ignores, as we have seen in chapter 3, the narrative and historical nature of our moral lives and our social existence. Such a notion of expressive individualism is a product of political liberalism, which, as MacIntyre has shown, is itself a communal tradition, one that is highly problematic for the developing world given its lack of concern for social solidarity, authenticity, and development (see chapters 8 and 9). Thus, faith-based diplomacy sees religion as a resource for conflict resolution and peacebuilding because it recognizes the narrative and historical structure to the lives of its participants, and the narrative structure of the violent conflict in which the community is embedded.

The virtue-ethics approach emphasizes that what constitutes authentic existence for the Muslim as well as for the Christian, or even the member of any other religious tradition, is not the idea that religion is a form of private existence. Religious existence is a public and a corporate existence lived out in the local mosque or lived out in the church and in society as the *umma* or the body of Christ.

Thus, the emergence of faith-based diplomacy is part of a growing recognition that the truthfulness of the convictions of faith communities cannot be separated from the kind of communities they are and should become, and that this recognition needs to be a part of diplomacy and peacebuilding. Indeed, it is the absence of this recognition, as it was mentioned earlier, that makes it so difficult to reconcile culture and religion with the approaches to peace studies and conflict resolution when they are embedded within the individualistic discourse of secular liberalism.

What is so important about a virtue–ethics perspective on faith-based diplomacy? The failure of so many cease-fire agreements, peace accords, and so on, are well documented, as are the problems with post-conflict reconstruction and development.[47] What a virtue–ethics perspective on faith-based diplomacy and peacebuilding indicates is that it is only by acting corporately, as the local mosque, temple, or church, can the individual members of these congregations and communities be sustained in those practices — such as hospitality, works of mercy, and reconciliation, by means of virtues such as hope, courage, beneficence, and forbearance, can peace and reconciliation be maintained over the long haul.

Peacebuilding and the Global Resurgence of Religion

The concept of peacebuilding emerges from the more holistic understanding of peace found in many of the main world religious traditions. Peace, as the concept is used in the literature on international relations, is more than the absence of war or armed conflict between states. This basic understanding is largely what the Romans meant by peace in antiquity. The word *pax* is derived from the same root as pact, simply an agreement not to fight, and so it was associated with *tranquilitas* and *securitas*.[48] Israel's peace agreements with Egypt and Jordan are examples of this more limited definition of peace.

The Arabic word *sulah*, which means a truce or the end of open hostilities, reflects a similar understanding of peace. The absence of war or an unstable peace is often called negative peace in the peace studies literature. It is enforced by all the realist's tools of statecraft— the fear, uncertainty, and insecurity of others generated by military force, alliances, deterrence, and the balance of power to reduce the potential for military conflict through arms control or disarmament.[49]

What is called a stable peace or positive peace is the absence of the preparation for war or the expectation that war will take place, and is often associated with reducing what are considered to be the causes of violent conflict—economic deprivation and structural violence.[50] The notion of positive peace is expressed by the Arabic word *salaam*, which means an enduring and peaceful relationship based on mutual respect and well-being, and is similar to the Hebrew or Jewish concept of *shalom*, in which well-being is almost synonymous with economic prosperity. "Peace be within your ramparts and prosperity in your palaces" (Psalm 122:7). A stable peace is what now exists between the countries that are apart of the OECD and the European Union.

What is regarded as positive peace or sustainable peace is not only the laying down of arms, signing of a cease-fire, negotiating a peace agreement, and implementing a peace accord. One of the most sustainable ways of promoting peace within states is through good governance, which can respond to the root causes of conflict because it offers social groups a voice in resolving grievances at an early stage before they turn into violent conflict or regenerate destabilizing tensions. It is also necessary to safeguard human rights and promote a fairer distribution of resources. Good governance can be assisted by good regional or international governance, which can be promoted by international organizations such as the Organization for Security and Cooperation in Europe, the Organization of American States, and by NGOs, such as the Carter Center.[51]

Sustainable peace requires something far more difficult to achieve, a profound repentance and reconciliation that will endure in a society. It is sustained by a network of relationships and mechanisms throughout society that promote justice. Good governance gives voice to grievances before they grow into larger problems. In other words, the goal of sustainable peace and reconciliation is the creation of the conditions for a stable peace.

Peacebuilding

In the aftermath of the end of the Cold War the U.N. Secretary General Boutros Boutro-Ghali proposed "An Agenda for Peace," which included four main areas of U.N. activity: preventative diplomacy, peacemaking, peacekeeping, and postconflict peacebuilding. The Secretary-General connected peacebuilding exclusively to the postconflict support of peace accords and the rebuilding and reconstruction of war-torn societies.[52]

Peacebuilding is increasingly understood in a more dynamic, less mechanistic, and a more comprehensive way. It can be distinguished from the more narrowly focused concept of peacemaking which is the attempts to resolve a dispute or armed conflict between states or other actors, often using the methods set out in Chapter VI of the U.N. Charter on the "Pacific Settlement of Disputes," including negotiation, mediation, conciliation, and adjudication.[53]

Peacebuilding does not start or stop with the launch or termination of a UN peacekeeping operation, or with establishing political parties, or with the holding of elections. Peacebuilding addresses the structural issues, long term relationships between the social groups, and the cultural contradictions that can be at the root of a conflict.[54] Peace is conceived of as a social process or dynamic social construct, something people build in their society. What is called peacebuilding is a comprehensive concept that includes, generates, and sustains a full array of social processes, approaches, and stages needed to transform conflict toward more sustainable and peaceful relationships.

Peacemaking is often understood in a similarly more comprehensive way. Peacemaking can refer to the concrete activity related to a specific dispute to make peace between parties. The concept also has been applied to a whole range of activities that contribute to the prevention, management, and resolution of conflicts—healing, reconciliation, dialogue, negotiation, and mediation.[55]

John Paul Lederach has developed the concept of peacebuilding from an analogy with house building—how is it possible to build and maintain the house of peace? Building peace is like building a house in so far as it requires an investment of materials, architectural design and coordination of labor, laying a foundation, and detailed finished work and continued maintenance. He says peacebuilding is different from building a house in one important respect. There is no mechanical formula for tackling peacebuilding in deeply divided societies, as if with the right foreman or director overseeing the job, and with the right plan, skill, and resources, peace—like all the parts of a house—will simply fall into place. "What we must acknowledge and address from the start," he says, "are the unique human dimensions of the types of conflict under consideration."[56]

Lederach argues, in a way that is contrary to the positivism of the social sciences, that peacebuilding is not amenable to rational and mechanical processes and solutions. It is aimed at, and is to help restore, broken relationships between individuals and communities. Thus, peacebuilding in this broader perspective is about relationships and reconciliation, and involves subjective and experiential realities that have shaped people's needs and perspectives.

The global resurgence of religion is also transforming our understanding of peacebuilding in international relations. We have already seen how the concept itself is in many ways deeply influenced, if not embedded, in the more holistic understanding of peace found in many religious traditions. We have also seen how religion, identity, and globalization are changing the nature of diplomacy and international conflict.

Religion may be a part of the solution as well as the problem of international conflict. We have seen how religious actors represent a potentially powerful source for peace and political stability. Governments have often undervalued the contribution they can make to resolving conflicts peacefully. Religious groups often have strong links at the grass roots level as well as to governments, and they recognize that sustainable reconciliation and sustainable development are related in societies divided along ethnic and religious lines. Conflict, security, and development are now more interrelated than ever before and many faith-based NGOs have come to peacebuilding through their work on relief and development.[57]

Peacebuilding and sustainable reconciliation are larger, more complicated, and more long term objectives that conflict resolution. It is recognized that building peace involves a long-term commitment across all levels of society. Therefore, it is increasingly recognized that religious groups may have an important role in peacebuilding and conflict resolution.

A virtue-ethics perspective helps us to see why Lederach's analogy between house building and peacebuilding is an important one. It might be useful to see peacebuilding not as a practice but as a set of diverse but interconnected social practices. This perspective directly confronts the fact that peacebuilding deals with, as he says, the uniquely human dimensions of conflict in communities. It is, as we saw in chapter 5, the fear, loss, grievance, anger, hatred, and stereotyping of others that makes repentance and reconciliation so difficult in peacemaking and conflict resolution.

House building nor peacebuilding take place through a mechanistic formula (forgetting for the moment the existence of prefabricated housing). Both can be described as social practices, that is, socially established cooperative activities as MacIntyre understands this term. They are not the activities of isolated individuals or work men, but as practices, they are more than group activities because they require the active participation of not only other likeminded people, but the practices themselves are complex enough to require a clear goal in a unified fashion. There are also virtues—qualities of excellence—that are required to perform the practice well, and so unlike other kinds of group activities, individuals do not create the practices of house building or peacebuilding, but they participate in them, and so from MacIntyre's perspective this is the profound truth behind the analogy between house building and peacebuilding.

Understanding peacebuilding as a practice, or as a set of interconnected practices, is also useful because the objective of peacebuilding—healing, sustainable reconciliation, and conflict transformation require what in virtue–ethics is called the practice of community formation. Why is this the case? Recall that for MacIntyre practices are not only socially embodied in the traditions of particular faith communities, but they are also historically and systematically extended. The standards of the practices and qualities necessary to sustain them take place day after day, and year after year, and go on for generations. "One swallow," as Aristotle said, "does not make a spring; neither one fine day."

The practice of building a house, like the practice of peacebuilding, or like the practice of medicine, are indebted to previous practitioners. It is not only a matter of gaining better materials or technical skills (Lederach's notion of following a mechanical formula). It is a recognition that such social practices are not self-contained activities but are part of a larger system or tradition, each with their own epistemologies, authoritative texts, structured communities and institutions, and histories of their development, and so to participate in house building or peacebuilding is really to *co-participate* in these social practices as part of a larger community.

It is for this reason that MacIntyre's understanding of practice, tradition, and community is partly reminiscent of Maire Dugan and John Paul Lederbach's "nested theory of conflict." What this theory indicates is that the narrow focus on a particular dispute needs to be broadened to see how it is nested or situated in the context of the relationships that need to be reconciled in the community, and how the relationships themselves are part of the larger social structures in society, which also may need to be transformed if violence and conflict are to be avoided in the future.[58]

Peacebuilding is about helping to establish the conditions that are necessary for a community to be a viable polity. What a virtue–ethics perspective shows us is that the form and substance of these relationships and social structures are themselves dependent on the narrative of the community in which they are embedded. The beginning of the reconciliation and transformation of these distorted relationships and social structures, as we have seen, is about retelling the narrative of the community or communities and the stories of the individuals within them.

Another way of saying this is to recognize that the practice of reconciliation requires a narrative account of individual and social identity that is part of the practice of truthfulness. Only in this way can the members of a community give an adequate account of their existence, for only when we tell the story or narrative in this way can we truly answer the kind of social science question asked in chapter 3, "How can we understand what is going on in this conflict situation?"

Conclusion

In this chapter we have examined why religious NGOs are coming to play a much larger role in diplomacy, conflict resolution, and peacebuilding. Although religion has been identified as one of the most important forms of multitrack diplomacy, we have seen that the rather narrow focus of track-seven diplomacy, motivated by the concerns of pacifism and nonviolence, as important as these are, needs to be broader in order to account for the rise of faith-based diplomacy.

Faith-based diplomacy is part of a wider recognition of the way the global resurgence of religion is transforming our understanding of diplomacy and peacebuilding. The real existing communities in world politics are the faith communities that make up much of the developing world. Religion may be only one of the factors involved in the conflicts that divide these communities, but at the same time religious non-state actors often have the most extensive contacts in them. They provide a key way of transforming the politics of these communities in a sustainable way because the impetus for peace and reconciliation come from the transforming power of their faith.

CHAPTER 8

FUNDING VIRTUE? RETHINKING RELIGION, CIVIL SOCIETY, AND DEMOCRACY

The concepts of civil society and social capital generated a cornucopia of expectations for social change, democracy, and economic development among foreign aid agencies and Western governments in the aftermath of the Cold War. These concepts were used to explain a wide variety of social and political changes, including the fraying of the social fabric in the United States and in other mature democracies, the rise of "pro-democracy" demonstrations in China, the transition to democracy in Eastern Europe, and the relative wealth of northern Italy compared to the rest of the country.

This chapter examines the impact of culture and religion on foreign aid policy to promote civil society and democracy in developing and transitional countries. For some time now, a reappraisal had been going on among the foreign aid agencies and Western governments regarding their programs to promote democracy. It turns out that support for a narrow range of NGOs that fit the secular, rational, and utilitarian concepts of civil society and democracy used by Western donors is not the same thing as supporting democracy. They left out some of the most important associations in developing countries, many of which are based on religion or ethnicity, even though they have the deepest roots in society. Therefore, this chapter considers how religion can be brought back into a foreign policy that supports civil society and democracy in a way that takes cultural and religious pluralism seriously. It focuses on the activity of foreign aid agencies, Western governments, and the Office of International Religious Freedom in the U.S. State Department.

Mission Accomplished? Civil Society Revisionism and Modernization Theory

After September 11 the promotion of democracy was absorbed into the dangers posed by failing or collapsed states in the war on terrorism, and so the idea of nation-building has come back on to the foreign policy agenda.[1] In the United States these objectives are now part of an ambitious, neo-Wilsonian project to spread freedom and democracy around the world. What was once dismissed as "foreign policy as social work" has now become a key goal of U.S. foreign policy.[2]

Unfortunately, the United States has had a very low rate of success in nation-building when it has used military force to bring democracy to foreign countries. In a study of sixteen attempts at democracy promotion over the past century by the Carnegie Endowment for International Peace, democracy was sustained in only four cases—Germany, Japan, Grenada, and Panama (if the last two even qualify)—and then only ten years after the departure of U.S. forces.[3] What Amitai Etzioni has called "dud democracies" have appeared in countries as different as Haiti, Cambodia, Nicaragua, and South Vietnam.[4]

The re-appraisal among the foreign aid agencies and Western governments regarding their programs to promote civil society and democracy can be called civil society revisionism.[5] In making the promotion of democracy "the bedrock of the war against terrorism" the United States is not entering new or uncharted territory in foreign policy. We've all been through this once before. In many ways the skepticism toward civil society and democracy promotion resembles the modernization revisionism of an earlier era. This was the first wave of scholarship in the late 1960s, which began to reconsider how modernization theory could support democracy, although then it was called political modernization or political development.[6]

Samuel Huntington's *Political Order and Changing Societies*, published at the end of the 1960s, is widely regarded to have signaled this first wave of democratic revisionism, written in the aftermath of a raft of military coups and growing political instability in the developing world.[7] What followed was a collapse of this early democratic ideal for U.S. foreign policy, and a greater concern for political order and political institutions. The United States began to support dictatorships or authoritarian governments, but only ones that opposed communism.[8] A variety of people are worried this is happening all over again as part of the war against terrorism.[9]

Fareed Zakaria's *The Future of Freedom* represents this second wave of democratic disillusionment. It dissents from the democratic faith Western governments have placed over the past decade in open, free, and fair elections as a universal panacea for the developing world. He calls for a return to an older political tradition, what he calls "mixed" or republican government. Zakaria argues that the emphasis on multi-party elections has given rise to "illiberal democracies" in places like China, Egypt, Russia, South Korea, Haiti, Venezuela, and Serbia. Countries like these have popularly elected leaders, but they are unconstrained by habits of law-abiding liberalism or well-established political institutions, and have trampled on civil and political rights. This has led to more democracy, but to less liberty, and so there is a greater dissatisfaction with democracy.[10]

What are the characteristics of civil society revisionism? In the first instance it recognizes that after a decade of promoting democracy through foreign aid this has not turned out to be the same thing as supporting civil society. One of the main problems with donor-sponsored civil society programs has been their tendency to equate support for NGOs with the growth of civil society, and this has not turned out to be the same thing. What constitutes civil society in many countries is complex and contested, and simply does not neatly fit the definitions of nonprofit or voluntary agencies found in the West.

Western governments have ended up assisting the building up of an NGO sector by supporting a narrow range of donor-sponsored (and dependent) organizations. What were called democracy assistance programs made "civil society" synonymous with a narrow range of human rights, civic education, and advocacy groups favored by them.[11]

Western donors conceived of the state and civil society in a way that left out some of the most important associations in developing or transitional countries, many of which were based on religion, ethnicity, or other kinds of affective ties, although these associations often had the deepest roots in their society since religion is still deeply woven into the fabric of everyday life. This is the case in Africa, but it is also true elsewhere.[12] Muslim associations in Turkey, Jordan, or Syria, for example, that might be an informal way of empowering women, were not considered to be part of civil society because they were based on religion.[13] The same thing could be said about associations in Iran, Malaysia, and Indonesia.[14]

A second aspect of civil society revisionism more widely recognizes the elite character of local development NGOs, and what Western donors called civil society. What has occurred is that the global spread of NGOs and non-state actors involved in policy, service delivery, or advocacy examined in chapter 4 are often dominated by Western elites or Western-educated elites from the developing world. Sometimes they have only tenuous ties to the people in their countries on whose behalf they claim to be operating, and work in NGOs that are kept going mainly by foreign money.

A third aspect of civil society revisionism recognizes that external actors—development agencies and Western donor governments, do not provide technical or apolitical advice to promote democracy, any more than the promoting of political development and modernization was apolitical in the 1960s. It is an illusion to think that civil society aid to promote democracy or development is non-partisan, either in a political sense or in a moral or a cultural sense, in relation to the values or assumptions of liberal modernity.

The social change development brings is inherently political—it changes power relationships—and so any proposed change in social relationships that NGOs or building civil society brings inevitably affects a society's cultural or religious traditions. The participation of women in the interim neighborhood advisory councils USAID tried to start up in Baghdad, for example, often ran up against conflicting interpretations of the role of women in Islamic culture and society.[15] A women's micro-finance program in Bangladesh must break the grip of money lenders, and may even need to overcome the resistance of local clerics or gain their support, if it is going to give women more say in the household.

A fourth aspect of civil society revisionism recognizes that the "state-versus-civil society" model coming from Eastern Europe does not fit many developing countries. Western donors decided by the late 1980s that Africa's economic failure was mainly a failure of politics rather than economics (authoritarianism and one-party states). Now, given the role of civil society in overthrowing communism in Eastern Europe, what was advocated for Africa, as well as elsewhere, was the need for an active civil society.

However, this state-versus-civil society model does not always hold up under scrutiny. In China, like in Africa, there is not such a clear boundary between state and society. Unlike in Africa, however, in China civil society can still be seen as a network of affective ties, an expression of moral discourse created through local identity and historical memory. The state seeks to co-opt this kind of civil society as a part of its plans for community development, rather than to subvert it, which is what has taken place in Africa and the Middle East.[16]

What the donors did not realize was that the explosion in the number of NGOs did not indicate the flowering of civil society, but only the adaptation of the existing patron–client or neo-patrimonial relationships among political actors—peasants, land lords, shop keepers, factory workers, and so on. In Africa, for example, there was a change in the source of their resources from the state to NGOs funded by Western aid, but they used these resources in the same way, to reinforce the same neo-patrimonial relationships that have always existed in society.[17]

Thus, as a result of these confusions about NGOs and civil society, after a decade of civil society aid to promote democracy, it is not clear how sustainable many of the democratic transitions are which have taken place over the past decade. The spread of democratization seems to have stalled, and many countries are failing to consolidate their first steps toward democracy. The UNDP, for example, has now recognized there is a crisis of governance in many parts of the world. Citizens everywhere are loosing faith in the capacity of their governments to tackle their problems.[18] Therefore, it may be time to reconsider the role of religion in promoting democracy, given the saliency of religion to civil society in the politics of developing countries. Before we can do this we have to understand why religion was ignored or marginalized in the policy debates over civil society and democracy in the first place.

The Invention of Civil Society

The concept of civil society can be traced back to the ancient Greeks, and to the Romans, but the modern concept of civil society developed in the secular, scientific, and capitalist societies that emerged in the wake of the Scottish Enlightenment, the Continental Enlightenment, and the Industrial Revolution. The concept of civil society was used to describe the new kind of society emerging out of the changing economic realities of Europe in the eighteenth century, with the rise of private property, market competition, and the capitalist class.

The "Scottish moralists"—Adam Ferguson, Adam Smith, David Hume, and John Hutcheson—called the new social formation of capitalist modernity a "civil society" to distinguish it from the "savage and barbarous" societies observable in less developed countries. A civil society was "civil" or "civic" since it was ordered by the rule of law, it was larger than tribal societies, and also unlike them, it was held together by contractual ties or impersonal bonds of interest rather than kinship, lineage, or ethnicity.

What is important about this new kind of society, from the vantage point of this book—culture and religion, is not only what many scholars have emphasized, the mediating institutions that are a part of civil society. Civil society was also based on renegotiating the boundaries of the sacred and the profane, something which still distinguishes the West from many developing countries.[19]

The characteristics of this new society fit the core assumptions of modernization theory examined in chapter 2 in relation to international relations theory. Civil society was a secular society since religious pluralism and toleration are required for the spirit of free inquiry that inspires the capacity for innovation in a capitalist economy, and sustains democracy and political freedom. Civil society was also a commercial society, with a market economy bursting through mercantilist state regulations, and it was an industrial society, with a new division of labor developing along side it.[20]

Now, many commentators recognize John Locke is central to the civil society tradition. What is often missing from their analysis, however, is the extent to which he was a theist, deeply influenced by Calvinism, as well as a theorist of natural law. Locke considered the freedom and autonomy of individuals to be bounded by a moral order rooted in natural law—ordered liberty—which regulated both society and individual conscience. What should be recognized is that *before* the full impact of the Scottish moralists, the early modern concept of civil society was a blend of both reason and revelation.[21]

Therefore, what the literature on foreign aid and development has not emphasized is that the modern concept of civil society going back to the Scottish Enlightenment altered the concept of identity on which civil society was based. It was Hume and

Ferguson (and Diderot in France), who helped transform both the concept of the individual and the concept of civil society. They did this by rejecting the Aristotelian conception of morality, with its concept of the *telos* or ultimate governing principles that guide the moral life, and posited the notion of autonomous individuals motivated by moral sentiments—passions, emotions, and desires. Civil society simply became the arena in which each person pursues their own idea of the good life in a utilitarian way.[22]

It is Ernst Gellner who has emphasized more strongly than most commentators that a new kind of person, with a new kind of human identity, accompanied the development of civil society in the eighteenth century. Gellner calls "modular man" the new kind of person with the new human identity in the civil society created by capitalist modernity. The "modern self," with all these associations and attachments, is "modular," that is, there is something inorganic, bolted-on about them. People who are "modern" freely enter and leave them, and are constantly renegotiating their involvement in them, and yet they take them for granted since these bolted-on attachments are what we call modern life.[23]

The modern concept of civil society is part of a self-congratulatory form of political liberalism. John Hall argues it is one of the unique accomplishments of the West.[24] Many people consider Habermas's celebrated theory of the public sphere to reflect at its best this concept of civil society.[25] However, what Gellner celebrates as modular man, we see later on Michael Sandel deplores as the "unencumbered self" of liberal modernity. Civil society is inevitably a normative concept as well as an analytical one. In civil society a new kind of person, with a "modular" or bolted-on identity, unencumbered by ethnicity, religion, or other kinds of affective ties, is embedded in a new kind of culture, the culture of liberal democracy and capitalist modernity.[26]

If this is the case, then the idea of building civil society in developing countries has to be seen as part of the wider debates over modernization and Westernization. Civil society cannot be examined as a value-free, mechanistic, or technical way for Western donor governments and aid agencies to promote freedom, democracy, or economic development. The debate over civil society is part of the struggle over the boundaries of the sacred and the profane, and the battles over authenticity and development taking place throughout the developing world.

The English Pluralists:
Rediscovering the Religious Roots of Civil Society

Although things are now changing, the absence of the role of religion in the discourse on civil society and democracy in foreign policy and the foreign aid industry reflects the absence of the study of religion more generally in the study of democracy in political science. A climate exists in which the secular foundations are assumed to be the only ones important to modern democracy.[27]

The role of religion in the politics and civil society of developing countries today can be seen more clearly by examining the rise of civil society and associational life in early modern Europe. The relevance of early modern Europe rather than the Scottish Enlightenment for our understanding of civil society and democracy is that the religious roots of civil society and democracy go back to this time. This is where key questions about how civil society emerges, and how it creates a system of rights or a culture of association developed. What has happened is that concepts have been stripped from their cultural and religious context, which is what makes them intelligible and meaningful, as if this has no bearing on their usefulness today, particularly given the global resurgence of religion. Guilds, civil society, and the common good, for example, are talked about in development discourse without any notion of the moral life or the religious and political debates in which these concepts were embedded.[28]

The period of political and religious conflicts we are talking about took place between the Council of Constance (1414–1418) and the attempt by the Dutch Protestant lawyer and scholar Hugo Grotius to establish the foundations for a law of war and peace among nations. Oddly, given this violent background, Robert Putnam, Theda Skocpol, and other scholars are only now starting to emphasize the impact of war on social capital and associational life.

The English Pluralists, a group of historians, philosophers, and theologians prominent in the late nineteenth and early twentieth centuries, help us to see the way religious freedom has contributed to civil society and political freedom.[29] Their account of civil society can be distinguished from the American "pluralist" conception of liberal democracy. In the American interest-group model society is conceived of as an aggregate of rational, free, and autonomous individuals who organize themselves into interest groups and pressure groups for common purposes. They each have their own agendas, and compete with each other in the political arena to influence the national government to adopt polices in the interest of their members.

It is thought freedom is preserved in the cross-cutting membership between conflicting social groups, and this also ensures a degree of stability in the political system. There is no "common good" or "public interest" which the government tries to impose on society. The government acts as an "arena" where contending interest groups meet and reach a compromise, or it acts as a "referee," and seeks an acceptable compromise between them. In other words, social groups or associations are conceived of as means for the aggregation and articulation of specific interests, but they have little intrinsic worth in themselves.

The English Pluralists developed a concept of pluralism different from this one. What their account of civil society shows is the importance of social groups and intermediate associations as both a necessary means to other goals in the political process as well as ends in themselves, as a part of the *summum bonum* in the life of the community. Humans are social beings, as Aristotle said so long ago, and so living with other people in groups is what life is about, and is a fundamental aspect of human flourishing.

What is important for this chapter is the empirical account they give of the origins of civil society, toleration, and democracy. The English Pluralists were also known as the British guild socialists, and what they liked most about the early modern guild tradition was the freedom and autonomy of guilds and associations from state authority. They believed the strict dichotomy between the state and the individual failed to grasp the social complexity of society, and were one of the sources of the early tradition of Christian Socialism in Britain before the Labor Party adopted its collectivist traditions. The normative claims of English Pluralism go beyond its history of the origins of civil society examined in this chapter. How they also relate to concepts such as subsidiarity and the common good in Catholic social thought is also outside this chapter's concern.[30]

The English Pluralists argue ideas about democracy, representation, and the development of social pluralism goes back to the Middle Ages and to early modern Europe. What they rather awkwardly called "corporations" are what we now call voluntary associations, and they included craft, merchant, or political guilds, cathedral schools, and the mendicant orders, such as the

Franciscans and Dominicans. How corporations like these were related to the state were also a part of the early theories of popular sovereignty and representation.

Most people participated in public affairs at this time through guilds, lay fraternities, and village associations. A whole range of community associations that produced beneficial social capital in social life vanishes when it is restricted to the realms of the state or the family.[31] The model of small groups that make up associational life was later used by theorists of the conciliar movement, a reform movement within the Catholic Church, to support the rule of law and popular sovereignty. They tried to oppose the monarchical theory of governance with the age-old guild and communal values of consent, election, and majority rule.[32]

Thus, this social pluralism played an important role in the development of the civil society tradition. Social pluralism is an important part of the story of civil society because these social changes, *and cultural and religious context in which they occurred are what helped to create and legitimate the social space for the voluntary associations of civil society*. They also helped to create the values, principles, or what might better be called the virtues of fraternity or brotherhood, friendship, and mutual aid among craftsmen, as well as the virtues or standards of excellence and sense of honor they had as a part of a craft tradition.

What is being argued here is not a warm and fuzzy romantic notion of the guilds as agencies of social capital, craft honor, and solidarity (going back to German romanticism), but an alternative to a rule or principle-based account of the guilds, confraternities, and other guild-like associations. It is an account that interprets their ethos and doctrine within what Alasdair MacIntyre has called a tradition, one comprising Aquinas, Cicero, and Aristotle, and so an account of the virtues and social practices, and how the guilds fit within an understanding of the kind communities necessary for them to live well as craftsmen and as Christians in medieval Christian society. Many of these guilds or confraternities formed under ecclesiastical influence for pious or charitable purposes have been compared to grassroots organizations of clergy and lay people today, and even to the base ecclesial communities in Latin America.[33]

The religious roots of civil society can be seen more clearly if the question is asked, "*How was the social space for civil society*, with its voluntary associations, non-governmental organisations (NGOs), nonprofit organizations, or mediating institutions *created in the*

West? (emphasis added)"³⁴ This has become a crucial policy question today. How Western donor governments and aid agencies can *help to create and sustain such a social space* in developing or transitional countries is an important part of democratic transformation and consolidation.

The Pluralist account shows how the creation of a social space— as a prerequisite for the creation of a political space—takes us back to the religious and political debates of late medieval and early modern Europe, to the redrawing of the boundaries of the sacred and the profane over a variety of economic, social, and political issues. What was at stake then, and arguably what is at stake now, is a recognition that these are not simply debates in policy arenas in which various social groups try to shape policy (the interest-group model of liberal democracy followed by the World Bank and the aid agencies).

At stake was "the basic moral order, and the very structure within which the rights and wrongs of every day social behavior should be determined." Other questions include, "Who has the right to interpret the scriptures? Who is to be respected over others? What system of property rights will prevail? How will water and land be distributed within the context of the prevailing system of property rights?"³⁵ Thus, what makes this history of the West so important, as we have already seen in chapter 1, is that the redrawing of the boundaries between the sacred and the profane is a crucial part of the politics of developing countries today.

In the first instance the social space for civil society developed through the medieval theory of corporate or community life. The state was conceived of as a *communitas communitatum*, that is, as a "community of communities," a community composed of social groups rather than individuals. One of the most important medieval legal debates was on the nature of this associational life: were these voluntary associations, craft guilds and other social groups "entitled" to an existence on their own, or were they only "allowed" an autonomous existence by the power of the ruler or the state? A corporative view of society developed in which canon law justified the self-authenticating or inherent powers of voluntary associations as part of a social space—the public square, which effectively *limited* the activities of the growing national states.³⁶

The English Pluralists also help us to see that the debates in politics and theology in early modern Europe are similar to those that are at the heart of the debates in the Islamic world today. They remain at the heart of any faith-based approach to economics or international development, and can be seen in the debates over civil society, democracy, women's rights, and Islamic economics. The medieval debate over usury, interest, and the just price, for example, may seem obscure and unintelligible from a modern point of view. The reason is that we in the West have lost since the Scottish moralists and the Enlightenment Aristotle's conception of justice, moral order, and teleology in which such debates were embedded.[37] Thus, the rise of business ethics, corporate social responsibility in recent years, and the recognition of the role of culture and religion in development examined in the next chapter, are all indications (if we follow MacIntyre's analysis) of a return in the West to the remnants and fragments of these earlier, often forgotten, debates about the moral life in early modern Europe that are still central to politics and religion in the Islamic world, and to most other non-Western approaches to international development.

In the second instance the social space for associational life developed through the corporatist or communal ideas of the conciliar movement in the Catholic Church in the fourteenth and fifteenth centuries. The corporatist principles on election, corporate personality, representation, and consent were developed by canon law *giving voluntary associations a distinctive social and legal existence with rights, duties, and possessions which belonged to each association as a whole and not to its individual members.*[38]

Thus, the English Pluralists offer an alternative account of the origins of civil society in early modern Europe. It was through these ancient and obscure political and theological battles between pope and emperor, ecclesiastical and economic elites, craft guilds and arts, and through the distinctive histories of religious associations, heretical sects, and later on by the marginalized faiths like the Anabaptists and the Puritans the social space for civil society, and the principles of religious freedom and toleration were carved out of the existing order of European society.

Authenticity and Development: Foreign Aid and Liberal Communitarianism

We have seen that the struggle for authenticity and development is a key aspect of the global resurgence of religion. What does the recovery of the religious roots of civil society and democracy mean for the debates about promoting civil society and democracy in developing countries? The debate over social capital, civil society, and faith-based organizations that has emerged in the mature democracies in the West is about ways ordinary people, by coming together in new social networks or civic associations can help their own communities as well as local and state governments solve a variety of pressing social problems.[39]

After the Cold War these same concepts started to be applied to developing countries by NGOs, the World Bank, and Western governments to help them confront the problems of democracy and development. However, the broad range of topics and issues that make up the rich debate in the United States on civil society and social capital, apart from the ideas of Robert Putnam or Francis Fukuyama, have been largely neglected in the development literature.[40]

One of the main reasons for this is the dominance of the American "interest-group model" of pluralism among scholars and policymakers in the foreign aid industry. It is with this model in mind, in the aftermath of the political changes in Eastern Europe, that they assumed that multiple political parties, a vibrant civil society, and a diffuse supply of social capital were important for the transition and consolidation of democracy.[41] However, it is clear from civil society revisionism that it is time to move beyond secular Western models. Any conception of civil society which does not integrate religion into a broader discourse on what civil society is, how it functions, and how it may be supported, misunderstands what constitutes civil society and what makes it sustainable in developing countries.

Communitarian liberalism is part of the broader debate over social capital and civil society in the United States. Its critical analysis of the pluralist and interest group approach to liberal democracy makes clear why there has been so much difficulty in building civil society and promoting democracy in the developing countries. Communitarianism is a broadly based social and political movement, even though some of its participants reject this label, which seeks to move public debate away from a preoccupation with rights, to a balance between individual rights and social responsibilities, and it challenges the liberal and individualistic conception of the common good.[42]

Communitarians argue there is a tendency for liberal modernity to have an overly individualistic conception of the self, and so it concentrates on individuals as free agents that are rational and autonomous without recognizing that individuals are constituted by a variety of social attachments and communities in which they are embedded. We have already seen from our study of Rene Girard's theory of mimetic desire in chapter 5 that what people pick up from these attachments and communities are as much a part of them even as they may rebel against them.

Communitarians also recognize what some political scientists have ignored or forgotten. The rational and utilitarian ideology behind the technical-regulative interest-group model of American pluralism was itself embedded in a set of fundamental religious and moral understandings about what is right and wrong in the realm of individual and social action. Indeed, early American political debates are only intelligible within this recognition.[43] It is these moral, religious, and cultural dimensions that have been ignored in the rational and utilitarian conception of pluralism used by aid agencies and Western governments. It is this very American, allegedly value-free, model of civil society and interest group pluralism that is being exported around the world—as if culture and religion do not matter to civil society or democracy.

A liberal communitarian approach to foreign aid policy is a plea for humility and caution, and for openness, and a willingness to learn from people in other parts of the world. The goal of building civil society in developing countries should not be to reproduce a Western interest group model of democratic pluralism nor a "rights-based" form of liberal democracy. The experience of the established democracies indicates the problems of governance associated with this concept of liberal democracy even in countries with well developed social and political institutions.[44] The purpose of foreign aid is not simply to help countries develop in ways that lead their societies to fall apart like ours.

The interest-group model has created a society, what Sandel calls a "procedural republic," in which individuals increasingly organize themselves into interest groups or civic associations—civil society— with each one scrambling to pressure the government to such an extent they choke the working of the institutions of representative democracy. The state itself has become an impotent player—an arena or a referee—to guarantee fair procedures for social groups to compete without a larger public purpose or set of values to inform political debates and guide public life.

What the pluralist, interest group conception of liberal democracy has done is paralyze even the best-intentioned public officials, stifling attempts to cut or improve government programs, and distorting policy outcomes. The greatest goodies (in Putnam's words) go to the rich, the well-connected, or the best organized in society, and so people wonder whether politics changes anything. People want to engage more directly with the powers that shape their lives from city councils, local authorities, to state and national governments.[45] We have already seen that the UNDP's *Human Development Report* on deepening democracy has examined the global dimensions of this problem.

There is now a growing recognition of the need for a larger "public philosophy," a limited consensus on a community's goals, aspirations, ideals, and character that can impose some direction on this pluralistic understanding of liberal democracy.[46] Thus, what the experience of the Western democracies indicates is that the kind of pluralism and liberal democracy exported to the developing world is based on impoverished concepts of identity, freedom, and citizenship, and so may lack the civic resources to sustain democracy over the long haul.

It is a mystery why development NGOs and Western governments have adopted a rights-based approach to development given how this discourse has distorted democracy in the West.[47] An emphasis on rights rather than responsibilities has reduced political discourse to the "rights talk" of the narrow, self-centeredness of individuals and interest groups. At first the rights-talk of classical liberalism was about immunities, protecting rights-bearing individuals within civil society from the power of the state so they could each pursue within certain boundaries their differing understandings of the objective good for human flourishing. Rights-talk is now about individuals, with their entirely subjective understanding of the good, in which personal autonomy is the principle value. There is an expansive notion of entitlements, interpreted in highly individualistic terms, apart from an individual's wider responsibility in society.

However, a human rights regime cannot be sustained by rights alone. Its effectiveness depend on the appropriate political culture with dimensions of sociality and responsibility, in what the English Pluralists called the larger "community of communities" to which all citizens belong. In other words, the language of rights is morally incomplete. The right to act in a particular way without the interference of the state or other people (Mill's classic understanding of liberalism) provides insufficient reasons to act in that way. A richer moral vocabulary involving duty, decency, responsibility, and the common good is required, and was presupposed by the earlier forms of liberalism.[48]

Given the social and political difficulties of mature liberal democracies, and the English Pluralists' account of the rise of associational life, what might this tell us about building and supporting civil society in developing countries? First, the interest-group model of liberal democracy has the potential to turn rights-talk into rights-fights, to reduce the politics of developing countries further into acrimony and factionalism rather than promote the social space and tolerance required for civil society.

This problem is already emerging in developing or transitional countries. After the end of communism in Poland, for example, there is a concern that the revival of civil society can lead to anarchy rather than to a mature political society because of the endless claims by a large number of interest groups.[49] In Kenya the better organized groups in civil society are concentrated in the Kikuyu and Luo tribes, and so from the former KANU government's point of view, what these organizations represented (along with the mainline Protestant churches) was the entrenched ethnic interests of the opposition.[50]

One the one hand, the pluralist, interest-group model of civil society, with its differentiation, organizational independence, and tolerance of dissent is being applied to societies where these characteristics are weak, are an underdeveloped part of the political culture, or have even been destroyed by dictatorship or authoritarianism.[51] The crime, corruption, inequality, and ethno-nationalism in many developing and transitional countries indicates the low levels of virtue, civility, and morality there is on which to build civil society.[52] On the other hand, the problem in some developing countries is that pluralism may be stunted or distorted by a few powerful political actors—Africa's Big Men, who prevent other actors from entering the political arena—businesses, environmentalists, women, or the rural poor.

Second, one of the reasons the debate over the concept of civil society took place is because the key policy question for aid agencies and Western governments has been what kind of associations in civil society should they support to bring about democracy? In contrast, the perspective of English Pluralism suggests that the legal and political *legitimacy* of this social space, and the *interactions* of social groups, through which they can learn trust, tolerance, and reciprocity are in the short term more fundamental than cherry-picking the kind of associations that should make up the public square.

Why is this the case? Because the public square is where the debate, the dialogue about the good life of the community takes place, drawing on the cultural and religious traditions within which the community in embedded. Indeed, Sandel has argued "public life is diminished if it is cut off from the religious sources of the culture." Certainly, as Sandel, Putnam, Elshtain, and other communitarians have acknowledged, there is a "dark side" as well as "noble strands" present in any religious tradition. It is in the public square, however, where those traditions are tapped, contested, interpreted and reinterpreted to provide the ingredients for the public philosophy of a country.[53]

Now, in the developing world, it might very well be the case that that such a public philosophy is oriented toward development. It is for promoting economic growth and alleviating poverty. But as we see in the next chapter, if sustainable development is going to take place, and not lead to policy failure, revolution, or religious extremism, then it must be in accordance with a country's moral base, its cultural, and religious traditions. It is in the public square, as Sandel has indicated, where the debate over the on-going relevance of these religious traditions takes place. Therefore, the lesson from the English Pluralists' is that it is this public space that needs to gain legal and physical security as well as political strength and legitimacy.

The most that external interventions by aid agencies and Western donors may be able to do are two things. The first thing they can do is help to secure the legal and political legitimacy and physical security of the social space for civil society. In Kenya, for example, legislation in the early 1990s for greater state control of NGOs was one way of curbing the legitimacy of the social space for civil society, and there is similar legislation in many other countries.

Therefore, assisting and monitoring the state's protection of the social space for civil and political rights may be more important in the short term to prevent illiberal democracy than an early emphasis on multi-party elections, although there is room for debate over the sequence and time frame for these objectives.[54] The paradox of civil society is that the social space for associational life requires a strong state to support the kind of legal and political reforms which entrench the rule of law (and not only rule by law).[55]

Religion as Soft Power?
The Office of International Religious Freedom

The second thing Western donors can do to promote civil society and democracy is influence through public or cultural diplomacy the kind of debates, social habits, and discourses that take place in civil society. J. N. Figgis famously stated, "political liberty is the fruit of ecclesiastical animosities." What he recognized is that political freedom was a result of the debates and struggles for the liberty and legitimacy *of one group among a society of groups*, and this is what is so different from the liberal emphasis on individual liberty or freedom of religion or conscience, although the English Pluralists also affirmed this was part of liberalism.[56]

Fiery Jesuits or Protestant Reformers like Robert Bellarmine or John Knox, nor the English Puritans were really interested in religious or political liberty as such, any more than some Islamic clerics or Hindu priests today. It was not the liberal claim to freedom of speech or conscience that led to toleration, but the claims of social groups to freedom of assembly. However, religious freedom and toleration, as Herbert Butterfield reminds us, came about through political expediency *before* they came to be seen as ideals by religious groups to be defended on the basis of religious principles.[57] Indeed, it is in Iran, Iraq, Turkey, Pakistan, Nigeria, China, the Sudan, and elsewhere where such principles and animosities between religious groups are being worked out today, and so where the lessons of English Pluralism are relevant most of all.

Religious freedom uneasily came to the forefront of American foreign policy during the Clinton Administration through the pressure of a loose coalition of Jews and evangelical Christians, increasingly concerned about the persecution of Jews and Christians in foreign countries.[58] In order to stave off firmer legislation from Congress, Secretary of State Warren Christopher announced the creation of an Advisory Committee on Religious Freedom Abroad in 1996, and about the same time the U.S. Congress, faith-based NGOs, and the Department of State began discussing ways to integrate religious freedom initiatives into U.S. foreign policy. The result was the landmark International Religious Freedom Act of 1998.

The issue is whether religious freedom should be pursued separate from or as a part of a broader support for a human rights foreign policy. The problem is that liberals—political as well as theological—are more interested in human rights generally, and religious conservatives have been more interested in using religious freedom to attack countries hostile to the United States—China's persecution of Buddhists in Tibet, Muslims in Xinjiang, and the persecution of Christians in Islamic countries.[59] In spite of this kind of political bickering over religious freedom, reminiscent of the squabbles between liberals and conservatives over human rights during the Cold War, the global resurgence of religion has made the freedom of religion and religious persecution key issues in international relations.[60]

What does the Office of International Religious Freedom do as a part of U.S. foreign policy? The OIRF publishes an annual *International Religious Freedom Report.* This report labels those countries that have particularly severe violations of religious freedom as CPC's, that is, as "countries of particular concern," and so they can be subject to further action by the United States, including economic sanctions, something the U.S. business community is not entirely happy with. While most Americans may be oblivious to this report, its findings are widely reported abroad, and often cause a stir in the countries that it has criticized, such as China, Malaysia, or Indonesia.

The OIRF also does not seem to recognized that a rights-based approach to religious freedom can lead to a decline in political discourse because the effectiveness of a discourse on human rights depends on the political culture in which it is embedded. The United States, by using appeals to rights-based approaches, rooted in the universalistic assumptions of the Enlightenment, has no way out of the log-jam of relativism versus universalism human rights policy has been in for over a decade. Universal notions of human rights were challenged in the Bangkok Declaration in 1993 by Asian ministers in the run-up to the Vienna Conference on Human Rights held later that year.

Thus, the United States has made the case for religious freedom by relying on the principles of the Enlightenment, and this is helping to undermine the integrity and truthfulness of people's religious convictions. It is also alienating India, China, and Russia, some of the most important great powers of the twenty-first century, countries in the Pacific Rim with some of the most dynamic economies, and it has alienated much of the Islamic world.

Arguably, the American model of the separation of church and state has contributed to the vibrancy of American religious life.

The U.S. model shows that political secularization does not have to imply social secularization, and so the American experience can be contrasted with the decline of religion in Western Europe. A variety of surveys have shown that American patterns of religion are closer to those found in the Islamic world, and in much of the developing world.[61] Therefore, the religious vitality of American culture and civil society ought to provide the kind of soft power resources that could make a more positive contribution to religious freedom and the goals of U.S. foreign policy.

There is another way forward. Promoting religious freedom as if the truthfulness of people's religious convictions mattered. The promotion of religious freedom in this way, as chapter 9 shows, is part of a country's authenticity and development, and so is a part of its political stability and social integration in ways that will limit policy failure and diminish the possibility of revolution or religious extremism.

We have already examined MacIntyre's concept of tradition-dependent rationality, and his rejection of the Enlightenment's assumptions regarding religion and rationality. We saw in chapter 3 how his social theory has influenced the schools of narrative theology and "postliberal" theology. What is important about these approaches for diplomacy is that they offer a way of taking religion seriously in public and cultural diplomacy.

What would a postliberal approach to promoting religious freedom look like? First, as a general principle, it makes appeals to values, experiences, and even the discourse of particular faith communities, rather than appeals to rights-based principles of universal rationality. Indeed, for Lindbeck and Hauerwas, the heart of religion is the living out of a specific historical religious tradition and the way its ideas, values, and practices in the lives of individuals are mediated through history and in the common life of a faith community.

Postliberal diplomacy makes use of the deep pluralism that exists among different cultures and faith communities in world politics. We have also seen how the modern notion of civil society and the public sphere, going back to Habermas, have considered secular reason to be the only legitimate discourse in public life.

Contrary to this approach, for postliberals, truthfulness is regarded as fidelity to a distinctive religious doctrine and traditions of the faith community. This means the validity of a religious tradition is judged by reference to its own internal standards—what does it mean to be a good Muslim, Christian, Jew, or Hindu?—and not to some publicly agreed, rights-based criteria, dependent on the use in the public sphere of the rationality of the Enlightenment.

A second aspect of postliberal diplomacy to promote religious freedom is that it recognizes the role of religious non-state actors in world politics. Multitrack diplomacy, as we saw in chapter 7, should allow for multiple forms of rationality and moral reasoning depending on different cultural and religious traditions. How governments may speak to each other does not have to be the same as how faith-based organizations in different countries speak to each other. It is this dimension which may become more important, as we see in the next chapter, with the privatization of foreign aid as a part of U.S. foreign policy.

Religious groups are not only a key aspect of civil society, but as we saw in chapter 4, they have the deepest grassroots connections that bring together the local with the global in their communities. In relation to the Arab or Islamic worlds, there has been a tendency in the West particularly underlying modernization theory, to reify their societies and cultures, as if they are bounded, monolithic, or homogeneous entities. MacIntyre's notion of a religious tradition, as a historically extended and socially embodied dialogue regarding the goods of that tradition, offers a more accurate description of what is taking place within the Islamic tradition and in many Muslim countries.

Islam is today a contested, dynamic, and differentiated tradition, in which what constitutes the boundaries of "public Islam," or Islam in the public sphere, is itself highly contested—by religious scholars, self-ascribed religious authorities, secular intellectuals, Sufi orders, mothers, women, students, workers, engineers, and so on. They are all part of the debate in civil society over the issues mentioned earlier—democracy, women's rights, and Islamic economics.[62] Indeed, they are in many ways trying to work out a kind of "Islamic public philosophy" for their countries, as Sandel has examined for the West.

Now, as a part of the OIRF's mandate, it does have meetings with foreign officials at all levels, as well as with religious and human rights groups, but religious freedom is examined from within a Western discourse of rights-based liberalism. Postliberal diplomacy differs from this approach by bringing together the dialogue about religious practice and discourse with the debate over religious freedom. It seeks to more directly engage in a dialogue about the meaning of freedom, truthfulness, and faithfulness within different religious traditions with officials, religious leaders, and faith-based organizations.

In the Islamic world, for example, this might mean that cultural attaches at U.S. embassies as well as American Muslim intellectuals and Arab or Islamic organizations in the United States would have a greater and more prominent role in multitrack diplomacy. They would seek to encourage and facilitate the debate that already exists in the Islamic public square in some countries—and, is struggling to exist in other ones, over law, observance, and faithfulness to the Islamic tradition, and they would seek to expand the kind of social groups that constitute the public sphere in Muslim countries.

However, for a genuine dialogue to take place about religious freedom U.S. officials, human rights workers, and Americans in faith-based organizations also have to be open to learning from other countries and their religious traditions. The criticisms religious clerics and teachers from other countries make about the contradictions they see in the United States between wealth and poverty, and religiosity and materialism should be taken seriously. One Islamic teacher from India, after coming to the United States through the State Department's International Visitor program, complained that neither American teachers nor American diplomats were interested in listening to him. "The only time they will actually take anything from us is when they are ready. Right now," he said, "they are in a position when they think they are Superman and they don't need anything from anybody."[63] If diplomacy, religious freedom, and democracy are now part of a much wider dialogue between states, non-state actors, and faith communities, then may be it is about time we in the West start listening to people in other parts of the world.

CHAPTER 9

WHERE FAITH AND ECONOMICS MEET? RETHINKING RELIGION, CIVIL SOCIETY, AND INTERNATIONAL DEVELOPMENT

Another aspect of the global resurgence of religion is the growing recognition that religion, spirituality, and cultural authenticity are a part of international development. There are a variety of indicators of this shift in international relations, including the World Faiths Development Dialogue started a decade ago by James Wolfensohn, the president of the World Bank, and Dr. George Carey, then the Archbishop of Canterbury, head of the worldwide Anglican Church, the growing partnership between the World Bank and faith-based organizations and interfaith organizations on a variety of issues in development, and the higher profile of the world's religious leaders at the United Nations, and at the World Economic Forum in Davos, Switzerland.[1]

One of the things that has prompted this dialogue, at least from the World Bank's point of view, is that it has come to recognize that religious organizations are often the most trusted institutions in developing countries, and they are some of the most important social groups in civil society. Therefore, unlike the debate over charitable choice in the United States, which has become bogged down by legal and political problems, the World Bank, Western governments, and development NGOs increasingly recognize the key role faith-based groups can play in delivering social services and alleviating world poverty.[2]

In this book we have already examined MacIntyre's conceptual scheme—virtues, practices, narrative, and social tradition—and why it is important for the study of religion in number of issue areas in international relations. What this chapter seeks to do is examine the relevance of his social theory for a foreign aid policy that begins to take cultural and religious pluralism seriously, and how through the virtue–ethics tradition it can more fully involve faith-based organizations. In this way a virtue–ethics approach to foreign aid policy is akin to the faith-based diplomacy examined in chapter 7.

Evangelism or Social Action? Development and Faith-Based Organizations

The area of foreign policy where religious organizations already have had a widely acknowledged role is in providing relief and foreign assistance. Many religious or faith-based NGOs today such as Catholic Relief Services, World Vision, and Christian Aid, like missionary organizations over a century ago, have had a role in health and education in the developing world as a part of their understanding of Christ's "Great Commission" to preach the gospel and make disciples of all nations (Matt. 28:19–20), although they have often struggled with how to interpret their activity.[3] St. Francis of Assisi, for example, advised Christians who were going to live in Muslim lands, "Preach the gospel with all your heart, and, if necessary, use words." Christian mission agencies have had a central role in influencing the moral debates surrounding U.S. foreign policy, they have helped to shape the country's national interests, and they have provided relief and development assistance for years.[4]

Most Western governments and development agencies, however, have argued that "religion" gets in the way of helping the poor or promoting development. It is all right for faith groups to be inspired by the love, compassion, or sense of justice or moral obligation their faith brings them, but they should not use it to proselytize or influence the *content* of development. In other words, following Max Weber, it is fine for faith-based NGOs to provide "motives," "inner factors," or "the practical impulses" for participating in activity to promote relief and development.[5] Faith-based NGOs should not, however, interfere in what is effectively a secular development agenda, with its own understanding of what constitutes rationality, progress, social justice, and modern economic development.

Some faith-based NGOs seem to agree with this secular understanding. Christian Aid, for example, defines itself as an overseas development agency, sponsored by the mainline British and Irish Churches, to fund long term development projects, and it distinguishes itself from organizations that do what it calls "missionary work"—evangelism. If that is what you want, its web page directs you to Tearfund, the evangelical relief and development agency, the British and Foreign Bible Society, and Oscar, the UK Information Service for World Mission. The success of World Vision, founded as an evangelical development agency, is now attributed to its broadly secular approach to development.[6]

There has been, often still is, a hostile and dismissive attitude toward religion in the aid industry, and what is derisively called the "missionary model" of development assistance. The stereotype still persists of zealous, if well-meaning, but ill-informed, missionaries, often with the support of Western governments, providing the kind of goods to people in developing countries they don't really need, with little understanding of what is really required for long term development.[7]

Most Western donor governments, the foreign aid industry, and the secular media have accepted what Stephen L. Carter has called the "culture of disbelief" in public debates about social policy, and his argument can be extended to foreign aid policy. There is no naked public square. If religious values and beliefs cannot be brought into politics, then politics will be dominated by the secular values and beliefs of political liberalism. A public legal and political discourse has been constructed in which religion is trivialized, is meant to have little or no political or social significance, and so religious believers are forced to act as if their faith doesn't really matter.[8]

What is important to recognize about this culture of disbelief, as this book has argued, is that it is at odds with the way most people in the developing world live out their moral lives. Andrew S. Natsios, a former vice-president of World Vision in the United States, and the head of the U.S. Agency for International Development (USAID) under George W. Bush's administration, is well aware of this situation. He has aptly argued, "While most American and European foreign policy elites may hold a secular worldview, much of the rest of the world lives in one of the great religious traditions."[9]

We can now see that the culture of disbelief in the foreign aid industry is often part of the pluralist, interest-group model of liberal democracy examined in the last chapter, and is a key component of modernization theory. It is for this reason that culture, religion, and spirituality have had an uneasy relationship with development theory and practice, and have tended to be ignored or marginalized.[10] As we saw in chapter 8, this is also why they have often wanted to exclude religious groups from civil society.

The stereotype of the missionary model may fit well with the bias of scholars, the media, and many development practitioners. However, it is misinformed, and no longer reflects the practice of most faith-based relief and development agencies.[11] Most of them operate along the lines of what is called the "Oxfam model," the model, which is supposedly distinguished from the missionary model by its reliance on local communities to determine their own development needs.[12] Michael Taylor, the former director of Christian Aid, points out that most faith-based NGOs accepted some time ago the kind of criticisms that are often still made of the missionary model of development assistance.[13]

What is Development? Bringing Culture and Religion Back into Development

Among many scholars and development practitioners a debate over a more holistic understanding of development has been taking place for 30 years. This general view is associated with a criticism of capitalism and radical political economy in so far as it is a less narrowly conceived approach to a positive, that is, value-free, economic orthodoxy. It is really both radical and conservative in so far as it "recognizes that man is a social being whose arrangements for the production and distribution of economic goods must be, if society is to be livable, consistent with congruent institutions of family, political, and cultural life."[14]

It is now more widely recognized that successful development, no matter how it is defined, can only occur if social and economic change correspond with the moral basis of society. This view has sought to connect religious values both to the actual kind of development that takes place, and to the meaning of development.[15] When development does not correspond with a society's moral base, and a country makes a choice for development over authenticity, like the Shah's Iran, and promotes a distorted form of modernity and development, this cannot only lead to policy failure, but also to political instability, or even revolution (today we would add religious terrorism).[16]

A number of factors have contributed to a shift in the meaning of development over the last thirty years. First, scholars and practitioners have reassessed the emphasis on economic growth and industrialization. There has been much economic growth in developing countries, but it has been so unequally distributed that great areas of poverty remained in many countries. The mid-1970s brought a greater emphasis on "growth with equity" in economic development.

Second, it was also recognized that there were huge costs of social change, and the basic values of poor people were being cavalierly disregarded in the quest for a Western understanding of modernization and development. There were high human costs of underdevelopment as well—poverty, low infant mortality, life expectancy, and so on—and what Denis Goulet famously called the cruel choice between bread and dignity and authenticity or development that faced people in the developing world.[17] Peter Berger's *Pyramids of Sacrifice* (1974) signaled a growing realization, as he put it, that "not by bread alone does man live," and even by gaining the bread—Brazil's rapid economic growth in the 1960s, it may be a stone.[18]

There were also what Berger called cultural or religious costs to development that must be taken into account. Authenticity, cultural diversity, and multiple forms of authentic development started to be seen as a part of development, and can be interpreted as another aspect of the global resurgence of religion. People want to develop, they want the fruits of economic prosperity, but without losing their souls.[19]

Thus, a third aspect of the change in the meaning of development has been a fitful, if steady, retreat from a faith in positivism in international development similar to that we have already examined in chapter 2 regarding the theory of international relations. It was increasingly recognized that development is a type of secular "global faith," and can no longer be thought of as a positivist, value-free, activity led by economists and technicians to promote economic growth and industrialization.[20]

Any concept of development inevitably includes a concept of the good life and the good society, and is not only a problem of getting the expertise or know-how right in order to promote economic development. It is recognized that the concept of development used until now was inevitably value-laden, and embodied the values of the industrialized societies of the West, and so it requires a firmer moral or ethical foundation.[21] The reality of these ethical and cultural dilemmas is what led to the concept of "post-development" in the development literature.[22]

Now, there were always people who felt ethics and development—and, sometimes even religion—were related to each other, such as Ivan Illich, Denis Goulet, Paulo Freire, E. F. Schumacher, Dudley Seers, and Mahbub al Haq. Their early criticism of the meaning, practice, and experience of development was sometimes associated with the rise of liberation theology in Latin America. Thus, the ideas questioning the meaning of development which thirty years ago were considered to be radical, marginal, and a dissent from the reigning orthodoxy are starting to become more main stream.[23]

A fourth aspect of this shift in the meaning of development was signaled by culture becoming a part of the official development agenda. The World Commission on Culture and Development was sponsored by UNESCO as part of the World Decade for Cultural Development proclaimed by the United Nations (1988–1997). It was now recognized that many efforts at development had failed, as Javier Perez de Cuellar, the former U.N. secretary general put it, "because the human factor—the complex web of relationships and beliefs, values and motivations, which lie at the very heart of culture—had been underestimated in many development projects."[24]

The rise of the Pacific Rim also contributed to a change in the role of culture in development. The old debate, initiated by Max Weber and R. H. Tawney over the way religious values—the "Protestant ethic," can help to shape, direct, or even be a barrier to economic development, had come full circle with the rise of East Asian countries, and the end of the third world as a coherent idea.[25] Culture and religion matter for economic performance. Protestantism and Confucianism were now thought to encourage the entrepreneurial attitudes necessary for economic growth and prosperity.[26] The East Asian countries, whose peoples remained faithful to their values, showed that it was possible to develop without loosing your soul after all.

A fifth factor that has led to a change in the meaning of development, as we saw in chapter 1, was the larger crisis of modernity—postmodernism taking place in the developed world. It reflects a deeper and more widespread disillusionment with a "modernity" that has brought high levels of material progress and consumption amidst widespread unemployment, hunger, and deprivation. This situation has also helped to bring the concerns of culture, religion, and, spirituality on to the public agenda regarding the meaning of development.

Thus, for a variety of reasons the need for a broader understanding of development is being recognized by the international community. Economic criteria alone cannot determine human dignity or well-being. It almost seemed like some economists and social scientists were starting to recognize what the founders of the main world religious traditions have said all along—man does not live by bread alone, and the material prosperity of this world is an illusion.

Religion, Civil Society, and the World Bank

How has the World Bank responded to this changing consensus on the meaning of development? The idea the World Bank was becoming more sensitive to ethics and religion, or at least notions of humanistic development, needs to be placed in the wider context of the changes taking place in secular bureaucratic as well as religious organizations. There has been a trend for some time now for religious organizations to become internally "secularized" in their operations while a counter-veiling process of "sacralization" has been taking place in secular social service organizations in an attempt to create a more "holistic" corporate culture.[27]

The World Bank was also not the only international organization to become concerned with the matters of culture and religion. At the same time the World Health Organization (WHO) started to redefine health, well-being, or quality of life to include spiritual health. The WHO's Constitution was changed in 1999 to define health as "a dynamic state of complete physical, mental, spiritual and social well-being and not merely the absence of disease or infirmity."[28]

Staff members of the World Bank have been meeting formally for over 25 years to discuss among themselves the role of religious and ethical values in world development.[29] The World Bank as an institution also came to recognize, in the context of its large research project, "Voices of the Poor," that when people in poor communities did speak up, they often voiced a much higher degree of confidence in religious leaders and organizations than with their own corrupt governments, public sector welfare services, and they expressed more confidence in religious organizations than in secular NGOs since they often seemed to have narrower interests.[30]

David Beckmann was one of the economists who played a leading role in helping the World Bank to learn more about grassroots groups and nongovernmental organizations. "In retrospect," he says, "it's strange that the Bank's intelligent staff just could not see how important churches, mosques, unions, and farm groups are to development. The Bank was structured to work in a Cold War context with most developing countries under dictatorships. So, its staff just couldn't see all of these peoples' organizations and what they were doing. Now, working with nongovernmental organizations and popular participation is World Bank orthodoxy. It's now clear that those of us who were trying to get the Bank to pay attention to those things were getting up on a surfboard just before the big wave of global democratization arrived."[31]

What the World Bank, development NGOs, and development practitioners now recognized was the extent to which poor communities can also be described as faith communities. It turns out that religion—beliefs, rituals, practices, and institutions—is still central to the social, cultural, and moral life of these communities.[32] Indeed, as this book has argued from the beginning, they constitute the real existing communities in international relations.

Thus, by the 1990s, the World Bank, Western donors, foreign aid agencies, and many development NGOs recognized that faith-based communities can play a key role in reaching the poor in the developing world. What can be called the new orthodoxy regarding religion and development was stated by Kumi Naidoo, the general secretary of CIVICUS, a global alliance of NGOs committed to strengthening citizen's action and civil society (www.civicus.org). In a study on charitable giving in Islam he stated, "faith-based organisations probably provide the best social and physical infrastructure in the poorest communities. . . . [because] churches, temples, mosques, and other places of worship [are] focal points for the communities they serve."[33]

Religious Values and Development: The World Faiths Development Dialogue

The changing nature of development and a growing recognition of the key role faith-based organizations can play in eradicating world poverty contributed to the formation of the World Faiths Development Dialogue at a conference at Lambeth Palace, London (the seat of the Archbishop of Canterbury) in February 1998 by James Wolfensohn, the president of the World Bank, and Dr. George Carey, then the Archbishop of Canterbury, the head of the Anglican Church. The conference included leaders from a variety of religions, including the Bahá'í faith, Buddhism, Hinduism, Judaism, Muslim, Sikhism, and Taoism (www.wfdd.org.uk).

The conference was an entirely new initiative, followed up by another one in Washington, D.C., involving both secular and religious institutions that now recognize that religious organizations have an important role to play in promoting international development. At the time it appeared there might be a willingness of the World Bank to move beyond a purely economic or technical understanding of development, in much the same way that there is now a recognition that culture and religion need to come back into the study of international relations.[34] However, as we will see, in many ways the World Bank seems to have backed away from this understanding of values, ethics, and development even though it continues to work with a variety of faith-based organizations on development issues.[35]

One of the outcomes of these conferences was the creation of a small organization based in the United Kingdom, which moved to Washington, D.C. at the end of 2004, called the World Faiths Development Dialogue (WFDD). The WFDD is a global network with ties to over 80 staff members at the World Bank, to development agencies, and research institutes and universities, and to a variety of faith communities and interfaith organizations. Its purpose is to help promote a dialogue on a number of specific issues related to poverty and development, or on specific country activities both among the different faith traditions and between them and the development agencies.[36] However, it is important to recognize that the WFDD was not created by the World Bank nor by any religious institution. It is situated between faith-based organizations and development institutions, and is independent of both of them.[37]

Another outcome has been a set of new partnerships between the World Bank and a variety of faith-based development organizations on a whole range of issues in development, including health, education, HIV/AIDS, and post-conflict transformation.[38] The World Bank's dialogue and partnerships with faith-based organizations seem to cross the liberal–evangelical divide since it includes organizations such as the Oxford Center for Mission Studies, the World Council of Churches (WCC), and the Inter-faith Network. The straddling of this divide reflects, as we saw in chapter 1, that the more liberal mainline churches in the West, where the money and resources are concentrated, are often at odds with the much larger and more conservative faith communities in the global South.

What is this dialogue about and what has it accomplished? At a variety of levels a dialogue and a set of new partnerships are taking place with the World Bank, the WFDD, and a variety of faith-based development organizations through meetings, conferences, and personal contacts regarding the meaning of development, the reduction of world poverty, and the promotion of faith-based development cooperation.[39] The WFDD and those faith-based organizations in partnership with the World Bank can be distinguished from other religious non-state actors involved in the kinds of global advocacy for peace, justice, or interfaith dialogue examined in chapter 4. The WFDD and other faith-based development NGOs, to their credit, are trying to engage in the messy, imperfect world, of actual policy to end world poverty.

It is simply impossible to say, however, given the variety of interests groups and perspectives at the World Bank, how effective the WFDD or faith-based development NGOs have been compared to other groups, in influencing World Bank policy. The dialogue with the World Bank needs to be seen as part of its general concern for accountability and consultation with NGO constituencies and community organizations.[40] It might be argued that the World Bank, in its dialogue and partnerships with faith-based organizations is playing catch up, having had stronger links with women's groups and community associations for some time. The WFDD has tried to use the dialogue to both influence the ideas and theories behind the World Bank's policy, but, regardless of its impact, the WFDD has participated in the World Bank's approach to alleviating world poverty.

The dialogue among the WFDD, other faith-based development NGOs, and the World Bank takes place in four main areas. First, the WFDD seeks to be in dialogue over a more "holistic," "comprehensive," and "integrated" understanding of development.[41] All the religious leaders present at the WFDD's founding conference agreed that economic and social development should be judged within the framework of faith, beliefs, and values, and wanted to examine how their religious tradition could be related to economics and development.

The WFDD's approach to finding a place where faith and economics could meet was extremely innovative. Michael Taylor, for example, the WFDD's director until the middle of 2004, has argued that there was widespread skepticism among many Christian development NGOs regarding the relevance of Christian doctrine to development policy. The aim of the WFDD, however, was to do precisely this, to examine how the practices of faith communities were related to development.[42]

The WFDD seeks to develop a common theoretical grounding regarding what faith communities have to say about religion, spirituality, and development, and to relate this understanding to specific and practical development programs. The WFDD has pursued this objective through a variety of workshops and case studies of faith groups in actual development projects, and it has produced training manuals setting out the teaching of the main world religions on poverty and development.[43]

Second, the dialogue between the World Bank and faith groups is to demonstrate what interfaith dialogue and cooperation can do in *practice* to promote development. The WFDD and the World Bank's partnerships with a variety of faith-based development NGOs have produced concrete reports that examine interfaith development cooperation. Perhaps, this kind of grassroots research needs greater publicity because most news reports concentrate on religious violence or the clash between civilizations.

The delivery of social welfare services in developing countries is another area of dialogue between the World Bank, the WFDD, and other faith-based development NGOs. The World Bank recognizes that faith-based organizations have been particularly successful in providing primary education and health care (especially in recent years related to HIV/AIDS). There is also a recognition that they are often well placed to respond directly to disasters and emergencies.

Third, the WFDD has tried to develop a set of common criticisms of the existing economic, technocratic, and materialistic understanding of development. The interfaith perspective, from the very first meeting, indicated how much common ground there was on many key issues. They all agreed that material and spiritual well-being could no longer be separated. Its first project, for example, in the run-up to the *World Development Report* on world poverty (2000–2001), was a conceptual study of the meaning of poverty and development.[44]

Fourth, there was a growing awareness among some faith groups that dialogue with the World Bank and radical criticism of it were not always compatible objectives. The WFDD's contributions to the World Bank Development Reports are most often criticisms of its theories and policies, and at times this borders on outright opposition. One can legitimately ask, what have been the benefits of the dialogue so far?

It is very difficult to balance engaging the principalities and powers of this world as they seem to be represented by the IMF or the World Bank, and still speak the truth to power at the same time; indeed, for some faith-based NGOs engaging with the World Bank is little more than supping with the devil.[45] There is a concern faith-based organizations could become too close to the World Bank for their own good. This concern can be seen as part of the wider NGO debate about the close relations between development NGOs and Western donors since a large proportion of their funding often comes from governments.[46]

How has the World Bank responded to its dialogue with faith communities? There was a growing concern at the World Bank by the end of 2000 that its dialogue with faith-based organizations through the WFDD was taking it too far into the realm of politics. This was considered to be inconsistent with its original mandate to provide technical assistance to developing countries. When, for example, the World Bank recommends greater female education in Muslim countries, it has done so in the past by saying that educating girls brings higher economic returns, rather than by trying to justify the policy on the basis of some set of common global values.[47] However, as we saw in the last chapter, a shift in social policy unavoidably mixes politics, religion, and social policy, and this is one of the main aspects of civil society revisionism.

Thus, the World Bank has reasserted its "economic positivism," and maintains that the content *of* development—skills, knowledge, and technical expertise, and so on, is morally and politically neutral, and can be distinguished from the motives for the ethics and values to be involved *in* development. The World Bank has now formally withdrawn from the WFDD's governing structure (it no longer participates on the WFDD's board of trustees) even though it continues an active dialogue with the WFDD, and meets with faith and development leaders. It also has continued to develop partnerships with a variety of faith-based development organizations.

Whose Development, Which Rationality?
The Limits of the World Faiths Development Dialogue

In chapter 8 we saw that the new kind of identity required for the modern concept of civil society adopted by Western donor governments is unrecognizable in most parts of the developing world. Religious beliefs and the ascriptive aspects of clan, ethnic, or religiously based forms of identity remain a part of the modernization of tradition. Contrary to modernization theory, the intermingling of ethnic groups and professions in urban life is not leading to the bolted-on, individualized, social conditioning required for the modern kind of civil society Hall, Gellner, and Habermas have celebrated. Quite the opposite has occurred with the resurgence of these ethnic, religious, or regional forms of identity.

> Africans do not conceive of themselves as discrete individuals in the Western mould . . . Individuals are not perceived as being meaningfully and instrumentally separate from the (various) communities to which they belong. This means that individuals remain firmly placed within the family, kin, and communal networks which (s)he is issued . . . Africans do not now appear to feel that their "being modern" requires them to be single individuals whose life choices are essentially determined by their own private circumstances and desires. Difficult as it may be for us to conceive of modernity other than in our own terms, it is necessary to understand how Africans can be both modern and "non-individual(ist)" if we are to make sense of political events on the continent.[48]

In chapter 3 we examined MacIntyre's narrative conception of the self, and we can see now why he has argued this may be more consistent with the way most people in the developing world still understand their moral and social lives. MacIntyre argues that our values and ethical conceptions and the rationality on which they are based, are socially embodied in particular social traditions and communities. There is no rationality independent of tradition, no set of principles which will commend itself to all independent of their conception of the good. The self in this account is a self with a life story embedded in the story of a larger community. Character is displayed and developed when individuals are inducted into particular communities, which are themselves shaped by larger narratives and social traditions. This continues to be the case in Africa, but the same thing can be said about other parts of the developing world, and even of Japan and East Asia.[49]

Unfortunately, the WFDD's approach to religion and development at times seems to be based on the assumptions of Enlightenment rationality and liberal modernity, and often seems to resemble the WCC's approach to world poverty. Michael Taylor, the WFDD's former director, in a devastating critique of the WCC's strategy, has argued that it did little more than follow the latest fads of the secular development agencies. The churches turned out to be little more than Oxfam—with hymns.[50] If that is the case, why bother with the hymns? If what is often called the "social teaching" of the world religions, are really what the ICRC says they are, "common values in different disguises," why bother with the disguises? Why bother with culture, religion, or spirituality at all?[51]

A deeper, more coherent account of these relationships is provided by MacIntyre's social theory. If rationality is dependent on tradition, then morality is not detached from historical communities and cultural and religious traditions. Appeals to the virtues and moral judgments in religion, or to duty, charity, justice, compassion, and obligation are not free-floating moral propositions to which rational (autonomous) individuals simply give their intellectual assent. What they mean is shaped by the linguistic conventions of different faith communities, connected to the practices of a religious tradition, and are only intelligible because they are recognized types of behavior (social practices) passed on through the narratives that shape the identity of these communities.

The vast majority of people in the world, as the WFDD and the World Bank now seem to acknowledge, still experience the moral life, however imperfectly it is lived out, as MacIntyre has indicated. Although the WFDD does not use MacIntyre's concepts or language, it recognizes that this takes place within the virtues, social practices, and traditions of their faith communities.[52] However, as we have seen, given the culture of disbelief in foreign aid policy, faith-based organizations, often with the best of intentions, have been co-opted—wittingly or unwittingly—into what is effectively a secular development agenda.

We can now see the extent to which this approach is rooted in Western concepts of liberal modernity. Many of the missionaries of faith-based organizations and the secular missionaries of the development NGOs are both proselytizing, each according to their understanding of modernity and development. They have reduced the "thick" social practices embedded in the traditions of the main world religions and communities into "thin" practices, abstract moral rules, norms, or values, which can only be appealed to by a concept of Enlightenment "rationality" detached from religion, culture, and tradition In other words, they have turned what MacIntyre would call a practice-based morality into a rule or principle-based approach to the ethical dilemmas in development.

The WFDD, although it does not use MacIntyre's language, almost seems to recognize MacIntyre's tradition-dependent concept of rationality, and the problems this raises for faith-communities in their relations with the World Bank or secular development agencies. It has argued, for example, that poverty reduction projects will fail "unless due attention is paid to the *different ways in which people give meaning to the world and their existence in it*, and to the ways in which they order their societies and run their economies" (emphasis added).[53]

For all the WFDD's concern for religion and development, it is unable to take cultural and religious pluralism seriously because its basic approach is rooted in the assumptions of Enlightenment rationality and liberal modernity. What is being argued here is not that there are no universal moral values, but what is needed to take cultural and religious pluralism seriously is a "rooted cosmopolitanism," based on the common, thick social practices in different religious traditions rather than appeals to the universal rationality of the Western Enlightenment.[54]

Religion, Social Capital, and Faith Communities

Dr. George Carey, in the debate he tabled in the House of Lords two years before September 11, on "Religions and International Order," argued for a perspective different from a postmodern ideology of religious pluralism. This ideology, rooted in the Westphalian presumption, celebrates diversity and difference, and argues that any normative truth claims are to be censured as inherently divisive or intolerant in a society characterized by cultural and religious diversity.

After acknowledging the good work of the Inter-faith Network, he said, "At the same time, a commitment to seeking and sharing common ground does not mean compromising or disowning what is distinctive and special." He went on to emphasize, "Religions and faith communities do not exert influence merely through the resonance of an ethical framework," which as we have seen, is one of the aspects of Weber's notion of a religious ethic in the sociology of religion. "We trust," Dr. Carey said, "that at their best they also seek to provide examples and agents of such values."[55]

How do faith communities come to embody the values that they proclaim? How can they, as a recent WFDD report put it, over

come the credibility gap and be true to their teaching since this is
the only way to bring about changes in themselves and in their
world.[56] The ethics of the main world religions and the problems of
alleviating world poverty and promoting global security now come
together in this question. *What difference do religious convictions make
one way or another for promoting or even achieving these objectives in
international relations?*

Social capital can be defined as the networks of social connections and the norms of reciprocity and trustworthiness that arise
from them.[57] Faith-based communities, as Robert Putnam, and
other scholars have rightly acknowledged, are a crucial repository
of social capital in society.[58] The WFDD says this as well, arguing
that the World Bank has focused too much on the powerlessness
and material deficiencies of poor people, and not enough on their
resourcefulness, spiritual groundedness and their awareness of the
importance of personal and community relationships.[59]

This is what is called bonding (or exclusive) social capital, and
theorists argue that this form of social capital, while it involves
small group activities, mixing religion and socializing, and so an,
tends to be inward looking, and can reinforce exclusive identities
and the homogeneity of ethnic or religious groups. What is often
called bridging (or inclusive) social capital, is about forming
networks that are outward looking, and include people across class-
based or other kinds of social or religious divisions in society, such
as the civil rights movement, ecumenical gatherings, interfaith
cooperation, or in transnational religious organizations.

How each of these forms of social capital are related is an important part of community organization and development strategy.[60]
The point social capital theorists make is that a poor community
may be rich in localized or bonding social capital but it may lack the
kind of linking or bridging social capital, or the power to get or
create these forms of social capital, necessary to gain access to
economic resources or better opportunities, a better education,
access to credit systems, or wider markets.[61]

Some of the reasons why faith-based communities are a reservoir
of social capital, however, may be different from the ones given by
the World Bank or those found in the social capital literature. It
takes more than church, temple, or mosque attendance—bums on
pews as they say in Britain—for places of worship to be a reservoir
of social capital, and to play a role in civic revival in their communities. In this sense faith communities are only secondarily a source of

social capital because of the social connections that their places of worship and related activities provide for their members. The main reason why faith-based communities are reservoirs of bonding social capital or bridging social capital is the kind of communities they are or are struggling to become. It is because of the kind of communities they are that civic virtue can be embedded in these dense networks of reciprocal social relations.

Social capital theorists recognize that values and beliefs can be a powerful source for the motives and commitment of faith-based communities. Any attempt, however, in the study of social capital to disentangle the impact of religious ideas, beliefs, and doctrines from the impact of social ties or networks in an account of the volunteering and philanthropy of faith-based communities is misplaced. It is simply based on a variety of unstated assumptions regarding rationality, modernity, and autonomy that are part of a modern concept of religion which simply does not even exist in many developing countries.

The reason why religious doctrines cannot so easily be separated from social ties—the virtues and practices that are part of the formation of a community—is because bonding and bridging social capital presuppose each other or are mutually constitutive relations in faith communities. This is explained by rabbi Michael Goldberg with an aptly put phrase that should appeal to theorists of social capital: "its not what you know, its who you know." The reason for this, as we have seen already, is because there is no rationality independent of a social tradition, and so the values, norms, virtues, and moral judgements that are appealed to as part of social capital are not free-standing, moral statements or propositions the way liberal modernity would have it.[62]

Social capital's supporters recognize there is quite often a dark side as well as the positive side to religion as a source of social capital. MacIntyre's social concept of religion as a tradition also helps us to understand better this dark side. The role of religion in promoting ethno-national conflict as well as cooperation and peacebuilding shows how often there is an ambivalence of the sacred. If culture and religion produce *both* social solidarity—bonding social capital—*and* negative social capital that in their most extreme forms can lead to racism, violence, and intolerance, then it is not simply a matter, as Putnam suggests, of destroying the negative or non-bridging forms of social capital. It is a matter of transforming them into the kind of positive social capital for social integration, civic renewal, and community development. Social change is not the same thing as social destruction.[63]

How can negative social capital be transformed into positive social capital? What is important are not only the types of social connections that matter (bridging or linking social capital), but the ideas, virtues, and social practices that make up the *content* of the connections in social capital matter as well. What happens *to* those bums on the pews listening to the sermons being preached, and *in* those social connections is as important as the connections themselves, for this is what helps to *transform* negative social capital into positive social capital.

The civil rights movement shows another way to approach the role of religion and social capital in faith communities. MacIntyre's social theory also offers a way of interpreting this struggle as something other than what Putnam has suggested, as the transformation rather than the destruction of negative social capital. At its heart, as the most recent research shows, the civil rights movement was a religious movement with political dimensions rather than the other way around. Both white and black communities needed the cultural depth and moral authority rooted in their religious traditions. It was the authority of the Bible, and evangelical Christianity, rather than appeals to a secular liberal creed of pluralism and political equality, which bolstered the black community's resolution to oppose segregation, and at the same time undermined the convictions of white segregationists.[64]

Southern religion embodied the ambivalence of the sacred. Religion provided a deep reservoir of positive and negative social capital in the southern United States. The civil rights struggle provides an example of the vitality of a religious tradition in the way MacIntyre has defined it, as a historically extended and socially embodied dialogue on what are the goods that constitute that religious tradition. In this case it was the debate, dialogue, and struggle regarding the kind of moral reasoning the church should employ to understand racism (and segregation), to combat it, to end it, and to demand black political rights. What we can see being employed in the preaching Sunday mornings, in church meetings, sit-ins, bus boycotts, and demonstrations, and in the White Citizen's Councils, and the Southern Baptist Convention's Sunday School Board was a form of moral reasoning that was an integral part of both black and white faith communities.

In other words, in terms of MacIntyre's conceptual scheme—virtues, practices, tradition, and narrative, the issue regarding racism and segregation in the South was not in the first instance framed as an individual question, "What am I to do?"—regarding racism, segregation, police brutality, sit-ins, bus boycotts, marches, freedom rides, prayer pilgrimages, demonstrations, and so forth. These are the kind of single questions framed in what is called "quandary ethics," which emerges from the moral predicament of the rational and autonomous individual in secular modernity and political liberalism.[65]

At issue for both faith communities—black and white—was a more primary question, "Of which stories am I a part?" a question that is identified with MacIntyre's narrative understanding of human identity. There were, as David Burrell has argued regarding the Israeli–Palestinian conflict, "narratives competing for our souls."[66] Recall that Martin Luther King's famous "Letter from Birmingham Jail" was addressed to his "fellow clergymen," many of whom did not want to break the law and participate in nonviolent resistance.

The real Rosa Parks did not decide one fine day that she had had enough, and would no longer go to the back of the bus, and so set in motion the year-long bus boycott in Montgomery, Alabama, which turned a young Martin Luther King, Jr. into a national leader of the civil rights movement. This is to understand her social action as a matter of heroic individualism and as a quandary ethics problem. The real Rosa Parks, as a part of her faith community—the African Methodist Episcopal Church—had spent 12 years helping to lead her local NAACP chapter and attended summer training sessions at a labor and civil rights organizing school; therefore, she was a part of an existing faith community and a social movement.[67]

Thus, if we use MacIntyre's conceptual scheme, what we can see from this example of the civil rights movement is that the "good" of the Christian tradition is the formation of a particular kind of community, one that inculcates those virtues necessary for living out an authentically Christian life. In the black community, at this time in history, it was a question regarding an authentically Christian response to racism, segregation, and oppression. For the white community it became a recognition that racism, segregation, and white supremacy (negative social capital or "evil practices" in MacIntyre's language) were in some ways incompatible with, or were completely incompatible with, the living out of an authentically Christian life. In other words, as Dr. Carey indicated, how a faith community understands the truthfulness of its convictions matters for the kind of community it is and seeks to become in the world. Contrary to Weber, what is important are not only the religiously based values or motives for social change and community development, but the kind of moral reasoning that gives rise to the content of those convictions as well.

Building Communities of Character in Developing Countries

What is the relevance of the civil rights movement as it has been explained here using MacIntyre's conceptual scheme for a faith-based approach to development assistance? Francis Fukuyama has recently argued that we need to better understand how social capital and cultural change are related, and how this can occur through training, education, and the way norms are reinforced.[68] The civil rights struggle provides an example—a reading if you will—of how the virtues and practices of particular religious traditions can be a part of social change and development. It shows how bonding social capital can be turned into bridging or linking social capital, and how the radius of trust of cooperative groups can be powerfully transformed as part of a social movement.

What is distinctive about the virtue–ethics tradition in the aftermath of MacIntyre's social theory is the place it allows for the crucial role of churches, mosques, temples, and other places of worship in building what Stanley Hauerwas has called "communities of character" as a part of foreign aid policy. Virtue–ethics emphasizes that the truthfulness of religious convictions cannot be separated from the kind of community that the church, the mosque, or temple are or are trying to become in the world.[69]

The "good," therefore, of the Islamic, Christian, Jewish, Hindu, or Buddhist religious tradition, is the formation of a particular kind of community, one that inculcates those virtues and practices necessary for what it means to authentically live out life according to a particular religious tradition. There is nothing to indicate that building a community of character is easy. The issues faith communities must deal with in the developing world are complex—including, faith and development, gender and reproductive issues, HIV/Aids, religious approaches to work, wealth and poverty, usury and interest, corruption, state privatization, interfaith cooperation, and good governance.[70]

Religion, in so far as it can be a source of positive social capital at all, it is because of this collective attempt by a faith community to live out the moral life together. Therefore, a virtue–ethics approach to foreign aid policy is about the ways Western donor governments can help assist the capacity building of faith-based NGOs or of churches, mosques, and temples in faith communities more directly, so they can become the kind of communities of character that can generate the social capital that contributes to social change and development.

How does a virtue–ethics approach to foreign aid policy operate in practice, and how is it different from what is taking place already? A virtue–ethics approach to foreign assistance is not the same thing as aid agencies or faith-based organizations developing partnerships or simply working with and through local churches, mosques, temples, and so on. This is happening in a variety of ways already. Virtue–ethics is a different way of working with and being with faith-based communities. On some issues and in some countries a virtue–ethics approach is already being implemented. What is required is for faith-based organizations, aid agencies, and Western donors to see how it can be a more integral and effective part of foreign aid policy.

First, as a general principle, a virtue–ethics approach recognizes the deep pluralism that exists among the different associations and communities which make up civil society in developing countries. In order to build communities of character it begins by identifying and developing a dialogue in the community over those "thick" social practices that are a part of particular religious and cultural traditions, such as charity (*zakat* in Islam) and hospitality, and the virtues necessary to sustain them. Such a foreign aid policy seeks to support and cultivate them as part of the communities' collective attempt to live out the moral life according to its religious tradition. Any other approach is simply to understand development as a series of never ending problems in quandary ethics.

Faith-based NGOs can help to build communities of character in Muslim countries, by engaging with clerics and ordinary believers in debate and dialogue about social policy and what are the goods of the Islamic tradition. If the World Bank or development NGOs want to support female education or family planning in Muslim countries, for example, a virtue–ethics approach is an alternative to appeals using economic rationality or a secular liberal creed of pluralism and political equality.[71] The Family Planning Association of Bangladesh (FPAB), for example, devised an educational program to look at the role of family planning in Islam with a target audience of clerics, students, and opinion leaders.[72] The association of young Islamic women (Fatayat), and the Women's Welfare Association in Indonesia are both connected to the Nahdlatul Ulama, the world's largest Muslim association, has developed similar programs.[73]

Second, a virtue–ethics approach seeks to assist those faith-based organizations in faith communities articulate and formulate a social space in civil society where the virtues are displayed, and social practices can be put into action. It does so, however, in ways that build up communities in their faith—by trying together to determine and live out what is an authentically Muslim, Christian, Buddhist, or Hindu response to the particular problems of development before them, as well as to empower communities as part of a strategy of participatory development.

The Sarvodaya Shramadana Movement in Sri Lanka is an example of a movement that uses the social practices of Buddhism as a part of the moral formation of faith communities dedicated to helping those in poor villages. It is within an understanding of Buddhist practices that rich farmers may be persuaded to give up part of their land to the landless poor. Buddhist monks, like the black preachers in the American South, organize public meetings in the local temples to discuss development problems, whether they relate to disaster management, bio-diversity, environmental conservation, or special projects the villagers say are necessary to help meet their basic needs.

At the heart of the Sarvodaya Village Development movement is moral formation and not only economic activity and social empowerment. It is the changing of the conceptual and psychological aspects of society, by the unfolding of people's inward capacities for sharing, and a desire to help others in the community. It turns out that religion and spirituality are a part of authenticity and development. It is these kind of inward changes that help villagers to over come their sense of fear and powerlessness, and gain the strength necessary to solve the problems of poverty in their own way.[74]

Third, the virtue–ethics approach offers a way for people in poor faith communities to build up their faith as they try to influence the events and processes that shape their lives by participating in grassroots community-based activities. Arguably, this approach gives even greater force to the biblical admonition that the first— the experts, the technocrats, the educated, the outsiders, the missionaries, and so on, shall be last.[75]

The Sarkan Zoumountsi Association in the Cameroon is an example of such a faith-based community development association. The association was set up in the mid-1990s to promote development in the socially underprivileged sections of the population. The coming of multiparty democracy and the IMF's structural adjustment program had led to cut backs in state subsidies for local funding for health case, schooling, and other social services, and so there was an increase in poverty, crime, and unemployment.

The local imams, ulemas (scholars), religious counselors, and community leaders formed the association. The Islamic clerics and scholars give advice regarding the virtues and practices necessary for living out an authentically Islamic life as part of the development activity of the association. Financial resources came from cultural activities, such as theatrical plays the association produced, and grants came from the European Union for participatory development, and from the Islamic Development Bank for women's projects.

What did the association do? It constructed foot bridges in the city of Yaoundé to open up certain isolated parts of the city, it purchased a minibus to transport school children, gave talks to girls and housewives, and developed programs for collecting rubbish, cleaning out gutters, and street sweeping. A savings and credit cooperative was also created, although it was later closed because of a lack of finance, and an inability to manage it along Islamic principles. The association, interestingly, refused finance and partnerships from abroad in the fight against HIV/AIDS because it felt Islam placed a greater emphasis on changing personal life style, and faithfulness to a single partner. It was the way the virtues and practices of Islamic bonding social capital were interpreted, which led to the association's bridging social capital, its willingness to work with the members of other faith communities, and resolve disputes between traditional or conservative Muslims, and more Wahhabite or Muslim fundamentalists in their own faith community.[76]

A virtue–ethics approach not only recognizes, as Paulo Freire did a generation ago, the importance of using local knowledge, but also as we have seen, the building up of local character as a key aspect of successful development.[77] It is for this reason that the WFDD has criticized the World Bank for focusing too much on the powerlessness and material deficiencies of poor people, and not enough, as we have seen in these examples, with bonding social capital being transformed into bridging social capital, their resourcefulness and spiritual groundedness. Thus, the building of a community of character involves people responding to these issues and events in a faithful and truthful way, by displaying those virtues and practices that allow them to become the kind of faith community necessary for them to live well as Hindus, Muslims, Christians, or Buddhists.

Fourth, a virtue–ethics approach seeks to understand the notion of "partnerships," in the language of foreign aid policy, as a form of moral formation for development. Faith-based organizations are particularly well placed to implement this understanding. On the one hand the emphasis on partnership tries to put foreign aid on to a more equal basis between donor and recipient countries.[78] On the other hand, by transferring responsibility for achieving the purpose of foreign aid programs on to the recipients, there is an attempt by donors to get them to accept local "ownership" (in development jargon) of the values, policies, and programs, and this is crucial if they are going to be effectively implemented.[79]

At issue here is how the values, policies, and so on, are effectively transmitted and supported, and underlying this jargon of management practice is a thinly veiled recognition of the need for moral formation within an institution. This understanding of development partnerships fits with the wider goal of assisting faith-based organizations to help local churches, mosques, temples, and so forth, to become communities of character in developing countries.

Thus, what a virtue–ethics approach recognizes is that character, empowerment, and participation must go together if over the long haul there is going to be political stability, democracy, and development. So was Hilary Clinton right after all? It takes a village to raise a child, a church to raise a Christian, a synagogue to raise a Jew, and a mosque to raise a Muslim.[80]

Conclusion

Many people may object to a virtue–ethics approach to foreign aid policy by saying it is certainly not the role of the United States or other Western countries to "preach morality" as a part of foreign assistance. I want to respond to this objection in a way that may help make clear the advantages of the virtue–ethics approach to foreign aid policy.

You don't have to be secularist or a member of a religious minority to recognize that when the state starts to preach religion, the role of religion can have a negative influence in public life. The real question is how religion can contribute to the common good. However, this objection distorts the concept of a community of character, and misunderstands how different the virtue–ethics tradition is from the kind of post–Enlightenment ethics debates that dominate most public policy discussions. It also underestimates the extent to which religious groups are increasingly transnational actors in world politics.

States such as Pakistan and Thailand, for example, where state legitimacy rests on a kind of civic religion can easily distort and undermine faith-based approaches to development. While in Sri Lanka and Indonesia, where the state is less directly involved in religion, many development NGOs and community activists question the possibility of a secular approach to economic and social development. There is a greater recognition of the role of faith-based organizations to promote or work out Buddhist or Islamic approaches to social change and development.[81]

Therefore, a virtue–ethics approach to foreign aid policy recognizes the negative impact the state can have on the vitality of religion in civil society. This is why it only seeks to help faith-based organizations to influence the role of religion in the civil society of faith communities. What are the other advantages of a virtue–ethics approach to foreign aid policy?

First, as it was argued in the last chapter, the religiosity of American civil society and the vitality of American religion ought to provide untapped soft power resources for U.S. foreign policy. The virtue–ethics tradition opens up a way for the soft power resources of religion to become a part of foreign aid policy. It can do this because it takes seriously the religious and cultural traditions of other countries.

A virtue–ethics approach is the key to understanding the kind of broader agenda of cultural change — norms, training, and education — social capital theorists have advocated. It provides a way for aid agencies to assist faith-based organizations to help build up the churches, mosques, and temples in faith communities into the kind of communities of character that can produce the social capital useful for civic renewal and community development.

Second, the virtue–ethics approach to foreign aid policy makes better use of the changing landscape of foreign assistance. Most people tend to think of foreign aid as mainly publicly funded programs, but now most foreign assistance comes from private sources, and official development assistance (ODA) by Western donor governments is low and is declining.[82] Therefore, if money and personnel from aid agencies, development NGOs, and religious organizations are playing a much larger role in foreign aid, and faith-based organisations provide the best social and physical infrastructure in poor communities, then it is appropriate to form a foreign aid policy which can use these conditions more effectively.

Third, a virtue–ethics approach to foreign aid policy is also part of a better way to fight terrorism over the long haul. Simply promoting freedom, democracy, and development—the neoliberal agenda—is not necessarily going to improve national security. Our attempt to rebuild failed societies or promote development, as we saw in chapter 8, will not be successful if they do so in ways that unleash the same kind of disruptive forces of social change we have not been able to cope with in our own countries with stronger social and political institutions.

We have seen that this is what happens when development does not correspond with a society's moral base. We now know that when authenticity and development do not go together it cannot only lead to policy failure, but also to political instability, revolution, and religiously motivated terrorism. Building communities of character engages with these forces of social change in constructive ways by seeking to promote and facilitate the kind of dialogue and debate within a religious tradition in faith communities on the meaning and relevance of their tradition for today.

A cautionary note is in order at the end of this chapter. There is no reason to expect or to believe that by helping to build communities of character countries in the developing world will support the goals of U.S. foreign policy. Building communities of character, as the civil rights movement indicates, could also end up creating communities of conviction and constructive resistance. However, there is no reason why the United States should not be able to support such movements for positive social change and development. Much the rest of the world, in spite of the current hostility, is desperately looking for positive American leadership in this area.

For all of us—belonging to different faith communities or none—our political, social, and economic life is a form of confession. We make clear what we believe by the choices we make, and how we conduct our lives. Americans, as well as people in other developed countries, need to recognize that the choices they make regardless—or, even because of—their faith commitments affect the world in far greater ways than the actions of any peasant in Bangladesh or Mozambique.

Therefore, for faith-based organizations in developed countries to be able to help build communities of character in the churches, mosques, and temples abroad, they may need to develop those virtues and practices that enable them to live well—as Muslims or Christians or Jews or Hindus here at home. In our global era, however, they may not be able to do this without recognizing that how they conduct their lives in this country affects the people in faith communities in other parts of the world.

CONCLUSION: HOW SHALL WE THEN LIVE?

These are not mathematical symbols or hydrocarbon molecules that the scholars are studying; their subject matter consists of living, feeling men [and women]. It would be a melancholy comfort, if we were all blown up into a cloud of radioactive dust [or by weapons of mass destruction today], to realize that the scientific scholars knew exactly why this was happening. Men live by the things they cannot prove, and we lose much, if in our search for the reasons for human behavior, we forget the truth about man is not as important as the miracle that man exists at all.[1]

> —*Charles O. Lerche and Abdul A. Said*
> *School of International Service*
> *The American University*

It was stated at the outset this book seeks to examine the way the global resurgence of religion is challenging our understanding of how culture and religion influence international relations. At the heart of this challenge, at least for those of us in the West, is the way it challenges our understanding of what it means to be modern, opening up the possibility of multiple ways of being modern. We have to understand that the sacred, and considerations of religion and spirituality are an inherent part of a postmodern world.

Its purpose was to begin to sketch out—and, in the nature of things it can only be a sketch, worked out in dialogue with other scholars, colleagues, and friends some of the possible contours of what the discipline might be like if religion was brought back into our understanding of international relations. It has tried to do this by using the social theory of the philosopher Alasdair MacIntyre and the conceptual scheme he has developed—virtues, practices, tradition, and narrative—in a way that takes seriously cultural and religious pluralism in international relations. What does this mean in a practical way?

We have seen that the global resurgence of religion challenges the idea that has been with us since the Enlightenment that there is some kind of neutral or privileged social space from which to evaluate values, beliefs, and practices of others in international society.

This does not have to mean that there are no universal values, only that the Western Enlightenment is not the only way of arriving at them. I have called for a "deeper pluralism" between different cultures and civilizations, and have argued for a "rooted cosmopolitanism," one which sees that a genuine dialogue between religious traditions and civilizations can only take place within the virtues and practices of particular religious traditions among the real existing communities that make up world politics.

The study of culture and religion in international relations needs to consider the wider debates in social theory over modernity, postmodernity, and secularization. It is these debates that are behind the concepts, discourse, and language used to explain culture and religion in international relations—extremism, fanaticism, fascism, terrorism, or fundamentalism. We can now see how misleading it may be to view the global resurgence of religion through such lenses—as if the global resurgence of religion is an aberration in an otherwise modern world.

This is not the kind of world scholars within the rationalist world of international relations expected to be a part of in the twenty-first century. Postmodernity has challenged the idea that in our era Western modernity can determine the meaning of the overall character and direction of progress, modernity, or development for all countries. Our theories need to be able to account for the meaning and significance religious actors give for their social action. We have seen that so many of the concepts scholars have developed, and the hypotheses in which these concepts are framed, often rest on hidden, undeclared, and unstated assumptions about modernity and progress that are of doubtful resonance in view of the global resurgence of religion. This book has tried to grapple with the fact that rationalist approaches may be too embedded in the assumptions of Western modernity to fully understand the impact of culture and religion on international relations. It has also criticized some constructivist and postmodern approaches to international relations for the same reason.

An approach to theory that seeks to understand the action of religious actors through a narrative of their identity and the meaning they give to their actions will not allow us to formulate theories with predictive capacity or produce the kind of general conclusions social scientific scholars seek in international relations. If I can bring Abdul Said's comments up to date, it offers us no melancholy comfort to know exactly why highjackers fly airplanes into skyscrapers or why suicide bombers blow themselves up in cafes, nor why nationalist extremists consolidate their power through religious scapegoating.

If religion is best understood as a living tradition in the way that MacIntyre has described, then the key issue for policymakers is the nature of the debates within those traditions, and for the members of those traditions themselves—the key issue is really a normative question, as we have emphasized. It is to what narratives do they belong? The purpose of explanatory narratives rather than explanatory theories is to show that different choices and different circumstances could have led to different endings or outcomes for social action.

It is at those decision points where narrative explanations can lead to policy choices and various forms of policy intervention. The key thing to remember here is that not all but many of the key forms of intervention will be a part of public or cultural diplomacy. The interventions will contribute to the cultural and religious dialogue taking place within these faith communities. We saw some of these possibilities for a whole new variety of non-state actors given the way globalization has changed the nature of diplomacy, peacemaking, and international conflict as well as international development.

How do we know what is going on in the world? This sounds like a basic social science question. Both Rene Girard and Alasdair MacIntyre have a narrative conception of how identity is constructed. Girardians point to the underlying violence on which rests any social cohesion and political order. It is for this reason the relative peace and stability in the Balkans, Rwanda, or even our own society should not be overstated. Beautiful Georgian Bath and Bristol were built on the wealth of the slave trade, as was the wealth and beauty of the American South. The seeds of the civil rights struggle in the 1960s were sown in the myth of the "lost cause" spread after the Civil War, which united the white United States by sacrificing the rights of black Americans, denying right up to the end of the twentieth century, that the war was about slavery, morality, and justice. White Afrikaners and English-speaking South Africans were united after the Boer War in a new Union of South Africa only by sacrificing the rights of black South Africans.

In all of these events, the violence, or catastrophes on which our social cohesion, political stability, and worldly power rests, it is possible to say, "*we* weren't there," or "we didn't do *that*," and then wonder why there are riots in Birmingham (in England or Alabama), or "why the Muslims rage" or "why do they hate us so much?" What a Girardian perspective indicates most disturbingly is that all of us, in our own societies, in our thoughts, words, and deeds, through our negligence, or weakness, or through our own deliberate fault, participate in the rituals and practices of a social and political order maintained through violence.

What Girard and MacIntyre open up for us is a wider recognition that events such as these are not only about history and memory, but also about our own story or our own narrative. We will not know what is going on in the world—or interpret what is going on in this way—unless our identity is bound up in a narrative that is larger than our own story. A narrative that questions our agency or autonomy in liberal modernity, or our ability to freely choose what to include or exclude from our story; and one that recognizes we are, or need to be, embedded in the kind of community that trains us in those virtues and practices that help us to see what is going on in the world in this way. If we can do this then understanding what is going on in the world may also be a way of changing it.

NOTES

Introduction: The Struggle for the Soul of the Twenty-First Century

1. Fred Halliday, *Iran: Dictatorship and Development* (London: Pelican, 1979).
2. Barry Rubin, *Paved with Good Intentions: the American Experience and Iran* (New York: Oxford University Press, 1980); John Stempel, deputy chief of the Political Section, *Inside the Iranian Revolution* (Bloomington, IN: Indiana University Press, 1981).
3. Zbigniew Brzezinski, *Power and Principle* (New York: Farrar, Straus, & Giroux, 1983, 1985), 354–398.
4. Gary Sick, *All Fall Down: America's Fateful Encounter with Iran* (London: I.B. Tauris, 1985).
5. James E. Bill, *The Eagle and the Lion: The Tragedy of American-Iranian relations* (New Haven: Yale University Press, 1988), 417.
6. Moorhead Kennedy, *The Ayatollah in the Cathedral* (New York: Hill & Wang, 1986), 54–55.
7. Robert Wuthnow, "The World of Fundamentalism," *The Christian Century*, April 22, 1992, 426–429.
8. Ray Takeyh, "Iran's Emerging National Pact," *World Policy Journal*, 19, 3 (2002): 43–50.
9. Thomas Powers, *Intelligence Wars: American Secret History from Hitler to Al-Qaeda* (New York: New York Review of Books, 2002).
10. Richard K. Herrmann and Richard Ted Lebow (eds.), *Ending the Cold War: Interpretations, Causation and the Study of International Relations* (New York & London: Palgrave, 2004).
11. Robert V. Daniels, *The End of the Communist Revolution* (London: Routledge, 1993).
12. Ian Clark, *Globalization and Fragmentation: International Relations in the Twentieth Century* (Cambridge: Cambridge University Press, 1997).
13. George Weigel, *The Final Revolution: The Resistance Church and the Collapse of Communism* (Oxford: Oxford University Press, 1992); James Billington, "The Crisis of Communism and the Failure of Freedom," *Ethics and International Affairs*, 5 (1991): 87–97; John Clark and Aaron Wildavsky, *The Moral Collapse of Communism: Poland as a Cautionary Tale* (San Francisco: ICS Press, 1990).

14. Patrick Michel, *La societe retrouvee, politique et religion dans l'Europe sovietisee* (Paris: Fayard, 1988).
15. Maryjane Osa, "Creating Solidarity: The Religious Foundations of the Polish Social Movement," *East European Politics and Societies*, 11, 2 (1997): 339–365.
16. Ted G. Jelen and Clyde Wilcox, "Context and Conscience: The Catholic Church as an Agent of Political Socialization in Western Europe," *Journal for the Scientific Study of Religion*, 37, 1 (1998): 28–40.
17. Weigel, *The Final Revolution*, 111–119.
18. Ibid., 119–158.
19. Adam Michnik, *The Church and the Left*, edited, translated, with an introduction by David Ost (Chicago: University of Chicago Press, 1993).
20. George Weigel, *Witness to Hope: The Biography of Pope John Paul II* (New York: HarperCollins, 1999), 145–180.
21. Timothy Garton Ash, *The Polish Revolution: Solidarity* (New York: Vintage Press, 1985), 30.
22. Edward Stourton, *Absolute Truth: The Catholic Church in the World Today* (London: Viking, 1998), 85–106.
23. David Brooks, "Kicking the Secularist Habit," *The Atlantic Monthly*, March 2003.
24. V. S. Naipaul, "Our Universal Civilization," *The New York Review of Books*, November 5, 1990.
25. Fareed Zakaria, "The Return of History," in James F. Hodge and Gideon Rose (eds.), *How Did This Happen? Terrorism and the New War* (New York: Public Affairs/Council on Foreign Relations, 2001), 307–317.
26. Francis Fukuyama, "History Is Still Going Our Way," *Wall Street Journal Europe*, October 8, 2001; Robert L. Bartley, "Thirty Years of Progress—Mostly," *Wall Street Journal Europe*, November 29, 2002; Michael Mandelbaum, *The Ideas That Conquered the World: Peace, Democracy, and Free Markets in the Twenty-First Century* (Oxford: Oxford University Press, 2002).
27. Michael Walzer, "Can There Be a Decent Left?" *Dissent* (Spring 2002): 19–23.
28. S. Hashmi, "The Terrorists' Zealotry is Political, Not Religious," *Washington Post*, September 30, 2001; Fred Halliday, *Two Hours that Shook the World: Septmeber 11, 2001: Causes & Caonsequences* (London: Saqi Books, 2002).
29. Lael Brainard, "Textiles and Terrorism," *New York Times*, December 27, 2001; Richard Sokolsky and Joseph McMillan, "A Robust Foreign Aid Program," *International Herald Tribune*, February 13, 2002.
30. Christopher Hewitt, *Understanding Terrorism in America From the Klan to Al Qaeda* (New York and London: Routledge, 2003).

31. Steven Simon and Daniel Benjamin, "America and the New Terrorism," *Survival*, 42, 1 (2000), 59–75; Daniel Banjamin and Steven Simon, *The Age of Sacred Terror* (New York: Random House, 2002); Oliver McTerman, *Violence in God's Name: Religion in an Age of Conflict* (London: DLT, 2003).

32. *Congressional Record* (Washington, D.C.: House of Representatives), September 20, 2001.

33. Paul Berman, "Terror and Liberalism," *The American Prospect*, October 22, 2001; Paul Berman, *Terror and Liberalism* (London and New York: W.W. Norton, 2003).

34. Emilio Gentile, "The Sacralization of Politics: Definitions, Interpretations and Reflections on the Question of Secular Religion and Totalitarianism," *Totalitarian Movements and Political Religions*, 1, 1 (2000): 18–55; Roger Eatwell, "Reflections on Fascism and Religion," in Leonard Weinberg and Ami Pedahzur (eds.), *Religious Fundamentalism and Political Extremism* (London: Frank Cass, 2004), 145–166.

35. Daniel Bell, "Revolutionary Terrorism: Three Justifications," *Correspondence* (Council on Foreign Relations), 9 (2002): 15–16; Walter Laquer, "Left, Right, and Beyond: The Changing Face of Terror," in Hodge and Rose (eds.), *How Did This Happen?* 71–82.

36. Josef Joffe, "The Meaning of Spain," *Time*, March 29, 2004.

37. Robert Harris, "Forget Islam: Bin Laden Is No More Than a Spoilt Rich Kid," *The Daily Telegraph*, October 9, 2001.

38. Andrew McKenna, "Scandal, Resentment, Idolatry: The Underground Psychology of Terrorism," *Anthropoetics—The Journal of Generative Anthropology*, 8, 1 (2002) <http://theol.uibk.ac.at/cover>; "Bin Laden, Dostoevsky and the Reality Principle: An Interview With Andre Glucksmann," <www.opendemocracy.net/articles>.

39. Gabriel A. Almond, R. Scott Appleby, and Emmanuel Sivan, *Strong Religion: The Rise of Fundamentalisms Around the World* (Chicago and London: University of Chicago Press, 2003).

40. Robert O. Keohane, "The Globalization of Informal Violence, Theories of World Politics, and the 'Liberalism of Fear,'" *International Organization*, IO-Dialog (Spring 2002): 29–43.

41. Fabio Petito and Pavlos Hatzopoulos (eds.), *Religion in International Relations: The Return from Exile* (New York & London: Palgrave Macmillan, 2003).

42. Joseph Nye, "Soft Power," *Foreign Policy*, 80 (1990): 153–171; Judith Goldstein and Robert O. Keohane (eds.), *Ideas and Foreign Policy: Beliefs, Institutions, and Political Change* (Ithaca, NY: Cornell University Press, 1993); Pierre Hassner, "Le role des idees dans les relations interna-tionales," *Politique Estrangere*, 65, 3/4 (2000): 687–702.

43. Albert S. Yee, "The Causal Effects of Ideas on Policies," *International Organization*, 50, 1 (1996): 69–108; Michael C. Desch, "Culture

Clash: Assessing the Importance of Ideas in Security Studies," *International Security*, 232, 1 (1998): 141–170; Craig Parsons, "Showing Ideas as Causes: The Origins of the European Union," *International Organization*, 56, 1 (2002): 47–84.

44. Christian Smith (ed.), *Disruptive Religion: The Force of Faith in Social-Movement Activism* (London: Routledge, 1996).
45. R. Scott Appleby, *The Ambivalence of the Sacred: Religion, Violence, and Reconciliation* (Oxford: Rowan & Littlefield, 2000).
46. Richard John Neuhaus, *The Naked Public Square: Religion and Democracy in America* (Grand Rapids, MI: Eerdmans, 1986).
47. Harry Bauer and Elisabetta Brighi (eds.), *International Relations at LSE: A History of 75 Years*, foreword by James Mayall (London: Millennium Publishing Group, 2003).
48. Tim Dunne, *Inventing International Society: A History of the English School* (London: Macmillan, 1998); B. A. Roberson (ed.), *International Society and the Development of International Relations Theory* (London: Pinter, 1998).
49. Scott M. Thomas, "Faith, History, and Martin Wight: The Role of Religion in the Historical Sociology of the English School of International Relations," *International Affairs*, 77, 4 (2001): 905–929.

Chapter 1 "The Revenge of God?" The Twentieth Century as the "Last Modern Century"

1. Mary Pat Fisher, *Religion in the Twenty-first Century* (London: Routledge, 1999).
2. Timothy Fitzgerald, *The Ideology of Religious Studies* (Oxford: Oxford University Press, 2003).
3. Carl J. Nederman and John Christian Laursen (ed.), *Difference and Dissent: Theories of Tolerance in Medieval and Early Modern Europe* (London: Rowman and Littlefield, 1996).
4. William T. Cavanaugh, "The Myth of the State as Savior," in William T. Cavanaugh, *Theopolitical Imagination: Discovering the Liturgy as a Political Act in an Age of Global Consumerism* (London & New York: Continuum, 2002), 9–52.
5. John Bossy, *Christianity in the West, 1400–1700* (Oxford: Oxford University Press, 1985), esp. 170–171; Mack P. Holt, *The French Wars of Religion, 1562–1629* (Cambridge: Cambridge University Press, 1995); and Mack P. Holt, "Putting Religion Back into the Wars of Religion," *French Historical Studies*, 18 (1993): 524–551.
6. William T. Cavanaugh, "A Fire Strong Enough to Consume the House: The Wars of Religion and the Rise of the State," *Modern Theology*, 11, 4 (1995): 397–420; Diane B. Obenchain, "The Study of Religion and the Coming Global Generation," in Max L. Stackhouse and Diane B. Obenchain (eds.), *Christ and the Dominions of Civilization, God and*

Globalization, vol. 3 (Harrisburg, PA: Trinity Press International, 2002), 59–109.

7. Eamon Duffy, *The Stripping of the Alters: Traditional Religion in England, 1400–1580* (New Haven, CT: Yale University Press, 1992).

8. Roland Robertson, "Globalization and the Future of Traditional Religion," in Max L. Stackhouse and Peter J. Paris (eds.), *Religion and the Powers of the Common Life, God and Globalization*, vol. 1 (Harrisburg, PA: Trinity Press International, 2000), 53–68.

9. Robert Wuthnow, *The Restructuring of American Religion* (Princeton: Princeton University Press, 1988), 13; Robert Wuthnow, "Understanding Religion and Politics," *Daedalus*, 120, 3 (1991): 3–19; Danièle Hervieu-Léger, "The Twofold Limit of the Notion of Secularization," in Linda Wood head, Paul Heelas, and Daniel Martin (eds.), *Peter Berger and the Study of Religion* (London: Routledge, 2001), 112–125.

10. Jeff Haynes, *Religion in Global Politics* (Longman, 1998); John L. Esposito and Michael Watson (eds.), *Religion and Global Order* (Cardiff: University of Wales Press, 2000); Ken R. Dark (ed.), *Religion and International Relations* (London: Macmillan, 2000); Peter L. Berger (ed.), *The Desecularization of the World: Resurgent Religion and World Politics* (Washington, D.C./Grand Rapids: Ethics & Public Policy Center/William B. Eerdmans, 1999); Oliver McTernan, Violence in *God's Name: Religion in an Age of Conflict* (London: Darton, Longman, Todd, 2003).

11. John L. Esposito, Darrell J. Fasching, and Todd Lewis, *World Religions Today* (Oxford: Oxford University Press, 2002).

12. Kenneth Waltz, *Man, State and War* (New York: Columbia University Press, 1959); Martin Hollis and Steve Smith, *Explaining and Understanding International Relations* (Oxford: Clarendon Press, 1991).

13. Jan Aart Scholte, *Globalization: A Critical Introduction* (Basingstoke: Palgrave, 2000).

14. Peter Beyer, *Religion and Globalization* (London: Sage, 1994); Benjamin R. Barber, *Jihad vs. McWorld: How Globalism and Tribalism are Reshaping the World* (New York: Ballantine Books, 1995, 1996); Ian Clark, *Globalization and Fragmentation: International Relations In The Twentieth Century* (Oxford: Oxford University Press, 1997).

15. John Naisbitt and Patricia Aburdene, *Megatrends 2000: Ten New Directions for the 1990s* (New York: Avon Books, 1990); Ken R. Dark, "Large-Scale Religious Change and World Politics," in Ken R. Dark (ed.), *Religion and International Relations* (London: Macmillan, 2000), 50–82.

16. K. R. Dark, *The Waves of Time: Long-Term Change in International Relations* (New York: Continuum, 2001); James N. Rosenau, *Distant Proximities: Dynamics beyond Globalization* (Princeton: Princeton University Press, 2003).

17. Philip Jenkins, *The Next Christendom* (Oxford: Oxford University Press, 2002).

18. Walter LaFaber, "The Post September 11 Debate Over Empire, Globalization, and Fragmentation," *Political Science Quarterly*, 117, 1 (2002): 1–17.

19. Felepe Fernandez-Armesto, *Millennium: A History of the Last Thousand Years* (New York: Scribner, 1995); Jeffrey Paine, *Father India: How Encounters with an Ancient Culture Transformed the Modern West* (San Francisco: HarperCollins, 1998); Colin Campbell, "The Easternization of the West," in Bryan Wilson and Jamie Cresswell (eds.), *New Religions Movements: Challenge and Response* (London: Routledge, 1999).

20. Diana L. Eck, *A New Religious America: How a "Christian Country" Has Become the World's Most Religiously Diverse Nation* (San Francisco: Harper, 2002).

21. Philip Jenkins, *The Next Christendom: The Coming of Global Christianity* (Oxford: Oxford Univeristy Press, 2002).

22. David B. Burrell, "Aquinas and Islamic and Jewish Thinkers," in Norman Kretzmann (ed.), *The Cambridge Companion to Aquinas* (Cambridge: Cambridge University Press, 1993), 60–84.

23. Mark Juergensmeyer (ed.), *Global Religions: An Introduction* (Oxford: Oxford University Press, 2003); Irving Hexham and Karla Poewe (eds.), *New Religions as Global Cultures: Making the Human Sacred* (Boulder, CO: Westview, 1997).

24. Zadi Laidi, *A World Without Meaning: The Crisis of Meaning in International Politics* (London: Routlege, 1998).

25. Bayless Maning, "The Congress, the Executive, and Intermestic Affairs," *Foreign Affairs*, 57 (1979): 308–324; Scott M. Thomas, "The Global Resurgence of Religion and the Study of World Politics," *Millennium*, 24, 2 (1995): 289–299.

26. Robert Uhlig, "Ban Urged on Kosher and Halal Butchery," *Daily Telegraph*, June 11, 2003; Jonathan Petre, "Religious Leaders React Angrily to Council's Ruling," *Daily Telegraph*, June 11, 2003.

27. Peter J. Paris, "Moral Exemplars in Global Community," in Max L. Stackhouse and Don S. Browning (eds.), *The Spirit and the Modern Authorities*, God and Globalization, vol. 2 (Harrisburg, PA: Trinity Press International, 2001), 191–220.

28. Samuel P. Huntington, *The Third Wave: Democratization in the Late Twentieth Century* (Norman & London: University of Oklahoma Press, 1991).

29. "Better Business Through Buddhism—How the Dalai Lama Won the West," *Civilization*, December 1999/January 2000, 57–71; Michelle Conlin, "Religion in the Workplace: The Growing Presence of Spirituality in Corporate America," *Business Week*, November 1 1999, 151–158.

30. Samuel Huntington, "Religion and the Third Wave", *National Interest* (1991): 31–42.

31. Harvey Cox, *Fire From Heaven: The Rise of Pentecostal Spirituality and the Reshaping of Religion in the Twenty-First Century*

(New York: Addison-Wesley, 1995); Karla Poewe (ed.), *Charismatic Christianity as a Global Culture* (Columbia, South Carolina: University of South Carolina Press, 1994).

32. *Arab Human Development Report* (Oxford: Oxford University Press, 2002).
33. James N. Rosenau (ed.), *Linkage Politics* (New York: Free Press, 1968).
34. Ernest Gellner, *Postmodernism, Reason, and Religion* (London: Routledge, 1992).
35. Christopher Clapham, "The Collapse of Socialism in the Third World," *Third World Quarterly*, 13, 1 (1992): 13–26.
36. See Samuel P. Huntington, *Political Order and Changing Societies* (Cambridge, MA: Harvard University Press, 1968) and Ira William Zartman, *Collapsed States: The Disintegration and Restoration of Legitimate Authority* (Boulder, CO: Lynne Rienner, 1994).
37. Mark Juergensmeyer, *The New Cold War: Religious Nationalism Confronts the Secular State* (Berkeley, CA: University of California Press, 1993); Jeff Haynes, *Religion in Third World Politics* (London: Open University Press, 1994); and David Westerlund, ed., *Questioning the Secular State: The Worldwide Resurgence of Religion in Politics* (London: I.B. Tauris, 1996).
38. Hedley Bull, "The Revolt Against the West," in Hedley Bull and Adam Watson (eds.), *The Expansion of International Society* (Oxford: Clarendon Press, 1984), 217–228.
39. Robert Lee, *Overcoming Tradition and Modernity: The Search for Islamic Authenticity* (Boulder, CO: Westview Press, 1997).
40. Gilles Kepel, *The Revenge of God: The Resurgence of Islam, Christianity and Judaism in the Modern World* (Cambridge: Polity Press, 1994).
41. Darrell Jodock, *Catholicism Contending with Modernity: Roman Catholic Modernism and Anti-Modernism in Historical Context* (Cambridge: Cambridge University Press, 2000).
42. Thomas L. Friedman, *The Lexus and the Olive Tree: Understanding Globalization* (New York: Anchor Books, 2000), 468.
43. Kepel, *The Revenge of God*, 11.
44. William James, *The Varieties of Religious Experience* (London: Penguin, 1985), 135–136.
45. Charles Taylor, *Varieties of Religion Today* (Harvard: Harvard University Press, 2002), 47.
46. Jose Casanova, *Public Religions in the Modern World* (Chicago: University of Chicago Press, 1994), 43.
47. Charles Taylor, *The Malaise of Modernity* (Toronto: Anansi, 1991); John Gray, *In Enlightenment's Wake* (London: Routledge, 1996).
48. David Lyon, *Postmodernity* (Buckingham: Open University Press, 1994), 11, 27.
49. Naisbitt & Aburdene, *Megatrends 2000*, 50–86.
50. David Ray Griffin, "Postmodern Spirituality and Society," in D. R. Griffin (ed.), *Spirituality and Society* (Albany, New York: State

University of New York Press, 1988); Graham Ward (ed.), *The Postmodern God* (Oxford: Blackwell, 1997); Kevin J. Van hoozer (ed.), *The Cambridge Companion to Postmodern Theology* (Cambridge: Cambridge University Press, 2003).

51. S. N. Eisenstadt, "Multiple Modernities," *Daedalus*, 129, 1 (2000): 1–30.
52. "The Last Modern Century," *New Perspectives Quarterly*, 8, 2 (1991).

Chapter 2   Blind Spots and Blowback: Why Culture and Religion were Marginalized in International Relations Theory

1. Garry Wills, *Under God: Religion and American Politics* (New York: Simon & Schuster, 1990), 15.
2. David Lake, "Why Do They Hate Us?" *The New York Times*, January 15, 2002.
3. Gabriel A. Almond, *The Appeals of Communism* (Princeton: Princeton University Press, 1954).
4. Donald Eugene Smith, "The Limits of Religious Resurgence," in Emile Sahliyeh (ed.), *Religious Resurgence and Politics in the Contemporary World* (Albany: State University of New York Press, 1990), 33–48.
5. Grace Davie, *Europe: The Exceptional Case, The Parameters of Faith in the Modern World* (London: Darton, Longman, and Todd, 2002).
6. S. N. Eisenstadt, "Multiple Modernities," *Daedalus*, 129, 1 (2000): 1–30.
7. Grace Davie, *Europe: The Exceptional Case, The Parameters Of Faith in the Modern World* (London: Darton, Longman, and Todd, 2002); Linda Wood head with Paul Heelas and David Martin (eds.), *Peter Berger and the Study of Religion* (London: Routledge, 2001).
8. Robert Wuthnow, *Cultural Analysis: The Work of Peter L. Berger, Mary Douglas, Michel Foucault, and Jurgen Habermas* (London: Routledge and Kegan Paul, 1984).
9. Lawrence Freedman, *Kennedy's Wars: Berlin, Cuba, Laos, and Vietnam* (Oxford: Oxford University Press, 2000).
10. David C. Engerman, "The Romance of Economic Development and New Histories of the Cold War," *Diplomatic History*, 28, 1 (2004): 23–54.
11. Robert Wuthnow, "Understanding Religion and Politics," *Daedalus*, 120, 3 (1991): 1–20.
12. Vicky Randall and Robin Theobald, *Political Change and Underdevelopment* (London: Macmillan, 1998).
13. John Gray, *Al Qaeda and What it Means to be Modern* (London: Faber & Faber, 2003).
14. Peter L. Berger, *The Sacred Canopy: Elements of a Sociological Theory of Religion* (New York: Doubleday/Anchor Books, 1967); Donald Eugene Smith (ed.), *Religion and Political Modernization* (New Haven and

London: Yale University Press, 1974); Steve Bruce, *God is Dead: Secularization in the West* (Blackwell, 2002).

15. Wuthnow, "Understanding Religion and Politics," 3.

16. Emmanuel Sivan, "Democracy, Catholicism, and Islam," *Arab Reform Bulletin*, 2, 2 (2004).

17. Jose Casanova, *Public Religions in the Modern World* (Chicago: University of Chicago Press, 1994).

18. Peter L. Berger (ed.), *The Desecularization of the World: Resurgent Religion in World Politics* (Grand Rapids/Washington, D.C.: William B. Eerdmans/Ethics & Public Policy Center, 1999; Peter L. Berger, "Postscript," in Linda Woodward et al. (eds.), *Peter Berger and the Study of Religion* (London: Routledge, 2001), 189–198.

19. Will Durant, *The Age of Faith*, The Story of Civilization, vol. IV (New York: Simon & Schuster, 1950); Will and Ariel Durant, *The Age of Reason*, The Story of Civilization, vol. VIII (New York: Simon & Schuster, 1961).

20. Rodney Stark, "Secularization, R.I.P. (rest in peace)," *Sociology of Religion,* 60, 1 (1999): 247–273; Rodney Stark, "Secularization: The Myth of Religious Decline," *Fides et Historia*, 30, 2 (1999): 1–19.

21. Robert N. Bellah, "Between Religion and Social Science," in Robert N. Bellah (ed.), *Beyond Belief: Essays on Religion in a Post-Traditionalist World* (Berkeley, CA: University of California Press, 1970, 2nd edition, 1991), 237–259; Scott M. Thomas, "Religious Resurgence, Postmodernism and World Politics," in John L. Esposito and Michael Watson (eds.), *Religion and Global Order* (Cardiff: University of Wales Press, 2000), 38–65.

22. Leo Gross, "The Peace of Westphalia, 1648–1948," in Richard A. Falk and Wolfram F. Hanrieder (eds.), *International Law and Organisation: An Introductory Reader* (New York: J.B.L. Lippincott, 1968), 45–67; Daniel Philpott, "Westphalia and Authority in International Society," *Political Studies*, 47, 3 (1999): 566–589.

23. Roger Boyes, "Treaty that Created 'Soil of Dispair,'" *The Times* (London), October 24, 1998.

24. Philip Windsor, "The Justification of the State," in Michael Donelan (ed.), *The Reason of States* (London: George Allen & Unwin, 1978), 171–194.

25. Klaus Bussmann and Heinz Schilling (eds.), *1648: War and Peace in Europe*, vol. 1 (Munich: Bruckmann, 1998).

26. Daniel Philpott, "The Religious Roots of Modern International Relations," *World Politics*, 52 (2000): 206–245.

27. Carsten Bagge Laustsen and Ole Waever, "In Defence of Religion: Sacred Referent Objects for Securitization," *Millennium*, 29, 3 (2000): 705–739.

28. Martin Wight, *Power Politics* (London: Penguin, 1978); Michael Joseph Smith, *Realist Thought from Weber to Kissinger* (Baton Rouge: Louisiana

State University Press, 1990); Jack Donnelly, *Realism in International Relations* (Cambridge: Cambridge University Press, 2000).

29. Kenneth Waltz, *Theory of International Politics* (New York: McGraw-Hill, 1979).

30. Daniel Philpott, "The Challenge of September 11th to Secularism in International Relations," *World Politics*, 55, 1 (2002).

31. Roger Epp, "The 'Augustinian Moment' in International Politics: Niebuhr, Butterfield, Wight, and the Reclaiming of a Tradition," International Politics Research Paper no. 10 (Department of International Politics, University College of Wales, Aberystwyth, 1991).

32. Reinhold Niebuhr, *The Irony of American History* (New York: Charles Scribner's Sons, 1952), Reinhold Niebuhr, *Christian Realism and Political Problems* (New York: Charles Scribner's Sons, 1953); Eric Patterson (ed.), *The Christian Realists: Reassessing the Contributions of Reinhold Niebuhr and his Contemporaries* (New York: University Press of America, 2003).

33. Stanley Hauerwas, *With the Grain of the Universe: the Church's Witness to Natural Theology* (London: SCM Press, 2002); Michael Loriaux, "The Realists and Saint Augustine: Skepticism, Psychology, and Moral Action in International Relations Thought," *International Studies Quarterly*, 36 (1992): 401–420; Jean Bethke Elshtain, *Augustine and the Limits of Politics* (Notre Dame: University of Notre Dame Press, 1995).

34. George Kennan, "Foreign Policy and Christian Conscience," *The Atlantic*, 203, 5 (1959): 44–49.

35. Joel H. Rosenthal, "Private Convictions and Public Commitments: *Moral Man and Immoral Society* Revisited," *World Policy Journal*, 12, 2 (1995): 89–96.

36. David Brooks, "A Man On a Gray Horse," *The Atlantic*, September 2002.

37. Ian Hall, "History, Christianity and Diplomacy: Sir Herbert Butterfield and International Relations," *Review of International Studies*, 28 (2002): 719–736; Paul Sharp, "Herbert Butterfield, the English School and the civilizing virtues of diplomacy," *International Affairs*, 79, 4 (2003): 855–878.

38. Scott M. Thomas, "Faith, History and Martin Wight: The Role of Religion in the Historical Sociology of the English School of International Relations," *International Affairs*, 77, 4 (2001): 905–929.

39. Charles Jones, "Not Dead but Sleeping: The Eclipse of Christianity in Academic International Relations," Centre of International Studies, University of Cambridge (unpublished MSS).

40. Darryl S. L. Jarvis (ed.), *International Relations and the "Third Debate": Postmodernism and its Critics* (New York: Praeger Publishers, 2002).

41. James Gunnell, *The Descent of Political Theory* (Chicago: University of Chicago Press, 1993).

42. Craig Parsons, "Showing Ideas as Causes: The Origins of the European Union," *International Organisation*, 56, 1 (2002): 47–84.

43. Robert Wuthnow, *Cultural Analysis: The Work of Peter L. Berger, Mary Douglas, Michel Foucault, and Jurgen Habermas* (London: Routledge and Kegan Paul, 1984).

44. Edward Luttwak, "The Missing Dimension," in Douglas Johnston and Cynthia Sampson (eds.), *Religion, The Missing Dimension of Statecraft* (Oxford: Oxford University Press, 1994), 8–19.

45. Martin Wight, *Power Politics* (London: Penguin, 1946, 1979), 213.

46. Fred Halliday, "A Necessary Encounter: Historical Materialism and International Relation," in Fred Halliday, *Rethinking International Relations* (London: Macmillan, 1994), 47–73; Justin Rosenberg, *The Empire of Civil Society: A Critique of the Realist Theory of International Relations* (London: Verso Press, 1994).

47. Stephen Gill, *Gramsci, Historical Materialism and International Relations* (Cambridge: Cambridge University Press, 1993).

48. Colin Wight, "Philosophy of Social Science and International Relations," in Walter Carlsnaes et al. (eds.), *Handbook of International Relations* (London: Sage, 2002), 23–51.

49. Martin Hollis, *The Philosophy of Social Science* (Cambridge: Cambridge University Press, 1990).

50. Yosef Lapid and Friedrich Kratochwil, "Revisiting the 'National': Towards an Identity Agenda in Neorealism?" in Yosef Lapid and Friedrich Kratochwil (eds.), *The Return of Culture and Identity in IR Theory* (Boulder, CO: Lynne Rienner, 1996), 105–128.

51. Kristen Renwick Monroe, *The Economic Approach to Politics: A Critical Reassessment of the Theory of Rational Action* (New York: HarperCollins, 1991).

Chapter 3   In the Eye of the Storm: Explaining and Understanding Culture and Religion in International Relations

1. William T. Cavanaugh, "Disciplined Imaginations of Space and Time," in William T. Cavanaugh (ed.), *Theopolitical Imagination: Discovering the Liturgy as a Political Act in an Age of Global Consumerism* (London & New York: T & T Clark/Continuum, 2002), 1–8.

2. Yosef Lapid, "The Third Debate," *International Studies Quarterly*, 33 (1989): 235–254; Yosef Lapid, "Through Dialogue to Engaged Pluralism: The Unfinished Business of the Third Debate," *International Studies Review*, 5, 1 (2003): 128–131.

3. Donald Polkinghorne, *Narrative Knowing and the Human Sciences* (Albany: State University of New York Press, 1988).

4. Robert Wuthnow, "Understanding Religion and Politics," *Daedalus*, 120, 3 (1991): 1–20.

5. Ibid., 11.

6. Sean O'Neill, "Britons Fall Victim to an Islamic Dream," *The Daily Telegraph*, October 5, 2001; John Lichfield, "The Baker Street Connection," *The Independent on Sunday*, October 7, 2001.

7. Robert O. Keohane, "The Globalization of Informal Violence, Theories of World Politics, and the 'Liberalism of Fear,'" *International Organization, Dialog-IO* (2003): 29–43.

8. Kanan Makiya, "The Arab World After Sept. 11," *Dissent* (2002): 5–2; Kanan Makiya and Hassan Mneimeh, "Manuel for a 'Raid,'" *New York Review of Books*, January 17, 2002, 18–21.

9. Ken Booth and Tim Dunne, "Worlds in Collision," in Ken Booth and Tim Dunne (eds.), *Worlds in Collision: Terror and the Future of Global Order* (London: Palgrave, 2003), 1–26; Fred Halliday, *Two Hours that Shook the World: September 11, 2001: Causes and Consequences* (London: Saqi Books, 2002).

10. Martha Finnemore, *National Interests in International Society* (Ithaca, New York: Cornell University Press, 1996), 30–31.

11. Robert Ted Gurr and Barbara Harff, *Ethnic Conflict in World Politics* (Boulder, CO: Westview, 2000).

12. James F. Keeley, "Toward a Foucauldian Analysis of International Regimes," *International Organization*, 44 (1990): 83–105.

13. William E. Connolly, *Why I Am Not a Secularist* (Minneapolis, MN: University of Minnesota Press, 1999); John Keane, "The Limits of Secularism," in John L. Esposito and Azzaaam Tamini (eds.), *Islam and Secularism in the Middle East* (New York: New York University Press, 2000).

14. Tim Dunne, *Inventing International Society: A History of the English School* (London: Macmillan, 1998); Richard Devetak, "Critical Theory, and Postmodernism," in Scott Burchill et al. (eds.), *Theories of International Relations* (New York and London: Palgrave, 1996), 155–180 and 181–208.

15. Steve Smith, Ken Booth, and Marysia Zalewski (eds.), *International Theory: Positivism and Beyond* (Cambridge: Cambridge University Press, 1996).

16. John Milbank, *Theology and Social Theory: Beyond Secular Reason* (Oxford: Blackwell, 1990).

17. Rudolf Bultmann, *Jesus and the World* (New York: Charles Scribner's Sons, 1934, 1958), 3.

18. Richard Devetak, "The Project of Modernity and International Relations Theory," *Millennium*, 24, 1 (1995): 27–51.

19. William T. Cavanaugh, "The City: Beyond Secular Parodies," in John Milbank, Catherine Pickstock, and Graham Ward (eds.), *Radical Orthodoxy* (London: Routledge, 1999), 182–200.

20. Jacques Derrida, "Faith and Knowledge: the Two Sources of 'Religion' at the Limits of Reason Alone," in Jacques Derrida and Gianni Vattimo (eds.), *Religion* (Palo Alto, CA: Stanford University Press, 1998).

21. Wuthnow, "Understanding Religion and Politics," 14.
22. Jim George, *Discourses of Global Politics: A Critical (Re)Introduction to International Relations* (Boulder, CO: Lynne Rienner, 1994); David Campell, *Writing Security: United States Foreign Policy and the Politics of Identity* (Minneapolis, MN: University of Minnesota Press, 1998).
23. Wuthnow, "Understanding Religion and Politics," 14.
24. Fouad Ajami, *The Arab Predicament: Arab Political Thought and Practice Since 1967* (Cambridge: Cambridge University Press, 1981), 198.
25. "They have healed the wound of my people lightly, saying, 'Peace, peace,' when there is no peace" (Jeremiah 6:14; 8:11).
26. Peter J. Katzenstein (ed.), *The Culture of National Security: Norms and Authority in World Politics* (New York: Columbia University Press, 1996); Martha Finnemore, *National Interests in International Society* (Ithaca, New York: Cornell University Press, 1996).
27. Peter J. Katzenstein, "Alternative Perspectives on National Security," in Peter J. Katzenstein (ed.), *The Culture of National Security*, 1–32.
28. Yosef Lapid, "Culture's Ship: Returns and Departures in International Relations Theory," in Yosef Lapid and Friedrich Kratochwil (eds.), *The Return of Culture and Identity in IR Theory* (Lynne Rienner, 1996), 3–20.
29. Jutta Weldes, *Constructing National Interests: The United States and the Cuban Missile Crisis* (Minneapolis: University of Minnesota Press, 1999).
30. Alexander Wendt, "Identity and Structural Change in International Politics," in Yosef Lapid and Friedrich Kratochwil (eds.), *The Return of Culture and Identity in IR Theory* (Boulder, CO: Lynne Rienner, 1996), 47–64.
31. Bull, *The Anarchical Society*, 38–52.
32. Alexander Wendt, "Anarchy is What States Make of it: The Social Construction of Power Politics," *International Organization*, 46 (1992): 391–425.
33. Morton Kaplan, *System and Process in International Politics* (New York: Wiley, 1957).
34. Peter J. Katzenstein (ed.), *The Culture of National Security: Norms and Identity in World Politics* (New York: Columbia University Press, 1996).
35. Gary King, Robert O. Keohane, Sidney Verba, *Designing Social Inquiry* (Princeton: Princeton University Press, 1994), 36–40.
36. David Leheny, "Symbols, Strategies, and Choices for International Relations Scholarship After September 11," *Dialog IO*, Spring 2002, 57–70.
37. John G. Ruggie, "Epistemology, Ontology, and the Study of International Regimes," in John G. Ruggie, *Constructing the World Polity: Essays on International Institutionalization* (London and New York: Routledge, 1998), 93–95; Michael Dalton McCoy, *Domestic Policy Narratives and International Relations Theory* (London: Rowman & Littlefield, 2000).

38. Stanley Hauerwas and L. Gregory Jones (eds.), *Why Narrative? Readings in Narrative Theology* (Eugene, OR: Wipf and Stock Publishers, 1997).

39. Emery Roe, *Narrative Policy Analysis: Theory and Practice* (Durham: Duke University, 1994); P. K. Manning and B. Cullum-Swan, "Narrative, Content, and Semiotic Analysis," in N. K. Denzin and Y. S. Lincoln (eds.), *Handbook of Qualitative Research* (Thousand Oaks, CA: Sage, 1994), 187–200.

40. This group includes Peter Kreeft, Gilbert Meilander, Stanley Hauerwas, Robert C. Evans, Jonathan Wilson, David W. Gill, and Mary Ann Glendon. See Mary Ann Glendon and David Blankenhorn (eds.), *Seedbeds of Virtue* (New York: Madison, 1995); Nancy Murphy, Brad J. Kallenberg, and Mark Thiessen Nation (eds.), *Virtues and Practices in the Christian Tradition: Christian Ethics After MacIntyre* (Harrisburg, PA: Trinity Press, 1997); Roger Crisp and Michael Slote (eds.), *Virtue-Ethics*, Oxford Readings in Philosophy (Oxford: Oxford University Press, 1997); Rosalind Hursthouse, *On Virtue-Ethics* (Oxford: Oxford University Press, 2002).

41. Albert S. Yee, "The Causal Effects of Ideas on Policies," *International Organization*, 50, 1 (1996): 69–108; Michael C. Desch, "Cutlure Clash: Assessing the Importance of Ideas in Security Studies," *International Security*, 232, 1 (1998): 141–170; Craig Parsons, "Showing Ideas as Causes: The Origins of the European Union," *International Organization*, 56, 1 (2002): 47–84.

42. Alasdair MacIntyre, *After Virtue: A Study in Moral Theory*, 2nd edition (London: Duckworth, 1985) and *Whose Justice? Which Rationality?* (London: Duckworth, 1988).

43. Max Weber, "The Social Psychology of the World Religions," in H. H. Girth and C. Wright Mills (eds.), *From Max Weber: Essays in Sociology* (New York: Oxford University Press, 1946), 267–301; Clifford Geertz, "Religion as a Cultural System," in Clifford Geertz, *The Interpretation of Cultures* (New York: Basic Books, 1973), 87–125.

44. Alasdair MacIntyre, *Whose Justice, Which Rationality?* (London: Duckworth, 1988), 354–355.

45. Talal Asad, *Genealogies of Religion: Discipline and Reasons of Power in Christianity and Islam* (Baltimore & London: Johns Hopkins University Press, 1993); Bruce Lincoln, *Holy Terrors: Thinking about Religion after September 11* (Chicago: University of Chicago Press, 2003).

46. Hans W. Frei, *The Eclipse of Biblical Narrative* (New Haven: Yale University Press, 1974), George A. Lindbeck, *The Nature of Doctrine: Religion and Theology in a Postliberal Age* (Philadelphia: Westminster Press, 1984); Stanley Hauerwas, *A Community of Character: Towards a Constructive Christian Ethic* (Notre Dame: University of Notre Dame Press, 1981).

47. Friedrich Kratochwil, *Rules, Norms, and Decisions* (Cambridge: Cambridge University Press, 1989); Nicholas Onuf, *World of Our*

Making: Rules and Rule in Social Theory and International Relations (Columbia: University of South Carolina Press, 1989).

48. Charles Tilly, *The Politics of Collective Violence* (Cambridge: Cambridge University Press, 2003), 26–54.

49. Erik Ringmar, *Identity, Interest, and Action: A Cultural Explanation of Sweden's Intervention in the Thirty Years War* (Cambridge: Cambridge University Press, 1996).

50. MacIntyre, *After Virtue*, 205–221.

51. Ibid., 204–225.

52. Michael J. Sandel, *Democracy's Discontents: America's Search for a Public Philosophy* (New York: Belknop Press, 1996).

53. MacIntyre, *After Virtue*, 213.

54. Jacques Maritain, *The Dream of Descartes* (reprint, 1944, Port Washington, New York: Kinnikat Press, 1969).

55. Martin Hollis *The Philosophy of Social Science* (Cambridge: Cambridge University Press, 1994); Benjamin A. Most and Harvey Starr, *Inquiry, Logic, and International Politics* (Columbia: University of South Carolina Press, 1989).

56. Phillip Cary, *Augustine's Invention of the Inner Self* (Oxford: Oxford University Press, 2000).

57. Alasdair MacIntyre, "Epistomological Crises, Dramatic Narrative, and the Philosophy of Science," *Monist*, 60, 4 (October 1977), reprinted in Stanley Hauerwas and L. Gregory Jones (eds.), *Why Narrative? Readings in Narrative Theology* (Eugene, Oregon: Wipf and Stock, 1997), 138–157.

58. Gerald Sorin, *Irving Howe: A Life of Passionate Dissent* (New York: New York University Press, 2002).

59. Ibid., 3.

60. Ibid., *Irving Howe*, 26.

61. Paul Kowert and Jeffrey Legro, "Norms, Identity, and Their Limits: A Theoretical Reprise," in Peter J. Katzenstein (ed.), *The Culture of National Security: Norms and Identity in World Politics* (New York: Columbia University Press, 1996), 451–497; John Gerard Ruggie, "Multilateralism at Century's End," in John Gerard Ruggie (ed.), *Constructing the World Polity* (New York and London: Routledge, 1998), 102–130.

62. Martin Hollis and Steve Smith, *Explaining and Understanding International Relations* (Oxford: Clarendon Press, 1991): 82–88, 176–181.

63. Finnemore, *National Interests in International Society*; James G. Marsh and Johan P. Olsen, "The Institutional Dynamics of International Political Orders," *International Organization*, 52, 4 (1998): 943–969.

64. Michael Donelan (ed.), *The Reason of States* (London: George Allen & Unwin, 1978); James Mayall (ed.), *A Community of States* (London: Pinter, 1982).

65. Finnemore, *National Interests in International Society*, 29.

66. Alexander Wendt, *Social Theory of International Relations* (Cambridge: Cambridge University Press, 1999).

67. Oded Lowenheim, " 'Do Ourselves Credit and Render a Lasting Service to Mankind': British Moral Prestige, Humanitarian Intervention, and the Barbary Pirates," *International Studies Quarterly*, 47, 1 (2003): 23–48; Chaim Kaufmann and Robert Pape, "Explaining Costly International Moral Action: Britain's Sixty Year Campaign Against the Atlantic Slave Trade," *International Organization*, 53, 4 (1999): 631–668.

68. David Lumsdaine, *Moral Vision and International Politics, the Foreign Aid Regime, 1949–1989* (Princeton: Princeton University Press, 1993).

69. Steve Smith, "Wendt's World," *Review of International Studies*, 26, 1 (2000): 151–164.

Chapter 4   The Soul of the World? Religious Non-State Actors and International Relations Theory

1. Fred Halliday, "The Romance of Non-State Actors," in Daphne Josselin and William Wallance (eds.), *Non-State Actors in World Politics* (New York: Palgave, 2001), 21–37.

2. David Martin, "Living in Interesting Times," *First Things*, July/August, 2002, 61–64.

3. Robert Keohane and Joseph Nye (eds.), *Transnational Relations and World Politics* (Cambridge: Harvard University Press, 1970).

4. Robert Wuthnow and Virginia A. Hodgkinson (eds.), *Faith and Philanthropy in America: Exploring the Role of Religion in America's Voluntary Sector* (San Francisco: Jossey-Bass, 1990); Robert Wuthnow (ed.), *Between States and Markets: The Voluntary Sector in Comparative Perspective* (Princeton: Princeton University Press, 1991); Robert Wuthnow and John H. Evans (eds.), *The Quiet Hand of God: Faith-Based Activism and the Public Role of Mainline Protestantism* (Berkeley, CA: University of California Press, 2003).

5. Alexander F. C. Webster, *The Price of Prophesy: Orthodox Churches on Peace, Freedom, and Security* (Grand Rapids, MI, Washington, D.C.: Eerdmans/Ethics & Public Policy Center, 1995).

6. Robert Booth Fowler and Allen D. Hertzke, *Religion and Politics in America* (Boulder, CO: Westview, 1995); Steven V. Monsma and J. Christopher Soper, *The Challenge of Pluralism: Church and State in Five Democracies* (Oxford: Rowan & Littlefield, 1997).

7. Jeff Haynes, *Religion and Politics in Africa* (London: Zed Press, 1996).

8. Sulak Sirvaraksa, "Buddhism and Contemporary International Trends," in Kenneth Kraft (ed.), *Inner Peace, World Peace* (New York: State University of New York Press, 1992), 127–137.

9. Thomas Risse-Kappen, *Bringing Transnational Relations Back In* (Cambridge: Cambridge University Press, 1995).

10. Andrew S. Natsios, "Faith-Based MGOs and U.S. Foreign Policy," in Elliot Abrams (ed.), *The Influence of Faith: Religious Groups & U.S. Foreign Policy* (Oxford: Rowan & Littlefield/Ethics & Public Policy Center, 2001), 189–200.

11. Richard Hughs Seager (ed.), *The Dawn of Religious Pluralism: Voices from the World's Parliament of Religions* (LaSalle, Ill.: Open Court, 1993); R. H. Roberts, "Globalized Religion? The Parliament of the World's Religions (Chicago, 1993) in Theoretical Perspective," *Journal of Contemporary Religion*, 10, 2 (1995).

12. Kenneth Leech, *The Eye of the Storm: Spiritual Resources for the Pursuit of Justice* (London: Darton, Longman, and Todd, 1992).

13. Kenneth Fraft (ed.), *Inner Peace, World Peace: Essays on Buddhism and Nonviolence* (New York: State University of New York Press, 1992).

14. Hugh Williams, "Tighter Rules Agreed on Money Laundering," *Financial Times*, June 21–22, 2003.

15. Julia Clancy-Smith, "Saints, Mahdis, and Arms: Religion and Resistance in Nineteenth Century North Africa," in Edmund Burke, III and Ira M. Lapidus (eds.), *Islam, Politics, and Social Movements* (Berkeley, CA: University of California Press, 1988), 60–80.

16. Mir Zohair Husain, *Global Islamic Politics* (London: HarperCollins, 1995).

17. Ivan Vallier, "The Roman Catholic Church: A Transnational Actor," in R. O. Keohane and R. S. Nye, Jr. (eds.), *Transnational Relations and World Politics* (Cambridge, MA: Harvard University Press, 1971), 129–152.

18. Michael Walsh, "Catholicism and International Relations: Papal Inteventionism," in John L. Esposito and Michael Watson (eds.), *Religion and Global Order* (Cardiff: University of Wales, 2000), 100–118.

19. David Ryall, "The Catholic Church as a Transnational Actor," in Daphne Josselin and William Wallance (eds.), *Non-State Actors in World Politics* (New York: Palgave, 2001), 41–58.

20. Alec R. Vidler, *The Church in the Age of Reason* (London: Penguin, 1971), 32.

21. William Schweiker, *Power, Value, and Conviction: Theological Ethics in the Postmodern Age* (Cleveland, Ohio: Pilgrim Press, 1998).

22. See the articles on Zionism, the Catholic Church, and Nasserism in "A Design for International Relations," *Journal of International Studies*, 12 (1958).

23. John Rourke, *International Politics on the World Stage* (Sluice Dock, Conn.: Dushkin Publishing, 1993), 192–200.

24. Susan Hoeber Rudolph and James Piscatori (eds.), *Transnational Religion & Fading States* (Boulder, CO: Westview, 1997).

25. Gene Sharp, *Gandhi as a Political Strategist, with Essays on Ethics and Politics* (Boston: Porter Sargent, 1979), 23–41.

26. Judith Goldstein and Robert O. Keohane, "Ideas and Foreign Policy: An Analytical Framework," in Judith Goldstein and Robert O. Keohane (eds.), *Ideas and Foreign Policy: Beliefs, Institutions, and Political Change* (New York: Cornell University Press, 1993), 3–30.

27. Ernst B. Hass, *When Knowledge is Power: Three Models of Change in International Organization* (Berkeley, CA: University of California Press, 1990); Peter Haas, "Introduction: Epistemic Communities and International Policy Coordination," *International Organization*, 46, 1 (1992): 1–36.

28. Susanne Hoeber Rudolph, "Introduction: Religion, States, and Transnational Civil Society," in Susanne Hoeber Rudolf and James Piscatori (eds.), *Transnational Religion & Fading States* (Boulder, CO.: Westview Press, 1997), 1–26.

29. Judith Goldstein and Robert O. Keohane, "Ideas and Foreign Policy: An Analytical Framework," in Judith Goldstein and Robert O. Keohane (eds.), *Ideas and Foreign Policy: Beliefs, Institutions, and Political Change* (New York: Cornell University Press, 1993), 11.

30. Thomas Risse-Kappen, "Transnational Actors and World Politics," in Walter Carlsnaes et al., *Handbook of International Relations* (London: Sage, 2002), 266–267.

31. Friedrich Kratochwil, "The Monologue of 'Science,'" *International Studies Review*, 5, 1 (2003): 124–128.

32. Andreas Tzortzis, "African Healers Join the AIDS Fight," *Christian Science Monitor*, June 30, 2003; Linda Elaine Thomas, *Under the Canopy: Ritual Process and Spiritual Resilience in South Africa* (Columbia, South Carolina: University of South Carolina Press, 1999); Ifi Amadiume, Adbullahi A. An-Nai'im, *The Politics of Memory: Truth, Healing and Social Justice* (London: Zed Press, 2000).

33. Goldstein and Keohane, "Ideas and Foreign Policy," 11; Max Weber, *Economy and Society* (Berkeley: University of California Press, 1968), 85.

34. Joseph Nye, "Soft Power," *Foreign Policy*, 80 (1990): 160–164; Joseph Nye, "The Changing Nature of World Power," *Political Science Quarterly* (1990): 181–191.

35. Paul Ramsey, *Who Speaks for the Church?* (New York: Abingdon, 1967), 149; Richard John Neuhaus, "The Sounds of Religion in a Time of War," *First Things*, 133 (2003): 76–82.

36. Mark R. Amstutz, "Faith-Based NGOs and U.S. Foreign Policy," in Elliot Abrams (ed.), *The Influence of Faith: Religious Groups & U.S. Foreign Policy* (Oxford: Rowman & Littlefield, 2001), 175–202.

37. International Affairs and Religion at Boston University, Theological Studies and International Peace and Conflict Resolution, Wesley Theological Seminary and the School of International Service at the American University.

38. Ernst B. Hass, *When Knowledge is Power: Three Models of Change in International Organization* (Berkeley, CA: University of California Press, 1990).

39. Mary Evelyn Turner and John A. Grim, "The Emerging Alliance of World Religions and the Environment," in Mary Evelyn Turner and John A. Grim (eds.), "Religion and Ecology: Can the Climate Change," *Daedalus*, 130, 4 (2001): 1–22; Jurgen Multmann, "The Destruction and Healing of the Earth: Ecology and Theology," in Max L. Stackhouse and Don S. Browning (eds.), *The Spirit and the Modern Authorities, God and Globalization*, vol. 2 (Philadelphia: Trinity Press International, 2001), 166–190.

40. Sidney Tarrow, *Power in Movement: Social Movements and Contentious Politics* (Cambridge: Cambridge University Press, 1998).

41. Theodore E. Long, "A Theory of Prophetic Religion and Politics," in A. Shupe and J. K. Hadden (eds.), *Secularization and Fundamentalism Reconsidered* (New York: Paragon Press, 1989), 3–16.

42. Jeffrey K. Hadden and Anson Shupe (eds.), *Prophetic Religions and Politics: Religions and the Political Order* (New York: Paragon Books, 1986).

43. Martin Wight, "An Anatomy of International Thought," *Review of International Studies*, 13 (1987), 221–227.

44. Martin Wight, *International Theory: the Three Traditions* (Leicester: University of Leicester Press, 1991), 115.

45. Wight, *International Theory*, 205.

46. Ibid., 205.

47. Wight, "Traditions of International Thought," 224.

48. Wight, *International Theory*, 161.

49. Richard Falk, *Religion and Human Global Governance* (Palgrave, 2001), Mark W. Janis and Carolyn Evans (ed.), *Religion and International Law* (The Hague: Martinus Nijhoff, 1999).

50. Cox, *Fire From Heaven*, 105–106.

51. Ann M. Florini (ed.), *The Third Force The Rise of Transnational Civil Society* (Washington, D.C.: Carnegie Endowment for International Peace, 2000).

52. Special Issue, "Beyond International Society," *Millennium: Journal of International Studies*, 21, 3 (1992); Special Issue, "Social Movements and World Politics," *Millennium*, 23, 3 (1994); John Keane and Ian Shapiro (eds.), *Global Civil Society?* (Cambridge: Cambridge University Press, 2003).

53. Daphne Josselin and William Wallance, "Non-State Actors in World Politics: A Framework," in Daphne Josselin and William Wallance (eds.), *Non-State Actors in World Politics* (New York: Palgave, 2001), 1–20.

54. Mark Juergensmeyer, "Thinking Globally about Religion," in Mark Jergensmeyer (ed.), *Global Religions: An Introduction* (Oxford, 2003), 3–13; David R. Mapel and Terry Nardin (eds.), *International Society: Diverse Ethical Perspectives* (Princeton: Princeton University Press, 1998).

55. Thomas Risse-Kappen, "Transnational Actors and World Politics," in Walter Carlsnaes et al., *Handbook of International Relations* (London: Sage, 2002), 260.

56. Amy and Nicholas Pye, "The Typical Anglican: Learning from Today's New Majority," *Re:generation Quarterly*, 4, 4 (1998/1999): 16–20.

57. Roland Robertson, "Globalization and the Future of 'Traditional Religion,'" in Max L. Stackhouse and Peter J. Paris (eds.), *Religion and the Powers of the Common Life, God and Globalization*, vol. 1 (Philadelphia: Trinity Press International, 2000), 53–68.

58. Ann M. Florini, "Lessons Learned," in Ann M. Florini (ed.), *The Third Force*, 217–218.

Chapter 5   Wars and Rumors of War?
Religion and International Conflict

1. R. Scott Appleby, *The Ambivalence of the Sacred: Religion, Violence, and Reconciliation* (London: Rowman & Littlefield, 2000).

2. John Ferguson, *War and Peace in the World's Religions* (New York: Oxford University Press, 1978).

3. David Martin, *Does Christianity Cause War?* (Oxford: Clarendon Press, 1997).

4. See the webpage for the Colloquium on Violence and Religion (COV&R) set up in 1990 by the University of Innsbruck, Austria <theol.uibk.ac.at/cover/index.html>.

5. David C. Rapoport, "Some General Observations on Religion and Violence," in Mark Juergensmeyer (ed.), special issue on "Violence and the Sacred in the Modern World," *Terrorism and Political Violence* (1991), 125.

6. David Little, "Religious Militancy," in Chester Crocker, Fen Osler Hampson, with Pamela Aall (eds.), *Managing Global Chaos: Sources of and Responses to International Conflict* (Washington, D.C.: U.S. Institute of Peace, 1996), 79–92.

7. Jill Krause and Neil Renwick (eds.), *Identities in International Relations* (New York: St. Martin's Press, 1996).

8. Afshin Molavi, Roger Scruton, Mukul Kesavan, and Hugh Heclo, "Holy Wars," *The Wilson Quarterly*, 2003, 47–82.

9. Mark Juergensmeyer, *The New Cold War: Religious Nationalism Confronts the Secular State* (Berkeley: University of California Press, 1993).

10. Charles Tilly, *The Politics of Collective Violence* (Cambridge: Cambridge University Press, 2003).

11. Rene Girard, "Triangular Desire," in James G. Williams (ed.), *The Girard Reader* (New York: Crossroad/Herder, 1996), 33–44.

12. Richard Conniff, *A Natural History of the Rich* (London: Heinemann, 2003).

13. "[Mark] Shields and [David] Brooks," The Newshour with Jim Lehrer, transcript, Online Newshour, September 5, 2003.
14. Rene Girard, "The Goodness of Mimetic Desire," in James G. Williams (ed.), *The Girard Reader*, (New York: Cross road/Herder, 1996) 62–65.
15. Thomas Hobbes, *The Leviathan* (Cambridge: Cambridge University Press, 1991), 87.
16. Wolfgang Palaver, "On Violence: A Mimetic Perspective," February 23, 2002 <theol.uibk.ac.at/cover/index.html>.
17. Ibid.
18. Hans Magnus Enzensberger, *Civil Wars: From L.A. to Bosnia* (New York: The New Press, 1993).
19. Rene Girard, *Violence and the Sacred* (Baltimore: Johns Hopkins, 1977), *The Scapegoat* (Batimore: Johns Hopkins University Press, 1986).
20. Eric Gans, "The Sacred and the Social: Defining Durkheim's Anthropological Legacy," *Anthropoetics: the journal of generative anthropology*, 6, 1 (2000) <www.anthropoetics.ucla.edu/anthro.htm>.
21. Girard, *Violence and the Sacred*, 1–38.
22. Tim Judah, *The Serbs: History, Myth & the Destruction of Yugoslavia* (New Haven and London: Yale University Press, 1997), 135–136.
23. Gil Bailie, *Violence Unveiled: Humanity at the Crossroads* (New York: Crossroad Publishing Company, 1995).
24. Janice Gross Stein, "Image, Identity, and the Resolution of Violent Conflict," in Chester A. Crocker, Fen Osler Hampson, and Pamela Aall (eds.), *Turbulent Peace: The Challenges of Managing International Conflict* (Washington, D.C.: U.S. Institute of Peace, 2001), 189–208.
25. Nils Zurawski, "Girard Among the Paramilitaries of Ulster: Identity, History, and Violence," *Anthropoetics: The Journal of Generative Anthropology*, 8, 1 (2002) <www.anthropoetics.ucla.edu/anthro.htm>.
26. Rowan Williams, *Lost Icons: Reflections on Cultural Bereavement* (Edinburgh: T & T Clark, 2000), 107.
27. Andrew McKenna, "Scandal, Resentment, Idolatry: The Underground Psychology of Terrorism," *Anthropoetics: The Journal of Generative Anthropology*, 8, 1 (2002) <www.anthropoetics.ucla.edu/anthro.htm>.
28. Rene Girard, "Triangular Desire," 43.
29. Markus Muller, "Interview with Rene Girard," *Anthropoetics: The Journal of Generative Anthropology*, 2, 1 (1996) <www.anthropoetics.ucla.edu/anthro.htm>.
30. Tilly, *The Politics of Collective Violence*, pp. 26–54; Jacques Ellul, *Violence: Reflections From a Christian Perspective* (London: SCM Press, 1970).
31. Gil Bailie, *Violence Unveiled: Humanity at the Crossroads* (New York: Crossroad Publishing Company, 1995).
32. Ibid.
33. Ted Robert Gurr, "Minorities and Nationalists: Managing Ethnopolitical Conflict in the New Century," in Chester Crocker et al., *The Turbulent Peace*, 163–188.

34. John A. Vasquez, "Factors Related to the Contagion and Diffusion of International Violence," in Manus I. Midlarsky (ed.), *The Internationalization of Communal Strife* (London: Routledge, 1992), 149–172; Stuart Hill and Donald Rothchild, "The Congagion of Political Conflict in Africa and the World," *Journal of Conflict Resolution*, 30, 4 (1986): 716–735.

35. Michael E. Brown, "Ethnic and Internal Conflicts," in Chester Crocker et al. (eds.), *The Turbulent Peace*, 209–226.

36. Epilogue: The Anthropology of the Cross: A Conversation with Rene Girard, in James G. Williams (ed.), *The Girard Reader*, 266–267.

37. I. William Zartman (ed.), *Collapsed States: The Disintegration and Restoration of Legitimate Authority* (Boulder and London: Lynne Rienner, 1995); Gerald B. Helman and Steven R. Ratner, "Saving Failed States," *Foreign Policy*, 89 (1992–1993): 3–20.

38. Robert D. Kaplan, *The Ends of the Earth: A Journey at the Dawn of the 21st Century* (New York: Random House, 1996).

39. Girard, *Violence and the Sacred*, 39–67.

40. Girard, *Things Hidden*, 154–158, 451–452.

41. Paschalis M. Kitromilides, " 'Balkan Mentality': History, Legend, Imagination," *Nations and Nationalism*, 2, 2 (1996): 163–191.

42. Girard, *Violence and the Sacred*, 1–18, 39–44.

43. Juhah, The Serbs, 225, 226, 234–235; Rene Girard, "The Scapegoat as Historical Referent," in James G. Williams (ed.), *The Girard Reader*, 97–106.

44. Girard, *Violence and the Sacred*, 48.

45. Girard, *Violence and the Sacred*, 61

46. Girard, *Violence and the Sacred*, 4; James Alison, *Raising Abel: The Recovery of the Eschatological Imagination* (New York: Crossroad/Herder & Herder, 2000).

47. Girard, *Things Hidden*, 38–39, 144–149, 158–161.

48. Michael Ignatieff, *The Warrior's Honor: Ethnic War and the Modern Conscience* (New York: Vintage, 1999), 34–71; Anton Blok, *Honor and Violence* (Cambridge: Polity, 2001), 115–135.

49. Girard, *Violence and the Sacred*, 51.

50. Paul Collier, "Doing Well Out of War: An Economic Perspective," in Mats Berdal and David M. Malone (eds.), *Greed and Grievance: Economic Agendas in Civil Wars* (Boulder and London: Lynne Rienner, 2000), 91–111.

51. Paul Collier, "Economic Causes of Civil Conflict and Their Implications for Policy," in Chester Crocker et al., *Turbulent Peace*, 143–162.

52. Paul Collier, "Doing Well out of War: An Economic Perspective," in Mats Berdal and David M. Malone (eds.), *Greed and Grievance: Economic Agendas in Civil Wars* (Boulder and London: Lynne Rienner, 2000), 91–111.

53. Robert H. Nelson, *Reaching for Heaven on Earth: The Theological Meaning of Economics* (London: Rowan & Littlefield, 1991), and Robert H. Nelson, *Economics as Religion: From Samuelson to Chicago and Beyond* (University Park, Pennsylvania State University Press, 2001).

54. David Brooks, "The Elephantiasis of Reason," *Atlantic Monthly*, January/February 2003, 34–35.

55. Mark Juergensmeyer, *Terror in the Mind of God: The Global Rise of Religious Violence* (Berkeley, CA: University of California Press, 2000).

56. Mark Juergensmeyer, "Sacrifice and Cosmic War," in Mark Juergensmeyer (ed.), Special Issue on "Violence and the Sacred in the Modern World," *Terrorism and Political Violence* (1991): 101–117.

57. Rene Girard, "What is Occurring Today is a Mimetic Rivalry on a Planetary Scale," An Interview by Henri Tincq, *Le Monde*, November 6, 2001, translated for COV&R by Jim Williams <theol.uibk.ac.at/cover/index.html>.

58. Mohammed M. Hafez, *Why Muslims Rebel: Repression and Resistance in the Islamic World* (Boulder, CO: Lynne Reinner, 2003).

59. Fouad Ajami, "The Falseness of Anti-Americanism," *Foreign Policy*, September 2003, 52–61.

60. Fouad Ajami, *The Dream Palace of the Arabs: A Generation's Odyssey* (New York: Random Books, 1998), 61–62.

61. Ibid.

62. Rene Girard, "What is Occurring Today is a Mimetic Rivalry on a Planetary Scale," *Le Monde*, November 6, 2001 <theol.uibk.ac.at/cover/index.html>.

63. Josef Joffe, "Whose Afraid of Mr. Big?" *The National Interest* (Summer 2001).

64. Lawrence Freedman, "Blaming America," *The Prospect* (London), December 2001, 34–37.

65. W. M. Watt, *Islamic Fundamentalism and Modernity* (London: Routledge, 1988).

66. Albert Hourani, *Arabic Liberal Thought in the Modern Age, 1798–1939* (Oxford: Oxford University Press, 1970).

67. Robert D. Lee, *Overcoming Tradition and Modernity: The Search for Islamic Authenticity* (Boulder: Westview, 1997).

68. Fouad Ajami, "Beirut, Baghdad," *Wall Street Journal*, August 25, 2003; Girard, *Violence and the Sacred*, 43.

69. Martin Kramer, "Sacrifice and Fratricide in Shi'ite Lebanon," in Mark Juergensmeyer (ed.), Special Issue on "Violence and the Sacred in the Modern World," *Terrorism and Political Violence* (1991): 30–47.

70. Neil MacFarquhar, "Iraqi Shiites gripped by struggle," *New York Times*, August 26, 2003; Farnaz Fassihi, "Iraqi Shiites Are Split on Political Role," *Wall Street Journal*, September 2, 2003.

71. Eric Hoffer, *The True Believer: Thoughts on the Nature of Mass Movements* (New York: Harper & Row, 1951).

72. Mark Juergensmeyer, "Sacrifice and Cosmic War," in Mark Juergensmeyer (ed.), special issue on "Violence and the Sacred in the Modern World," *Terrorism and Political Violence* (1991): 101–117; David C. Rapoport, "Fear and Trembling: Terrorism in Three Religious Traditions," *The American Political Science Review*, 78, 3 (1984): 658–677.

73. Daniel Benjamin and Steven Simon, *The Age of Sacred Terror* (New York: Random House, 2002); Bruce Hoffman, "The Logic of Suicide Terrorism," *The Atlantic Monthly*, June 2003, 40–47.

Chapter 6   "Creating a Just and Durable Peace": Rethinking Religion and International Cooperation

1. Paul Tillich, "Christian Basis of a Just and Durable Peace (1943)," in Ronald H. Stone (ed.), *Theology of Peace* (Louisville, KY: Westminster Press/John Knox Press, 1990), 73–87.

2. Robert Keohane, "International Institutions: Two Approaches," in James Der Derian (ed.), *International Theory: Critical Investigations* (London: Macmillan, 1995), 279–307.

3. Barry Buzan, "From International System to International Society: Realism and Regime Theory Meet the English School," *International Organisation*, 47, 3 (1993): 327–352; Barry Buzan, Charles Jones, and Richard Little, *The Logic of Anarchy: Neorealism to Structural Realism* (New York: Columbia University Press, 1993).

4. "What is Europe?," *The Economist*, February 12, 2000; Michael Prowse, "Reason, not emotion, will be the foundation of a new Europe," *Financial Times*, October 11/12, 2003.

5. Alain Woodrow, "Europe without God," *The Tablet*, June 21, 2003: 8; Alain Woodrow, "Battlelines over the new Europe," *The Tablet*, May 24, 2003: 4–6.

6. Martin Wight, *Systems of States* (Leicester: Leicester University Press, 1977), 21–45.

7. Nicholas J. Rengger, "Culture, Society, and Order in World Politics," in John Baylis and Nicholas J. Rengger (eds.), *Dilemmas of World Politics* (Oxford: Oxford University Press, 1992).

8. Wight, *Systems of States*, 34.

9. Roger Epp, "The English School on the Frontiers of International Society: A Hermeneutic Recollection," *Review of International Studies*, 24, 3 (1998): 47–63.

10. Hedley Bull and Adam Watson, "Conclusion," in Hedley Bull and Adam Watson (eds.), *The Expansion of International Society* (Oxford: Clarendon Press, 1984), 425–435.

11. Wight, *Systems of States*, 35.
12. R. J. Vincent, "Edmund Burke and the Theory of International Relations," *Review of International Studies*, 10 (1984), 205–218; R. J. Vincent, "The Cultural Factor in the Global International Order," *The Yearbook of World Affairs*, 34 (1980): 252–264; Hedley Bull, *Justice in International Relations*, Hagley Lectures (Waterloo, Ontario: University of Waterloo, 1984).
13. John Finn, "Human Rights in Vienna," *First Things*, 37 (1993): 4–8; George Weigel, "What Really Happened at Cairo, and Why," in *The 9 Lives of Population Control*, ed. Michael Cromartie (Washington, D.C.: Ethics and Public Policy Center, 1995), 129–148; and Mary Ann Glendon, "What Happened in Beijing," *First Things*, 59 (1996): 30–36.
14. Mary Ann Glendon, *Rights Talk: The Impoverishment of Political Discourse* (New York: Free Press, 1991).
15. Stephen D. Krasner (ed.), *International Regimes* (Ithaca, NY: Cornell University Press, 1983); Andreas Hasenclever, Peter Meyer, and Volker Rittberger, *Theories of International Regimes* (Cambridge: Cambridge University Press, 1997).
16. Robert O. Keohane, "The Theory of Hegemonic Stability and Change in the International Economic Regimes, 1967–1977," in Ole R. Holsti, R. M. Siverson, and A. L. George (eds.), *Change in the International System* (Boulder, CO: Westview Press, 1980).
17. Charles P. Kindleberger, "Dominance and Leadership in the International Economy: Exploitation, Public Goods, and Free Rides," *International Studies Quarterly*, 25 (1981): 242–254.
18. Henry Kissinger, *White House Years* (Boston: Little, Brown and Company, 1979).
19. Walter Russell Mead, *Special Providence: American Foreign Policy and How It Changed the World* (New York: Alfred A. Knopf, 2001).
20. Peter Alexis Gourevitch, "The Second Image Reversed," *International Organization*, 32, 4 (1978): 161–178.
21. Keohane, "International Institutions," 178–179.
22. Ibid., 179.
23. Heather A. Warren, *Theologians of a New World Order, Reinhold Niebuhr and the Christian Realists, 1920–1948* (Oxford: Oxford University Press, 1997).
24. Richard Devetak, "The Project of Modernity in International Relations Theory," *Millennium*, 24, 1 (1995): 123–154.
25. John Gerard Ruggie, "Introduction: What Makes the World Hang Together?" in John Gerard Ruggie, *Constructing the World Polity* (London: Routledge, 1998), 1–40.
26. Ruggie, "Multilateralism at Century's End," in John Gerard Ruggie, *Constructing the World Polity*, 102–130; John G. Ruggie, "Interests, Identity, and American Foreign Policy," in John G. Ruggie, *Constructing the World Polity*, 203–239.

27. Robert Bellah, *The Broken Covenant: American Civil Religion in Time of Trial* (Berkeley, CA: University of California Press, 1975, 1992).

28. G. John Ikenberry, "Is American Multilateralism in Decline?" *Perspectives on Politics*, 1, 3 (2003): 533–550.

29. Sydney E. Ahlstrom, *A Religious History of the American People*, vol. 2 (Garden City, NY: Image Books, 1975), 599–620.

30. Henry P. Van Dusen (ed.), *The Spiritual Legacy of John Foster Dulles* (Philadelphia: The Westminster Press, 1959).

31. Suzanne Long (ed.), *Partners for Justice and Peace: Ways for Christians to support the United Nations* (London: CCBI, Inter-Church House/UNA-UK, 1998).

32. Graham Dale, *God's Politicians: the Christian Contribution to 100 Years of Labour*, foreword by Tony Blair (London: HarperCollins, 2000).

33. Warren, *Theologians of a New World Order*, 129.

34. Charles C. Brown, *Niebuhr and His Age: Reinhold Niebuhr's Prophetic Role and Legacy* (Harrisburg, PA: Trinity Press International, 2002).

35. David Brooks, "A Man On a Gray Horse," *The Atlantic*, September 2002.

36. Richard Fox, *Reinhold Niebuhr: A Biography* (San Francisco: Harper & Row, 1987), 232–233.

37. Warren, *Theologians of a New World Order*, 130.

38. Ibid., 131.

39. Alan Wilkinson, *Christian Socialism: Scott Holland to Tony Blair* (London: SCM Press, 1998).

40. Bernard K. Johnpoll, *Pacifist's Progress: Norman Thomas and the decline of American Socialism* (Chicago: Quadrangle Books, 1970).

41. Warren, *Theologians of a New World Order*, 113.

42. Ibid., 7

43. Ibid., 103–104.

44. H. G. Nicholas, *The United Nations as a Political Institution* (Oxford: Oxford University Press, 1975), 32–33.

45. Warren, *Theologians of a New World Order*, 104–105.

46. Ibid., 107.

47. Ibid., 107.

48. Ibid., 107–108.

49. Antje Wiener and Thomas Diez (eds.), *European Integration Theory* (Oxford: Oxford University Press, 2004), for example, makes no mention of Christian Democracy or Catholic Social thought.

50. The argument of this section is based on the research of a pathbreaking doctoral dissertation by Nelson Gonzalez, *Ideas, Causes, and Preference Formation: Christian Democracy, the ECSC, and European Institutional Design 1946–1954*) a Ph.D. student in the Department of Government at the London School of Economics, who is currently a research fellow at KADOC, the Institute for International and

European Policy, Catholic University, Leuven, Flanders, Belgium. I want to thank him for kindly making some of his research available to me for this section. Nelson Gonzalez, "Political Science's Theoretical Blindspots: Historical Institutionalism and the Puzzle of Christian Democratic European Federalism," LSE Comparative Politics Workshop, June 6, 1997; Nelson Gonzalez, "Christian Democracy and the 'Heresy' of National Sovereignty: Ideas, Culture, and Institutionalization in European Integration," Seminarie Religie en Samenleving 1750–2000, KADOC, March 20, 2003.

51. John G. Ruggie, "Interests, Identity, and American Foreign Policy," in John G. Ruggie, *Constructing the World Polity* (London: Routledge, 1998), 203–239; Craig Parsons, "Showing Ideas as Causes: The Origins of the European Union," *International Organization*, 56, 1 (2002): 47–84.

52. Nelson Gonzalez, "Back to the Future? Locating Christian Democratic Normative Theories of Federal Constitution— Implications for the European Convention," ECPR Joint Sessions, University of Edinburgh, March 28–April 2, 2003.

53. Gonzalez, "Political Science's Theoretical Blindspots," quoting Paul Pierson, "The Path to European Integration: A Historical Institutionalist Analysis," *Comparative Political Studies*, 29, 2 (1996): 123–163.

54. Gonzalez, "Political Science's Theoretical Blindspots," quoting Andrew Moravcsik, "Preferences and power in the European Community—a liberal intergovernmentalist approach," *Journal of Common Market Studies* 31, 4 (1993): 473–524.

55. Austen Ivereigh, "Europe of the Heart," *The Tablet*, May 15, 2004, 35–36.

56. Nelson Gonzalez, "Back to the Future?"

57. Gonzalez, "Political Science's Theoretical Blindspots."

58. Gonzalez, "Back to the Future?"

59. Daniel Philpott, *Revolutions in Sovereignty: How Ideas Shaped Modern International Relations* (Princeton: Princeton University Press, 2001), 261–262.

60. Nelson Gonzalez, "Back to the Future?"

61. Ibid.

62. Gonzalez, "Back to the Future?"

63. Ibid.

64. Ibid.

65. Gonzalez, "Political Science's Theoretical Blindspots."

66. John Ruggie, "Introduction: What Makes the World Hang Together," in John Gerard Ruggie, *Constructing the World Polity*, 22.

67. See Bryan Hehir, Michael Walzer, Charles Krathammer, Louise Richardson, and Shibley Telhami, *Liberty and Power: A Dialogue on Religion and U.S. Foreign Policy in an Unjust World* (Washington, D.C.: Brookings Institution, 2004).

68. Harriet A. Harris, "Theological Reflections on Religious Resurgence and International Stability: a Look at Protestant Evangelicalism," in Ken R. Dark (ed.), *Religion in International Relations* (London: Macmillan, 2000), 24–49.

Chapter 7   Soulcraft as Statecraft? Diplomacy, Conflict Resolution, and Peacebuilding

1. Michael Joseph Smith, "Liberalism and International Reform," in Terry Nardin and David R. Mapel (eds.), *Traditions of International Ethics* (Cambridge: Cambridge University Press, 1992), 201–224.
2. R. Scott Appleby, *The Ambivalence of the Sacred: Religion, Violence, and Reconciliation* (Oxford: Rowan & Littlefield, 2000).
3. Duane Ruth-Heffelbower, *The Anabaptists Are Back: Making Peace in a Dangerous World* (Scottdale, PA: Herald Press, 1991).
4. Mary Kaldor, *New & Old Wars: Organized Violence in a Global Era* (Oxford: Polity Press, 1999).
5. John Paul Lederach, *Building Peace: Sustaining Reconciliation in Divided Societies* (Washington, D.C.: U.S. Institute of Peace, 1997).
6. Jean-Marie Guechenno, "The Impact of Globalization on Strategy," in Chester A. Crocker, Fen Hampson, and Paula Aall (eds.), *Turbulent Peace: The Challenge of Managing International Conflict* (Washington, D.C.: U.S. Institute of Peace, 2001), 83–95.
7. G. R. Berridge, *Diplomacy: Theory and Practice* (London: Palgrave Macmillan, 2002); Adam Watson, *Diplomacy: the Dialogue Between States* (New York: McGraw-Hill, 1983).
8. David R. Smock (ed.), *Interfaith Dialogue and Peacebuilding* (Washington, D.C.: U.S. Institute of Peace, 2002).
9. Raymond Cohen, "Negotiating Across Cultures," in Chester A. Crocker et al. (eds.), *Turbulent Peace*, 469–482.
10. Raymond Cohen, *Negotiating Across Cultures: International Communication in an Interdependent World* (Washington, D.C.: U.S. Institute of Peace, 1991, 1997).
11. Joseph Monville, "Transnationalism and the Role of Track-Two Diplomacy," in W. Scott Thompson and Kenneth M. Jensen (eds.), *Approaches to Peace: An Intellectual Map* (Washington, D.C.: U.S. Institute of Peace, 1991), 259–269.
12. Louise Diamond and John McDonald, *Multi-Track Diplomacy: A Systems Approach to Peace* (West Hartford, CN: Kumarian Press, 3rd edition, 1995).
13. Virginia Haufler, "Is There a Role for Business in Conflict Management?" in Chester A. Crocker et al. (eds.), *Turbulent Peace*, 659–675.
14. Hedley Bull, *The Anarchical Society: A Study of Order in World Politics* (London: Macmillan, 1977), 280.

15. E. H. Carr and Michael Cox (eds.), *The Twenty Years' Crisis, 1919–1939* (London: Palgrave MacMillan, 2001, 1939).

16. Nicholas J. Wheeler, *Saving Strangers: Humanitarian Intervention in International Society* (Oxford: Oxford University Press, 2000).

17. Diamond and McDonald, *Multi-Track Diplomacy*, 97–107.

18. David P. Barach, "Religious Inspiration," in David P. Barach (ed.), *Approaches to Peace: A Reader in Peace Studies* (New York: Oxford University Press, 2000), 199–222; Hugh Miall, Oliver Ramsbotham, and Tom Woodhouse, *Contemporary Conflict Resolution* (Oxford: Polity Press, 1999), 39–64.

19. K. Avruch, P. Black, and J. Scimecca, *Conflict Resolution: Cross Cultural Perspectives* (Westport, CT: Greenwood Press, 1991); M. Ross, *The Cultures of Conflict: Interpretations and Interests in Comparative Perspective* (New Haven: Yale University Press, 1993).

20. David P. Barash, *Introduction to Peace Studies* (Belmont, CA: Wadsworth Publishing, 1991).

21. Paul Salem, "In Theory: A Critique of Western Conflict Resolution From a Non-Western Perspective," *Negotiation Journal*, 9, 4 (1993): 361–369; Paul Salem (ed.), *Conflict Resolution in the Arab World: Selected Essays* (New York: American University of Beruit, 1997); Abdul A. Said, Nathan C. Funk, and Ayse S. Kadayifici, *Peace and Conflict Resolution in Islam: Precept and Practice* (Oxford: Rowan & Littlefield, 2001).

22. Mohammed Ayoob, "State Making, State Breaking, and State Failure," in Chester Crocker et al., *Turbulent Peace*, 127–142.

23. I. W. Zartman (ed.), *Traditional Cures for Modern Conflicts: African Conflict Medicine* (Boulder, CO: Lynne Rienner, 1999).

24. Ray Takeyh, "Faith-Based Initiatives: Can Islam Bring Democracy to the Middle East?" *Foreign Policy*, November/December, 2001.

25. David R. Smock (ed.), *Perspectives on Pacifism: Christian, Jewish, and Muslim Views on Nonviolence and International Conflict* (Washington, D.C.: U.S. Institute of Peace, 1995).

26. Douglas Johnston (ed.), *Faith-Based Diplomacy: Trumping Realpolitik* (Oxford: Oxford University Press, 2003).

27. Martin Wight, edited by Gabriele Wight and Brian Porter, *International Theory: The Three Traditions* (London: Leicester University Press for the Royal Institute of International Affairs, 1991), 13–15.

28. Ronald H. Stone, "Introduction," in Paul Tillich, *Theology of Peace*, edited and introduced by Ronald H. Stone (Louisville, Kentucky: Westminster/John Knox Press, 1990), 9–24.

29. Wight, *The Three Traditions*, 108–110, 115, 254–255.

30. Douglas Johnston and Cynthia Sampson (eds.), *Religion, The Missing Dimension of Statecraft* (Oxford: Oxford University Press, 1994).

31. Douglas Johnston, "Introduction: Realpolitik Expanded," in Douglas Johnston (ed.), *Faith-Based Diplomacy*, 3–10.

32. Robert Cox, "Social Forces, States and World Order: Beyond International Relations," *Millennium*, 10, 2 (1981): 126–155.
33. Mohammed Abu-Nimer, "The Miracles of Transformation Through Interfaith Dialogue: Are You a Believer?" in David R. Smock (ed.), *Interfaith Dialogue and Peacebuilding*, 15–32; Marc Gopin, "Conflict Resolution as a Religious Experience: Contemporary Mennonite Peacemaking," in Marc Gopin, *Between Eden and Armageddon: The Future of World Religions, Violence, and Peacemaking* (Oxford: Oxford University Press, 2000), 139–166.
34. Brian Cox and Daniel Philpott, "CFIA Task Force Report—Council on Faith & International Affairs," *The Brandywine Review of Faith & International Affairs*, 1, 2 (2003): 31–40.
35. Max Weber, "The Social Psychology of the World Religions," in H. H. Gerth and C. Wright Mills (eds.), *From Max Weber: Essays in Sociology* (New York: Oxford University Press, 1946), 267–301.
36. Brian Cox and Daniel Philpott, "CFIA Task Force Report: Faith-based Diplomacy," in *The Bradywine Review of Faith & International Affairs*, 1, 2 (2003): 31–40; Douglas Johnston and Brian Cox, "Faith-Based Diplomacy and Preventative Engagement," in Douglas Johnston (ed.), *Faith-Based Diplomacy*, 11–32.
37. Brian Cox, "Kashmir Project: Faith-based Reconciliation," September 12, 2003, Bhurban, Pakistan, Pearl Continental Hotel (photocopy); Andrew Rigby, *Justice and Reconciliation: After the Violence* (Boulder, CO: Lynne Reinner, 2001); John W. de Gruchy, *Reconciliation: Restoring Justice* (Minneapolis, MN: Angsburg Press, 2003).
38. R. Scott Appleby, *The Ambivalence of the Sacred: Religion, Violence, and Reconciliation* (Oxford: Rowan Littlefield, 2000), 167–204.
39. Desmond Tutu, *No Future Without Forgiveness* (London: Rider, 1999); Donald W. Shriver, *An Ethic for Enemies: Forgiveness in Politics* (Oxford: Oxford University Press, 1995), Michael Battle, *Reconciliation: The Ubuntu Theology of Desmond Tutu* (New York: Pilgrim Press, 1997).
40. George Irani, "Rituals of Reconciliation: Arabic-Islamic Perspectives," *Mind and Human Interaction: Windows Between History, Culture, Politics, and Psychoanalysis*, 11, 4 (2000): 226–245; *Faith-Based NGOs and International Peacebuilding*, special report (Washington, D.C.: U.S. Institute for Peace, October 22, 2001); Marc Gopin, *Holy War, Holy Peace: How Religion Can Bring Peace to the Middle East* (Oxford: Oxford University Press, 2002).
41. Appleby, *The Ambivalence of the Sacred*, 153–154, 223; David A. Steele, "Christianity in Bosnia-Herzegovina and Kosovo," in Douglas Johnson (ed.), *Faith-Based Diplomacy*, 124–177.
42. *Faith-Based NGOs and International Peacebuilding*, special report (Washington, D.C.: U.S. Institute for Peace, October 22, 2001).
43. David Steele, "Contributions of Interfaith Dialogue to Peacebuilding in the Former Yugoslavia," in Smock (ed.), *Interfaith Dialogue and Peacebuilding*, 73–88.

44. Lyn S. Graybill, *Truth and Reconciliation in South Africa: Miracle or Model?* (Boulder, CO: Lynne Reinner, 2002); Charles Villa-Vincencio and Wilhelm Verwoerd (eds.), *Looking Back, Reaching Forward: Reflections on the Truth and Reconciliation Commission of South Africa* (London: Zed Press, 2000).
45. Robert Kaplan, *Balkan Ghosts* (New York: Vintage, 1994), 9–20.
46. Mitchell Cohn, "Rooted Cosmopolitanism," in Nicholaus Mills (ed.), *Legacy of Dissent: 40 Years of Writing from Dissent Magazine* (New York: Touchstone Books, 1994), 131–140.
47. Roy Licklider, "Obstacles to Peace Settlements," in Chester A. Crocker et al. (eds.), *Turbulent Peace*, 697–718.
48. Roland H. Hainton, *Christian Attitudes Toward War and Peace* (London: Hodder & Stoughton, 1960), 17–32; Terry Nardin (ed.), *The Ethics of War and Peace: Religious and Secular Perspectives* (Princeton: Princeton University Press, 1996).
49. David Barash, "Negative Peace," in David Barash (ed.), *Approaches to Peace: A Reader in Peace Studies* (New York: Oxford University Press, 2000).
50. David Barash, "Positive Peace," in David Barash (ed.), *Approaches to Peace: A Reader in Peace Studies* (New York: Oxford University Press, 2000).
51. Connie Peck and David A. Hamburg, *Sustainable Peace* (Oxford: Rowan & Littlefield, 1998); Richard Smoke, *Paths to Peace: Exploring the Feasibility of Sustainable Peace* (Boulder, CO: Westview, 1987).
52. Boutros Boutro-Ghali, *An Agenda for Peace: Preventative Diplomacy, Peacemaking and Peace-keeping* (New York: United Nations, 1992).
53. John Paul Lederach, *Building Peace: Sustainable Reconciliation in Divided Societies* (Washington, D.C.: U.S. Institute of Peace, 1997).
54. Miall, Ramsbotham, and Woodhouse, *Contemporary Conflict Resolution*, 56–61.
55. *Multi-Track Diplomacy*, 11–25.
56. Lederach, *Building Peace*, 23.
57. *Faith-Based NGOs and International Peacebuilding*, special report, U.S. Institute for Peace, Washington, D.C., October 22, 2001; Mark Duffield, *Global Governance and the New Wars: The Merging of Development and Security* (London: Zed Press, 2001); N. Dower, "Development, Violence and Peace: A Conceptual Exploration," *The European Journal of Development Research*, 11, 2 (1999): 44–64.
58. Lederbach, *Building Peace*, 55–61.

Chapter 8   Funding Virtue? Rethinking Religion, Civil Society, and Democracy

1. Chester A. Crocker, "Engaging Failed States," *Foreign Affairs*, 82, 5 (September/October 2003): 32–44.
2. Michael Mandelbaum, "Foreign Policy as Social Work," *Foreign Affairs*, 75, 1 (January/February 1996): 16–32.

3. Minxin Pei and Sara Kasper, "Lessons From the Past: The American Record on Nation Building" (Washington, D.C.: Carnegie Endowment for International Peace, May 2003).

4. Amitai Etzioni, "A Sociologists's Iraq Exist Strategy," *Christian Science Monitor*, November 18, 2003.

5. Marina Ottaway and Thomas Carothers (eds.), *Funding Virtue: Civil Society Aid and Democracy Promotion* (Washington, D.C.: Carnegie Endowment for International Peace/Brookings Institution Press, 2000); Alison Van Rooy (ed.), *Civil Society and the Aid Industry* (London: North-South Institute/Earthscan, 1998).

6. Omar G. Encarnacion, "Beyond Civil Society: Promoting Democracy after September 11," *Orbis*, 47, 4 (2003).

7. Vicky Randall and Robin Theobald, *Political Change and Underdevelopment: A Critical Introduction To Third World Politics* (London: Macmillan, 1998).

8. Donal Cruise O'Brien, "Modernization, Order, and the Erosion of a Democratic Ideal: American Political Science, 1960–1970," *Journal of Development Studies*, 8, 2 (1972): 351–378.

9. Thomas Carothers, "Promoting Democracy and Fighting Terrorism," *Foreign Affairs*, 83 (2003); Rosemary Foot, *Human Rights and Counter-terrorism in America's Asia Policy*, Adelphi Paper 363 (London: International Institute for Strategic Studies, 2004).

10. Fareed Zakaria, *The Future of Freedom: Illiberal Democracy at Home and Abroad* (New York & London: W.W. Norton, 2003).

11. Larry Diamond, "Toward Democratic Consolidation: Rethinking Civil Society," *Journal of Democracy*, 5, 3 (1994).

12. Michael Bratton, "Beyond the State: Civil Society and Associational Life in Africa," *World Politics*, 41, 3 (1989).

13. Jenny B. White, "Civic Culture and Islam in Urban Turkey," in Chris Hann and Elizabeth Dunn (eds.), *Civil Society: Challenging Western Models* (London: Routledge, 1996), 143–154; and Annika Rabo, "Gender, State and Society in Jordan and Syria," in Hann and Dunn (eds.), *Civil Society: Challenging Western Models* (1996), and 155–177; Amyn B. Sajoo (ed.) *Civil Society in the Muslim World: Contemporary Perspectives* (London: I. B. Tauris, 2002).

14. Robert W. Heffner, "A Muslim Civil Society? Indonesia Reflections on the Conditions of its Possibility?" in Robert W. Heffner (ed.), *Democratic Civility: The History and Cross-Cultural Possibility of a Modern Political Ideal* (New Brunswick and London: Transaction Publishers, 1998), 285–321.

15. Ilene R. Prusher, "Iraq's new challenge: civil society," *Christian Science Monitor*, October 8, 2003.

16. John Flower and Pamela Leonard, "Community Values and State Co-Optation: Civil Society in the Sichuan Countryside," in Chris Hann

and Elizabeth Dunn (eds.), *Civil Society: Challenging Western Models* (1996), 199–221.

17. Patrick Chabal and Jean-Pascal Daloz, *Africa Works: Disorder as Political Instrument* (Oxford: James Currey, 1999).

18. *Human Development Report 2002*, Deepening Democracy in a Fragmented World (New York: Oxford University Press/United Nations Development Program, 2002).

19. Adam B. Seligman, *The Idea of Civil Society* (Princeton: Princeton University Press, 1992).

20. Michael Ignatieff, "On Civil Society," *Foreign Affairs*, 74, 2 (1995): 128–135.

21. Nicholas Wolterstorff, *John Locke and the Ethics of Belief* (Cambridge: Cambridge University Press, 1996).

22. Alasdair MacIntyre, *After Virtue: A Study in Moral Theory* (London: Duckworth, 1985); Charles Taylor, *Sources of the Self: The Making of the Modern Identity* (Cambridge: Cambridge University Press, 1989).

23. Ernest Gellner, *Conditions of Liberty: Civil Society and its Rivals* (London: Hamish Hamilton, 1994).

24. John A. Hall, "In Search of Civil Society," in John A. Hall (ed.), *Civil Society: Theory, History, Comparison* (Cambridge: Polity Press, 1995), 1–31.

25. Jurgen Habermas, *The Structural Transformation of the Public Sphere: An Inquiry into a Category of Bourgeois Society* (Cambridge, Mass.: MIT Press, 1989).

26. June Howell and Jenny Pearce, "Civil Society, the State, and the Market: A Triadic Development Model for the Twenty First Century?" in Jude Howell and Jenny Pearce, *Civil Society and Development: A Critical Exploration* (Boulder and London: Lynne Rienner, 2001), 63–88.

27. Graham Maddox, *Religion and the Rise of Democracy* (London: Routledge, 1996).

28. Howell and Pearce, *Civil Society and Development*, 13–38.

29. The English Pluralists include Lord Acton, F. W. Maitland, J. N. Figgis, Harold Laski, and G. D. H. Cole. David Nicholls, *The Pluralist State: the Political Ideas of J.N. Figgis and his Contemporaries* (London: St. Antony's/Macmillan, 2nd edition, 1994), Paul Q. Hirst (ed.), *The Pluralist Theory of the State: Selected Writings of G.D.H. Cole, J.N. Figgis, and H.J. Laski* (London: Routledge, 1989).

30. Alan Wilkinson, *Christian Socialism: Scott Holland to Tony Blair* (London: SCM Press, 1998), Mark D. Chapman, "Tony Blair, J.N. Figgis and the State of the Future," *Studies in Christian Ethics*, 13, 2 (2000): 49–66.

31. Marjorie K. McIntosh, "The Diversity of Social Capital in English Communities, 1300–1640 (with a glance at Modern Nigeria)," *Journal of Interdisciplinary History*, 19, 3 (1999): 459–490.

32. Anthony Black, *Guilds and Civil Society in European Political Thought from the Twelfth Century to the Present* (London: Methuen, 1984), 76–85, 143–152.
33. Ibid., *Guilds and Civil Society*, 5.
34. Max Stackhouse, "Religion and the Social Space for Voluntary Institutions," in Robert Wuthnow and Virginia A. Hodgkinson (eds.), *Faith and Philanthropy in America: Exploring the Role of Religion in America's Voluntary Sector* (San Francisco: Jossey-Bass, 1990), 22–37.
35. Joel S. Migdal, *State in Society: Studying How States and Societies Transform and Constitute One Another* (Cambridge: Cambridge University Press, 2001), 108.
36. Otto von Gierke, "Community in Historical Perspective" (1868), in James W. Skillen and Rockne M. McCarthy (eds.), *Political Order and the Plural Structure of Society* (Atlanta, GA: Emory University Studies in Law and Religion/Scholars Press, 1991), 79–96.
37. Joan Lockwood O'Donovan, "The Theological Economics of Medieval Usury Theory," *Studies in Christian Ethics*, 14, 1 (2001): 48–64.
38. J. N. Figgis, *Studies in Political Thought from Gerson to Grotius, 1414–1625* (Cambridge: Cambridge University Press, 1916), 141–171; Francis Oakley, *The Conciliarist Tradition: Constitutionalism in the Catholic Church 1300–1870* (Oxford: Oxford University Press, 2003).
39. E. J. Dionne Jr. (ed.), *Community Works: The Revival of Civil Society in America* (Washington, D.C., 1998); Corwin Smidt (ed.), *Religion and Social Capital: Producing the Common Good* (Waco, Texas: Baylor University Press, 2002).
40. Michael Woolcock, "Social Capital and Economic Development: Toward a Theoretical Synthesis and Policy Framework," *Theory and Society*, 27, 2 (1998): 151–208; Michael Woolcock, *Using Social Capital: Getting the Social Relations Right in the Theory and Practice of Economic Development* (New Haven, Conn.: Princeton, 2000).
41. Harry Blair, "Civil Society and Building Democracy: Lessons from International Donor Experience," in A. Bernard, H. Helmich, and P. Lehning (eds.), *Civil Society and International Development*. (Paris: North-South Centre of the Council of Europe, Development Centre, OECD, 1998), 65–80; Diana Mitlin, "The NGO Sector and its Role in Strengthening Civil Society and Securing Good Governance," in Helmich Bernard and Lehning (eds.), *Civil Society and International Development*, 81–96; *Governance and Development* (Washington, D.C.: World Bank, 1992).
42. Amitai Etzioni, *The Spirit of Community: Rights, Responsibilities, and the Communitarian Agenda* (New York: Crown, 1994); Amitai Etzioni, *The Essential Communitarian Reader* (Oxford: Rowman & Littlefield, 1998).
43. Robert Bellah, *The Broken Covenant: American Civil Religion in Time of Trial* (Chicago: University of Chicago Press, 1975, 2nd edition, 1984);

John Patrick Diggins, *The Lost Soul of American Politics: Virtue, Self-interest, and the Foundations of Liberalism* (Chicago: University of Chicago Press, 1984).

44. Susan J. Pharr and Robert D. Putnam (eds.), *Disaffected Democracies: What's Troubling the Trilateral Countries?* (Princeton: Princeton University Press, 2000).

45. Theodore J. Lowi, *The End of Liberalism: the Second Republic of the United States* (New York: Norton, 1969, 2nd edition, 1979); Jonathan Rausch, *Demosclerosis: The Silent Killer of American Government* (New York: Times Books, 1994); Michael Sandel, "The Procedural Republic and the Unencumbered Self," Shlomo Avineri and Avner de-Shalit (eds.), *Communitarianism and Individualism* (Oxford: Oxford University Press, 1992), 12–29.

46. Michael J. Sandel, *Democracy's Discontent: America's Search for a Public Philosophy* (New York: Belknop Press, 1996).

47. Peter Uvin, *Human Rights and Development* (Bloomfield, CT: Kumarian Press, 2004).

48. Mary Ann Glendon, *Rights Talk: The Impoverishment of Political Discourse* (New York: Free Press, 1991); Jean Bethke Elshtain, *Democracy on Trial* (New York: Basic Books, 1995).

49. Grzegorz Ekiert and Jan Kubik, *Rebellious Civil Society: Popular Protest and Democratic Consolidation in Poland* (Ann Arbor, MI: University of Michigan Press, 1999).

50. Stephen N. Ndegwa, *The Two Faces of Civil Society: NGOs and Politics in Africa* (West Hartford, CN: Kumarian Press, 1996).

51. M. Olson, "Dictatorship, Democracy, and Development," *American Political Science Review*, 87, 3 (1993).

52. Elisa P. Reis, "Banfield's Amoral Familism Revisited: Implications of High Inequality Structures for Civil Society," in Jeffrey C. Alexander (ed.), *Real Civil Societies: Dilemmas of Institutionalization* (London: Sage, 1998), 21–39.

53. Michael Sandel, "Competing American Traditions of Public Philosophy," in *Toward a New Public Philosophy: A Global Reevaluation of Democracy at Century's End, Ethics & International Affairs*, 20 (1997): 7–12.

54. Neil J. Kritz, "The Rule of Law in the Postconflict Phase," in Chester A. Crocker et al. (eds.), *Turbulent Peace*, 801–820; Thomas Carothers, "The Rule of Law Revival," *Foreign Affairs*, 77, 2 (March–April 1998): 103–104.

55. Michael Walzer, "The Civil Society Argument," *Dissent* (Spring 1991): 293–304; Michael Foley and Brian Edwards, "The Paradox of Civil Society," *Journal of Democracy*, 7, 3 (1996): 39–52.

56. Lord Acton, "The History of Freedom in Christianity," in Lord Action, *Essays in the Liberal Interpretation of History*, edited with an introduction by William H. McNeill (Chicago: University of Chicago Press, 1967), 271–299.

57. J. N. Figgis, *Churches in the Modern State* (London: Longmans, Green and Co., 1914), 101–120; Herbert Butterfield, *The Historical Development of the Principle of Toleration in British Life* (London: Menthuen, 1957); Perez Zagorin, *How the Idea of Religious Toleration Came to the West* (Princeton: Princeton University Press, 2003).

58. William Martin, "The Christian Right and American Foreign Policy," *Foreign Policy* (Spring 1999); Allan D. Hertzke and Daniel Philpott, "Defending the Faiths," *The National Interest*, 61 (Fall 2000): 74–81; Allan D. Hertzke, "The Political Sociology of the Crusade against Religious Persecution," in Elliot Abrams (ed.), *The Influence of Faith: Religious Groups & U.S. Foreign Policy* (Lanham/Oxford: Rowan & Littlefield/Ethics & Public Policy Center, 2001), 69–92.

59. J. Bryan Hehir, "Religious Freedom and U.S. Foreign Policy: Categories and Choices," in Elliot Abrams (ed.), *The Influence of Faith: Religious Groups & U.S. Foreign Policy*, 33–54.

60. Samuel P. Huntington, "Religious Persecution and Religious Freedom in Today's World," in Elliot Abrams (ed.), *The Influence of Faith: Religious Groups & U.S. Foreign Policy*, 55–64.

61. "America's Image Further Erodes, Europeans Want Weaker Ties," Pew Research Center for the People and the Press, Washington, D.C., March 18, 2003.

62. John L. Esposito and Francois Burgat (eds.), *Modernizing Islam: Religion in the Public Sphere in Europe and the Middle East* (London: Hurst, 2002); Armando Salvatore and Dale F. Eickelman (eds.), *Public Islam and the Common Good* (Leiden, Netherlands: E.J. Brill, 2004).

63. Scott Baldauf, "When Islamic clerics meet 'The Great Satan' face to face," *Christian Science Monitor*, February 19, 2004.

Chapter 9   Where Faith and Economics Meet?
Rethinking Religion, Civil Society, and International Development

1. "World Faiths Development Dialogue," Development Dialogue Web Site, The World Bank Group," www.worldbank.org/developmentdialogue <www.weforum.org>.

2. E. J. Dionne and Ming Hsu (eds.), *Sacred Places, Civic Purposes: Should Government Help Faith-Based Charity?* (Washington, D.C.: Brookings Institution, 2001).

3. Paul E. Pierson, "The Rise of Christian Mission and Relief Agencies," in Elliot Abrahams (ed.), *The Influence of Faith: Religious Groups & U.S. Foreign Policy* (New York: Rowan & Littlefield/Ethics & Public Policy Center, 2001), 153–170.

4. Mark R. Amstutz, "Faith-Based NGOs and U.S. Foreign Policy," in Elliot Abrams (ed.), *The Influence of Faith: Religious Groups & U.S. Foreign Policy*, 175–187.

5. Max Weber, "The Social Psychology of the World Religions," in H. H. Girth and C. Wright Mills (eds.), *From Max Weber: Essays in Sociology* (New York: Oxford University Press, 1946), 267–301.
6. Rachel M. McCleary, "Taking God Overseas: Christian Private Voluntary Organizations in International Relief and Development," Harvard University, Weatherhead Center for International Affairs, paper presented to the International Studies Association, 17–20 March, Montreal, Quebec, Canada.
7. Joshua S. Goldstein, *International Relations* (London: Longman, 2004), 527.
8. Stephen L. Carter, *The Culture of Disbelief: How American Law and Politics Trivialize Religious Devotion* (New York: Basic Books, 1993); Richard John Neuhans, *The Naked Public Square: Religion and Democracy in American Politics* (Grand Rapids: William B. Eevdmans, 1986).
9. Andrew S. Natsios, "Faith-Based NGOs and U.S. Foreign Policy," in Elliot Abrahams (ed.), *The Influence of Faith: Religious Groups & U.S. Foreign Policy*, 189–200.
10. Kurt Alan Ver Beek, "Spirituality: a Development Taboo," in Deborah Eade (ed.), *Development and Culture* (London: Oxfam, 2002), 60–77.
11. Fred Kniss and David Todd Campbell, "The Effect of Religious Orientation on International Relief and Development Organisations," *Journal for the Scientific Study of Religion*, 36, 1 (1997): 93–103.
12. Goldstein, *International Relations*, 526–528.
13. Michael Taylor, *Not Angels but Agencies—The Ecumenical Response to Poverty* (London: SCM Press, 1995).
14. Charles K. Wilber, "Preface to the First Edition" (1973), in Charles K. Wilber and Kenneth P. Jameson (eds.), *The Political Economy of Development and Underdevelopment* (New York: McGraw-Hill, 1996, 6th edition), xv–xvi.
15. Charles K. Wilber and Kenneth P. Jameson, "Religious Values and the Social Limits to Development," *World Development*, 8, 7/8 (1980): 467–479; Thierry G. Verhelst, *No Life Without Roots: Culture and Development* (London: Zed Books, 1990); B. Haverkort, K. van't Hooft, and W. Hiemstra (eds.), *Ancient Roots, New Shoots: Endogenous Development in Practice* (Bloomfield, CT: Kumarian Press, 2003).
16. Manning Nash, "Islam in Iran: Turmoil, Transformation or Transcendence?" *World Development*, 8, 7/8 (1980): 555–561.
17. Denis Goulet, *The Cruel Choice: A New Concept in the Theory of Development* (New York: Atheneum, 1971).
18. Denis Goulet and Charles K. Wilber "The Human Dilemma of Development," in Charles K. Wilber and Kenneth P. Jameson (eds.), *The Political Economy of Development and Underdevelopment* (New York: McGraw-Hill, 1996), 469–476.
19. Todd M. Vandenberg, " 'We Are Not Compensating Rocks': Resettlement and Traditional Religious Systems," *World Development*, 27, 2 (1999): 271–283.

20. G. Rist, *The History of Development: from Western Origins to Global Faith* (London: Zed Books, 1997); Julian Saurin, "Globalization, Poverty and the Promises of Modernity," *Millennium*, 25, 3 (1996): 657–680.
21. See the web page of the International Development Ethics Association <www.developmentethics.org>.
22. Arthuro Escobar, *Encountering Development: The Making and Unmaking of the Third World* (Princeton: Princeton University Press, 1995).
23. Denis Goulet, " 'Development'. . . or Liberation," in Wilber and Jameson (eds.), *The Political Economy of Development and Underdevelopment* (New York: McGraw-Hill, 1996), 543–550; Paulo Freire, *Cultural Action for Freedom* (London: Penguin, 1972), Paulo Freire, *Pedagogy of the Oppressed* (London: Sheed and Ward, 1972); Denis Goulet, *Development Ethics: A Guide to Theory and Practice* (New York: The Apes Press, 1995).
24. Javier Perez de Cuellar, "President's Forward," *Our Creative Diversity*, Report of the World Commission on Culture and Development (Paris: UNESCO, 1995, 2nd revised edition, 1996), 7.
25. Nigel Harris, *The End of the Third World: Newly Industrialized Countries and the Decline of an Ideology* (London: Penguin, 1986).
26. Lucian W. Pye and Mary Pye, *Asian Power and Politics: The Cultural Dimensions of Authority* (Cambridge, MA: Harvard University Press, 1989); Daniel Bell and Hahm Chaibong (eds.), *Confucianism for the Modern World* (Cambridge: Cambridge University Press, 2001).
27. Don Grant, Kathleen M. O'Neil, and Laura S. Stephens, "Neosecularization and Craft Versus Professional Religious Authority in Non-religious Organizations," *Journal for the Scientific Study of Religion*, 42, 3 (2003): 479–487.
28. Kathryn A. O'Connell, "Spirituality, Religion and Personal Beliefs: A Dimension of Quality of Life" (Department of Psychology, University of Bath, unpublished Ph.D. dissertation, 2002).
29. David M. Beckmann, *Where Faith and Economics Meet: A Christian Critique* (Minneapolis: Augsburg Publishing House, 1981); David M. Beckmann et al., *Friday Morning Reflections at the World Bank: Essays on Values and Development*, foreword by Barber B. Conable (Washington, D.C.: Seven Locks Press, 1991).
30. Deepa Narayan, *Voices of the Poor: Can Anyone Hear Us?* (Washington, D.C.: Oxford University Press, for the World Bank, 2000).
31. David Beckmann, President, Bread for the World, remarks as the recipient of the fifth Annual Leadership Award from the Center for Public Justice, Washington, D.C., March 1, 2001 <www.cpjustice.org>.
32. Deryke Belshaw, Robert Calderisi, and Chris Sugden (eds.), *Faith in Development: Possibilities for Partnership between the World Bank and the Churches in Africa* (Oxford: Regnum Books/Oxford Centre for Mission Studies, 2001).
33. Kumi Naidoo, The Charities Aid Foundation (CAF), *Alliance*, 5, 1 (2000).

34. Katherine Marshall, "Development and Religion A Different Lens on Development Debates," <www.wfdd.org.uk>.

35. "Development Dialogue: The Faiths in Development," Development Dialogue Web Site, the World Bank Group <www.worldbank.org/developmentdialogue>.

36. At the time this chapter was written the WFDD was going through a great period of transition. Michael Taylor, the former director of Christian Aid in Britain, and Professor of Social Theology at the University of Birmingham became the WFDDs' first executive director in 2000. When his tenure came to an end on July 31, 2004, the board of directors agreed to move the organization to Washington, D.C. <www.wfdd.org.uk>.

37. "Development Dialogue: The Faiths in Development," Development Dialogue Web Site, the World Bank Group <www.worldbank.org/developmentdialogue>.

38. Katherine Marshall and Richard Marsh (eds.), *Millennium Challenges for Development and Faith Institutions* (Washington, D.C.: World Bank, 2003); Katherine Marshall and Lucy Keough (eds.),; *Mind, Heart, and Soul in the Fight Against Poverty* (Washington, D.C.: World Bank, 2004).

39. "WFDD Work Plan," October 2002–December 2003 <www.wfdd.org.uk>.

40. Jonathan Fox and David L. Brown (eds.), *The Struggle for Accountability: The World Bank, NGOs, and Grassroots Movements* (Cambridge: MIT Press, 1998).

41. "Development Dialogue: The Faiths in Development," Development Dialogue Web Site <www.worldbank.org/developmentdialogue>.

42. Michael Taylor, *Poverty and Christianity* (London: SCM Press, 2000).

43. "WFDD—The Future: A Discussion Paper," September 24, 2003 <www.wfdd.org.uk>.

44. *Poverty and Development: An Inter-faith Perspective* (Oxford: World Faiths Development Dialogue, 2000, June 1999).

45. "WFDD—The Future: A Discussion Paper," September 24, 2003 <www.wfdd.org.uk>.

46. Michael Edwards and David Hulme, *NGOs, States and Donors: Too close for Comfort?* (New York & London: Earthscan/Save the Children, 1997); T. Tvedt, *Angels of Mercy or Development Diplomats: NGOs and Foreign Aid* (New York: Africa World Press, 1998).

47. Jessica Einhorn, "The World Bank's Mission Creep," *Foreign Affairs*, 80, 5 (2003): 22–35.

48. Patrick Chabal and Jean-Pascol Daloz, *Africa Works: Disorder As Political Instrument* (London: James Currey, 1999), 52–53.

49. Joanne Baldine, "Is Human Identity an Artifact?: How Some Conceptions of the Asian and Western Self Fare During Technological and Legal Development," *Phil & Tech*, 3, 2 (1997): 25–36.

50. Michael Taylor, *Not Angels but Agencies: The Ecumenical Response to Poverty— A Primer* (London & Geneva: SCM Press/WCC Publications, 1995).

51. *World Disasters Report*, Focus on ethics in aid (Geneva: International Federation of Red Cross and Red Crescent Societies, 2003).

52. World Faith's Development Dialogue (WFDD), "The Provision of Services for Poor People: A Contribution *to World Development Report 2004*," <www.wfdd.org.uk>.

53. "A New Direction for World Development?" Comment on the first full version of the *World Development Report 2000/2001*, occasional paper, no. 3, WFDD <www.wfdd.org.uk>.

54. Mitchell Cohn, "Rooted Cosmopolitanism," in Nicholaus Mills (ed.), *Legacy of Dissent: 40 Years of Writing from Dissent Magazine* (New York: Touchstone Books, 1994), 131–140.

55. "Religion and International Order," *House of Lords* (official report), parliamentary debates (Hansard), 605, 135, October 15, 1999, United Kingdom.

56. Report of a workshop in Accra, Ghana arranged by Religious Bodies Forum of Ghana and World Faiths Development Dialogue to explore the relation between the Islamic and Christian faiths and development, October 28–29, 2003, <www.wfdd.org.uk>.

57. Robert Putnam, *Bowling Alone: The Collapse and Revival of American Community* (New York: Simon & Schuster, 2000), 19–28.

58. Ibid, *Bowling Alone*, 408–410.

59. "A New Direction for World Development?" Comment on the first full version of the *World Development Report 2000/2001*, occasional paper, no. 3 <www.wfdd.org.uk>.

60. Ross Gittell and Avis Vidal, *Community Organizing: Building Social Capital as a Development Strategy* (Thousand Oaks, CA: Sage, 1998).

61. Deepa Narayan, *Bonds and Bridges: Social Capital and Poverty* (Washington, D.C.: World Bank, 1999).

62. Michael Goldberg, "Discipleship: Basing One Life on Another-Its Not What You Know, Its Who You Know," in Stanley Hauerwas, Nancy Murphy, and Mark Nation (eds.), *Theology Without Foundations: Religious Practice & the Future of Theological Truth* (Nashville: Abingdon Press, 1994), 289–304.

63. Putnam, *Bowling Alone*, 362.

64. David L. Chappell, *A Stone of Hope: Prophetic Religion and the Death of Jim Crow* (Chapel Hill, NC: University of North Carolina, 2003).

65. Edmund Pincoffs, "Quandary Ethics," in Stanley Hauerwas and Alasdair MacIntyre (eds.), *Revisions: Changing Perspectives in Moral Philosophy* (South Bend, IN: University of Notre Dame Press, 1983), 92–112.

66. David B. Burrell, "Narratives Competing for Our Souls," in James P. Sterba (ed.), *Terrorism and International Justice* (Oxford: Oxford University Press, 2003), 88–100.

67. Paul Rogat Loeb, "The Real Rosa Parks," *The Los Angeles Times*, January 14, 2000; Stewart Burns, *To the Mountain: Martin Luther King, Jr.'s Sacred Mission to Save America, 1955–1968* (New York: Harper/Collins, 2004), 18–29.

68. Francis Fukuyama, "Social Capital and Development: The Coming Agenda," *SAIS Review*, 22, 1 (2002).
69. Stanley Hauerwas, *A Community of Character: Toward a Constructive Christian Social Ethic* (Notre Dame, Ind.: University of Notre Dame, 1981).
70. Report of a Workshop in Dar-es-Salaam, Tanzania arranged by Tanzania Inter-Faith Forum (TIFF) and World Faiths Development Dialogue to explore the relation between the Islamic and Christian faiths and development, November 11–13, 2003 <www.wfdd.org.uk>.
71. Jessica Einhorn, "The World Bank's Mission Creep," *Foreign Affairs*, 80, 5 (2003): 22–35.
72. Owais Tohid, "Bangladeshi Clerics Back Family Planners," *Christian Science Monitor*, June 17, 2003.
73. Christopher Candland, "Faith as Social Capital: Religion and Community Development in Southern Asia," in John D. Montgomery and Alex Inkeles (eds.), *Social Capital as a Policy Resource* (Boston: Kluwer Academic Publishers, 2001), 129–148.
74. George D. Bond, *Buddhism at Work: Community Development, Social Empowerment, and the Sarvoyada Movement* (Bloomfield, CT: Kumarian Press, 2004); Kamla Chowdhry, "The Sarvoyada Shramadana Movement in Sri Lanka," December 19, 2001; September 24, 2002 <www.wfdd.org.uk>.
75. Robert Chambers, *Whose Reality Counts? Putting the First Last* (London: Intermediate Technology Publications, 1997).
76. "Study of the Organization and Functioning of a Development Association: The Case Study of Sarkan Zoumountsi in Yaounde, Cameroon <www.wfdd.org.uk>.
77. Paulo Freire, *The Pedagogy of the Oppressed* (New York: Seabury, 1970).
78. Peter Burnell, "Britain's New Government, New White Paper, New Aid?" *Third World Quarterly*, 19, 4 (1998): 787–802.
79. Tony Killick, with Ramani Gunatilaka, Ana Marr, *Aid and the Political Economy of Policy Change* (London: Routledge and Overseas Development Institute, 1998).
80. Tod Bolsinger, *It Takes a Church to Raise a Christian: How the Community of God Transforms Lives* (Waco, Texas: Brazos Press, 2004).
81. Christopher Candland, "Faith as Social Capital: Religion and Community Development in Southern Asia," 129–148.
82. Carol C. Adelman, "The Privatization of Foreign Aid," *Foreign Affairs*, 82, 6 (November–December 2003): 9–14.

Conclusion   How Shall We then Live?

1. Charles O. Lerche and Abdul A. Said, *Concepts of International Politics* (Englewood Cliffs, NJ: Prentice-Hall, 1970), 15–16.

INDEX